MW01628219

ROCK BANNED

PAUL FREEMAN

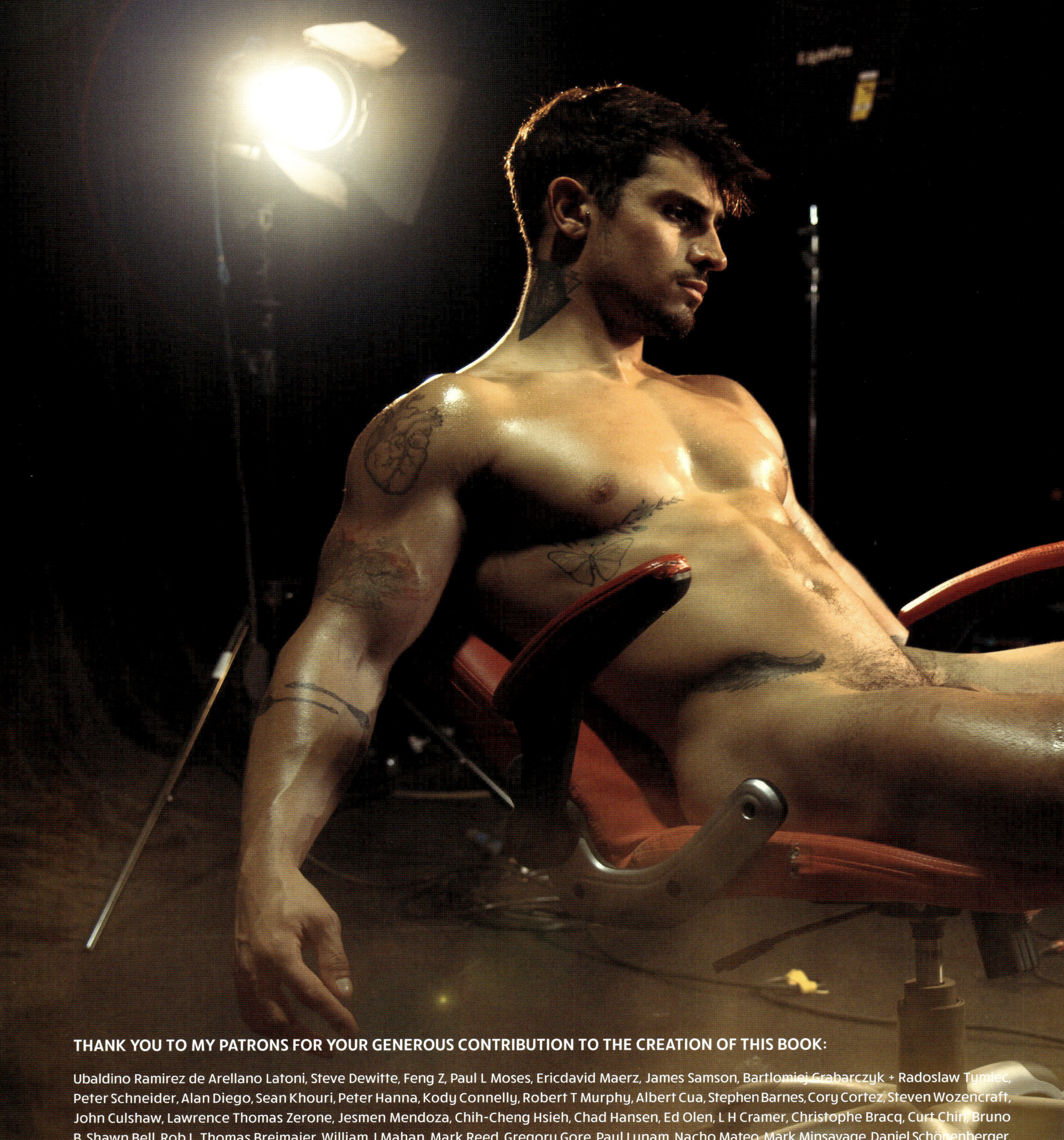

THANK YOU TO MY PATRONS FOR YOUR GENEROUS CONTRIBUTION TO THE CREATION OF THIS BOOK:

Ubaldino Ramirez de Arellano Latoni, Steve Dewitte, Feng Z, Paul L Moses, Ericdavid Maerz, James Samson, Bartlomiej Grabarczyk + Radoslaw Tymiec, Peter Schneider, Alan Diego, Sean Khouri, Peter Hanna, Kody Connelly, Robert T Murphy, Albert Cua, Stephen Barnes, Cory Cortez, Steven Wozencraft, John Culshaw, Lawrence Thomas Zerone, Jesmen Mendoza, Chih-Cheng Hsieh, Chad Hansen, Ed Olen, L H Cramer, Christophe Bracq, Curt Chin, Bruno B, Shawn Bell, Rob L, Thomas Breimaier, William J Mahan, Mark Reed, Gregory Gore, Paul Lynam, Nacho Mateo, Mark Minsavage, Daniel Schönenberger, Chris Kattelus, David Borst, John R, Justin Hicks, Vincent Ruer, Jay Sokolik, Michael Cole, Gari Billiot, Bruce Ladd, Dan Jung, Mitchell Chessman, Chris Metzger, David Dewenter, Hans Reiss, Patrick Devenney, Jim Gauthier, Mackenzie Pearce, Antony Lloyd, Ian Tan, Michael J Hatton, Steven Soh, David Rieunier, Keith Angle, Matthew Hamilton, Brian Finstad, Alan Geoghegan, Joe Spears, Alfredo Gutierrez, Shenandoah Bunn, William Lewis, Lee David Packer, Greg Cawthorn, Noah Wright, François Renaud, Benjamin Brugiere, Jeff Henderson, Michael J Glasgow, Steven Soh , Barry Ringland, Scott P Valentine, Jacques Berthier, Mark Van Dorn, Michael Filardo, Brandon Griggs, Gerard de Leon, Dean Smith, Phil Tottie, Conrad Hechter, Stefano, Daniel Ashley, Marco Toppi, Theron Puccinelli, Manor Van Zetta, Ed Kinsella, Mark Cameron, Rafael Quezada, R S Donat, Thomas Phillips, Scott Erickson, Mitchell Herbel, Jeffrey Sauer, Gordon Ulrickson, Jeff Leatham, Rocco L Buonpane, Ed Kinsella, Rodgers McCowan, Jeffery Egan, Todd M Palumbo, Brenton Creed.

ROCK BANNED

PAUL FREEMAN

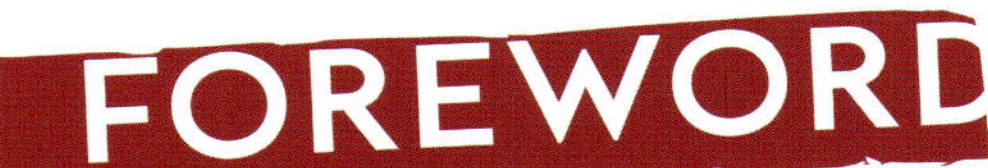

The idea for a book of rock portraits came about during the first Covid lockdown in 2020. I was friends with the lead singer of a local Sydney band and he had been keen for me to shoot his band during rehearsal, including some nudes, for publicity. He told me he and his fellow band members often rehearsed naked, (usually under the influence of various creative stimulants like 'shrooms'.) As it turned out our plans were stymied by their rehearsal space getting flooded and then, later, by the band being forced to split up due to lockdowns. But the seed had been planted for some kind of rock-music themed book and so, despite restrictions, I managed to do some shoots and have fun with the concept. I shot men that fit the bill, either with a music background or having that rock or roadie experience or look. The resulting collection is a homage to those sexy rock industry types, notorious for their on and off-stage provocative antics. Naturally I delve into the realm of sensual fantasy and capture them in rehearsal, in performance and behind the scenes perhaps a little more blasé and risqué in their various states of undress than you would find them in reality.

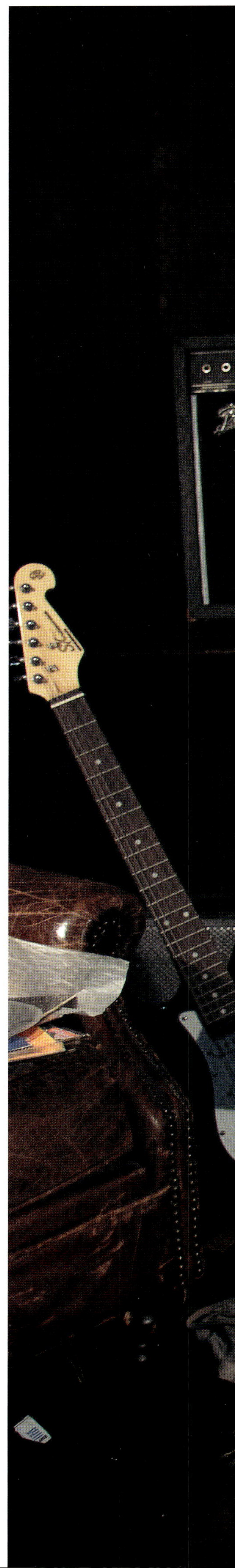

PUBLISHED BY PAUL FREEMAN PTY LTD (ABN: 26 298 037 520) PRINTED IN ITALY.

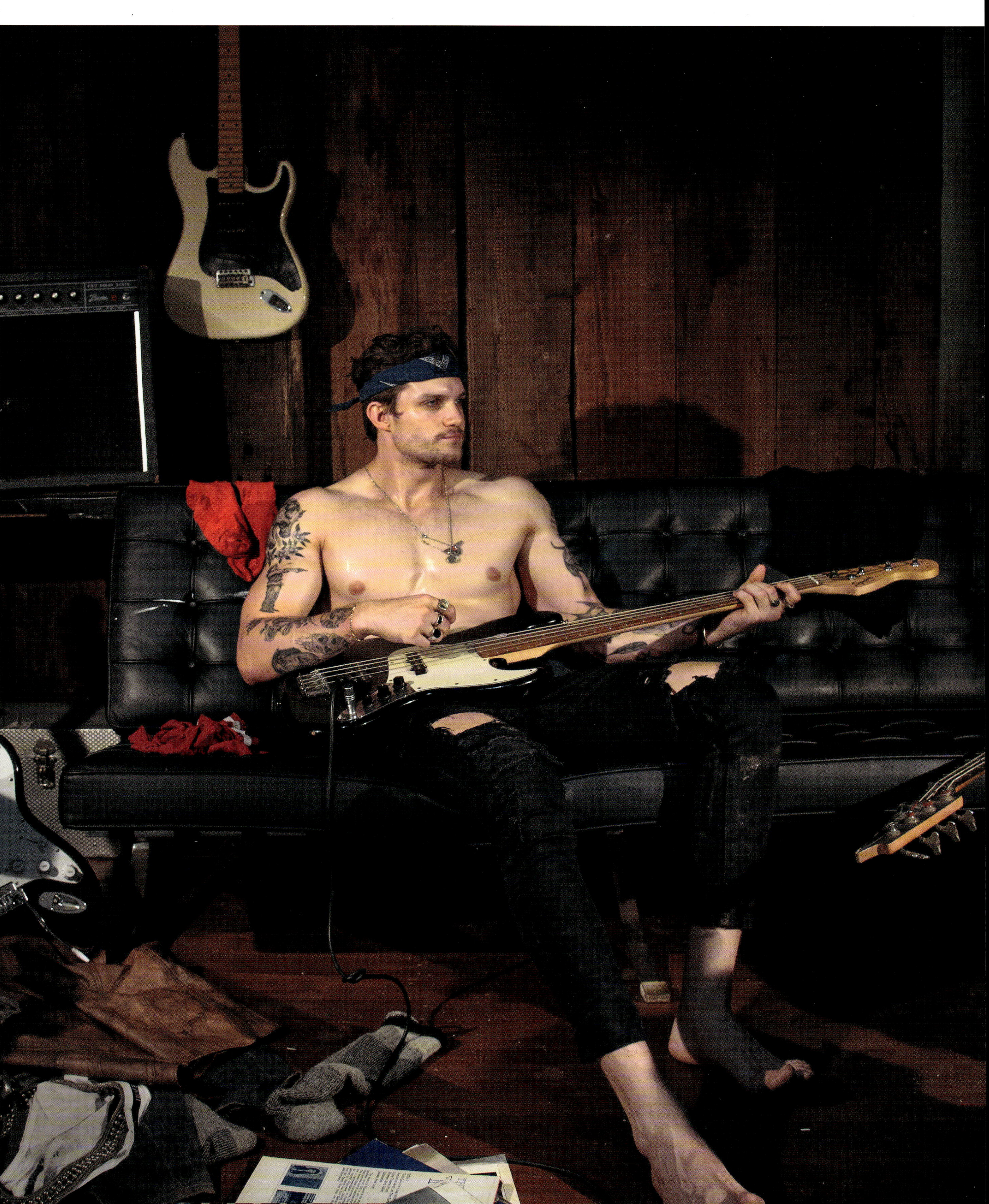

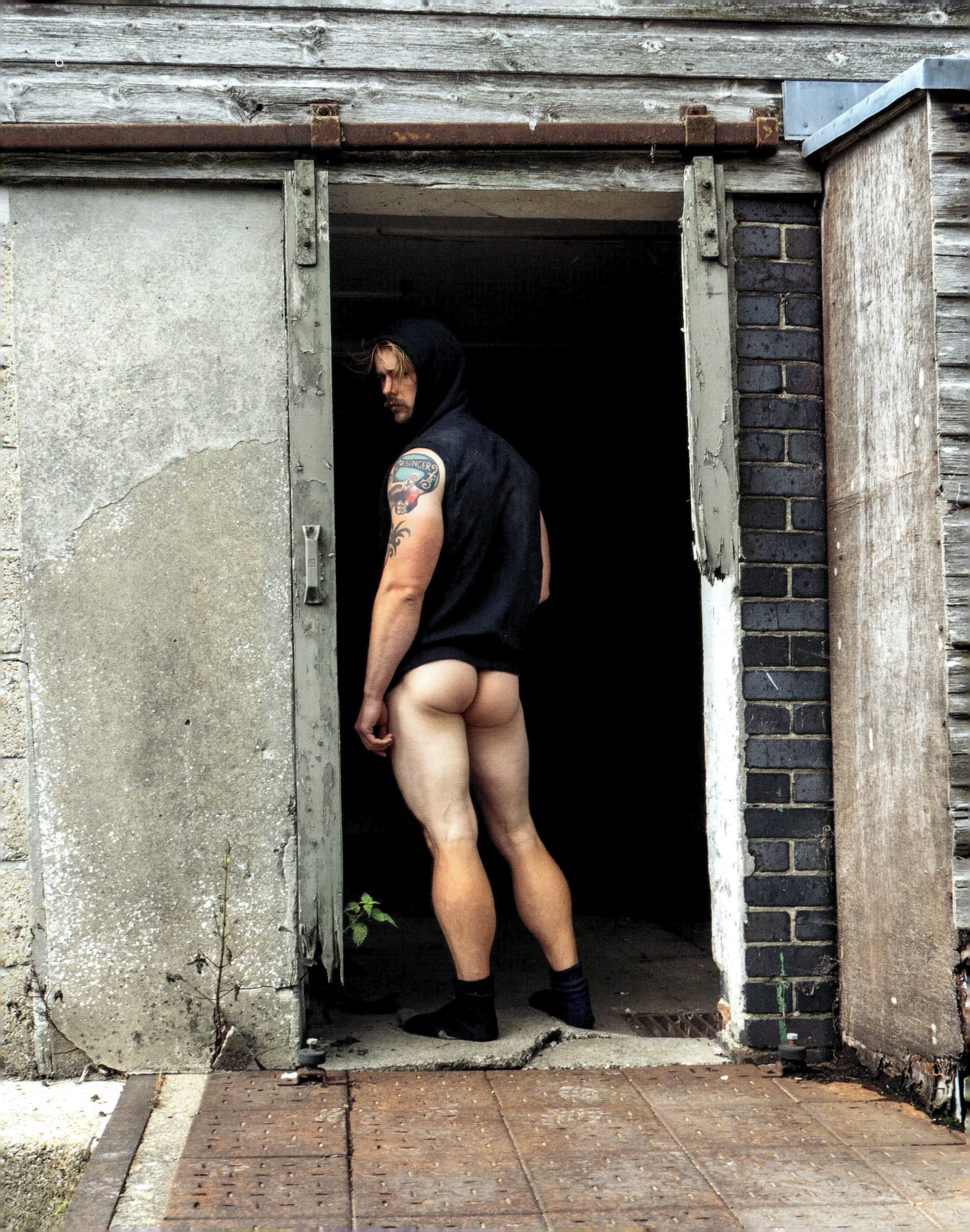
SINGER

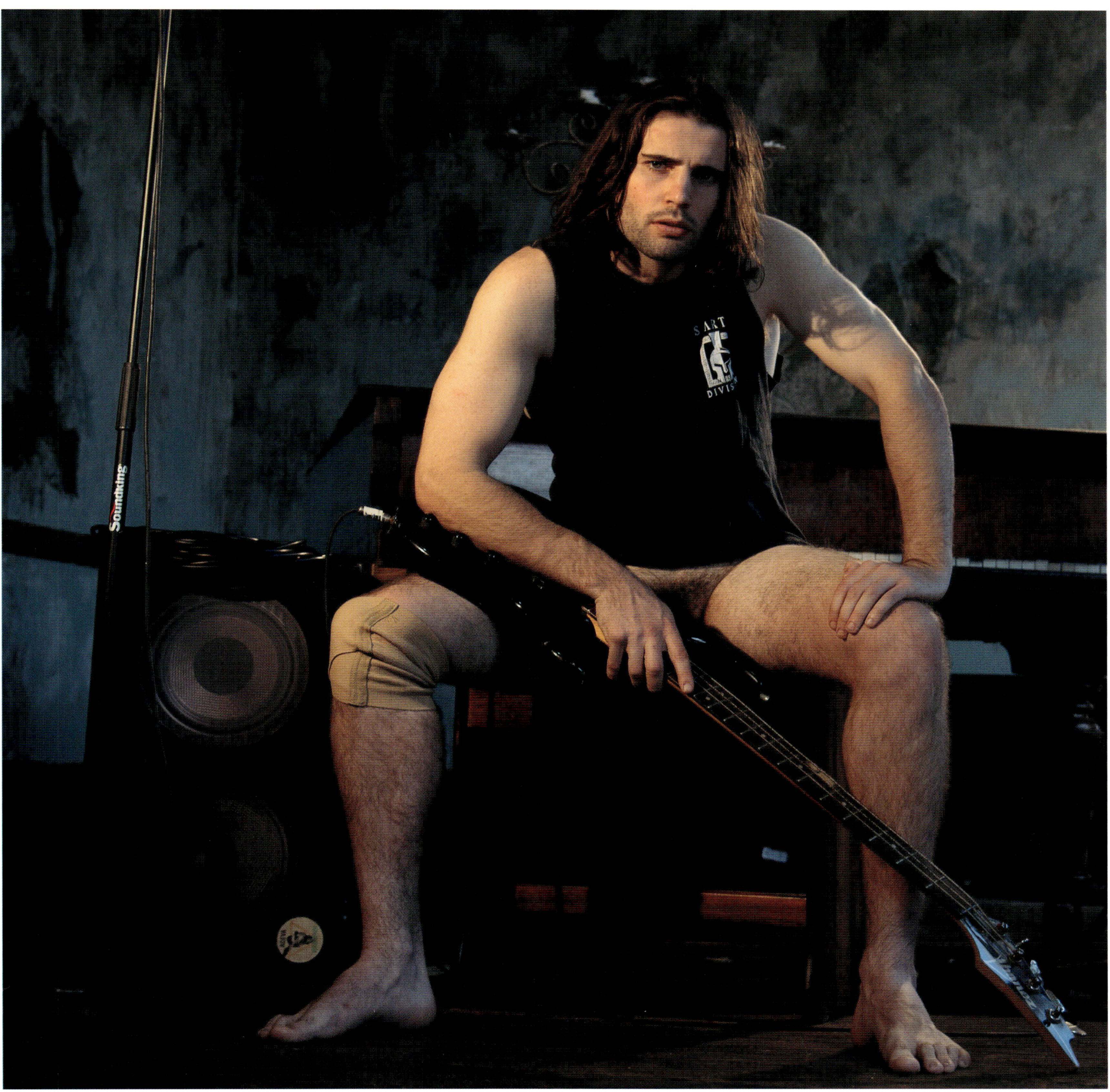
Soundking

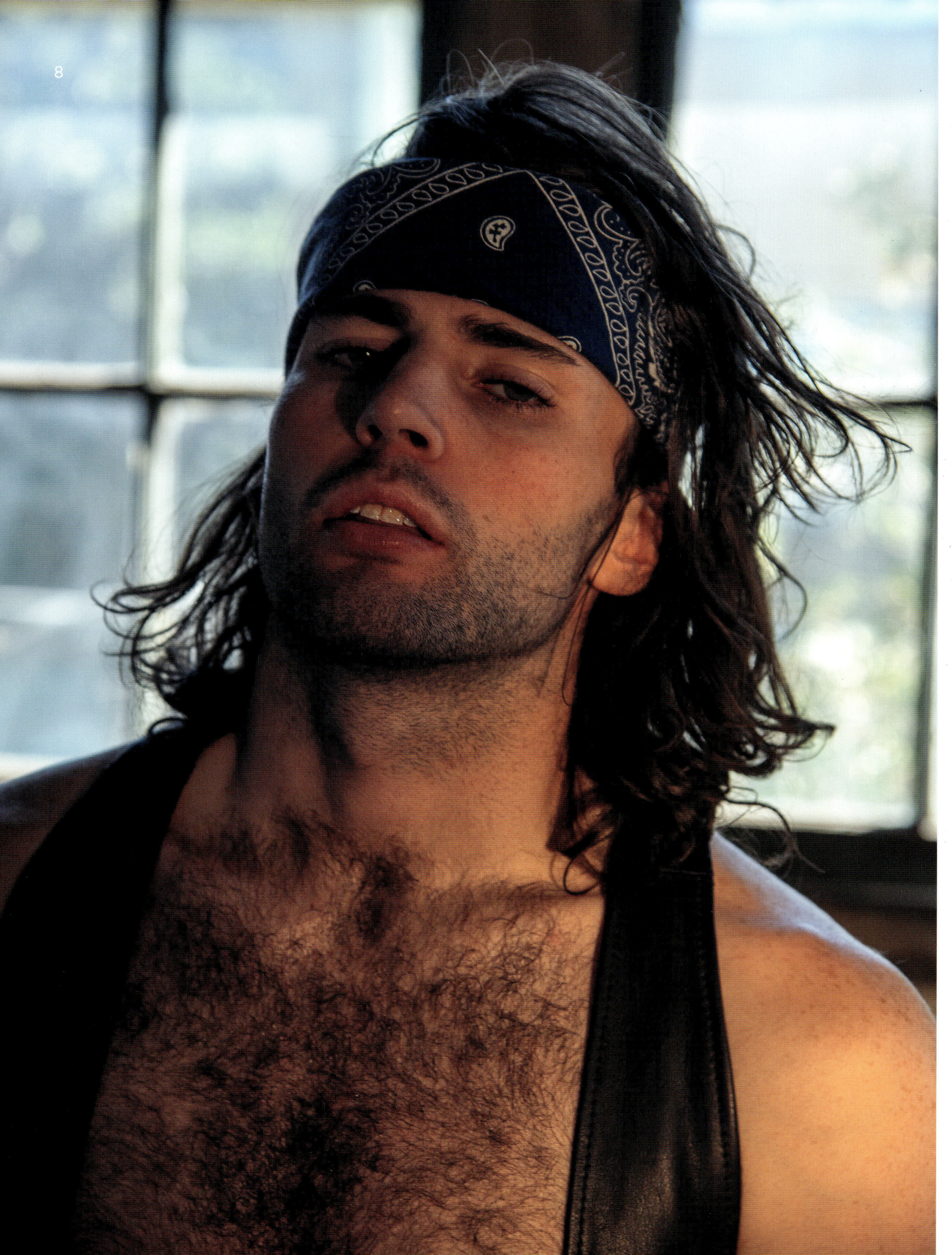

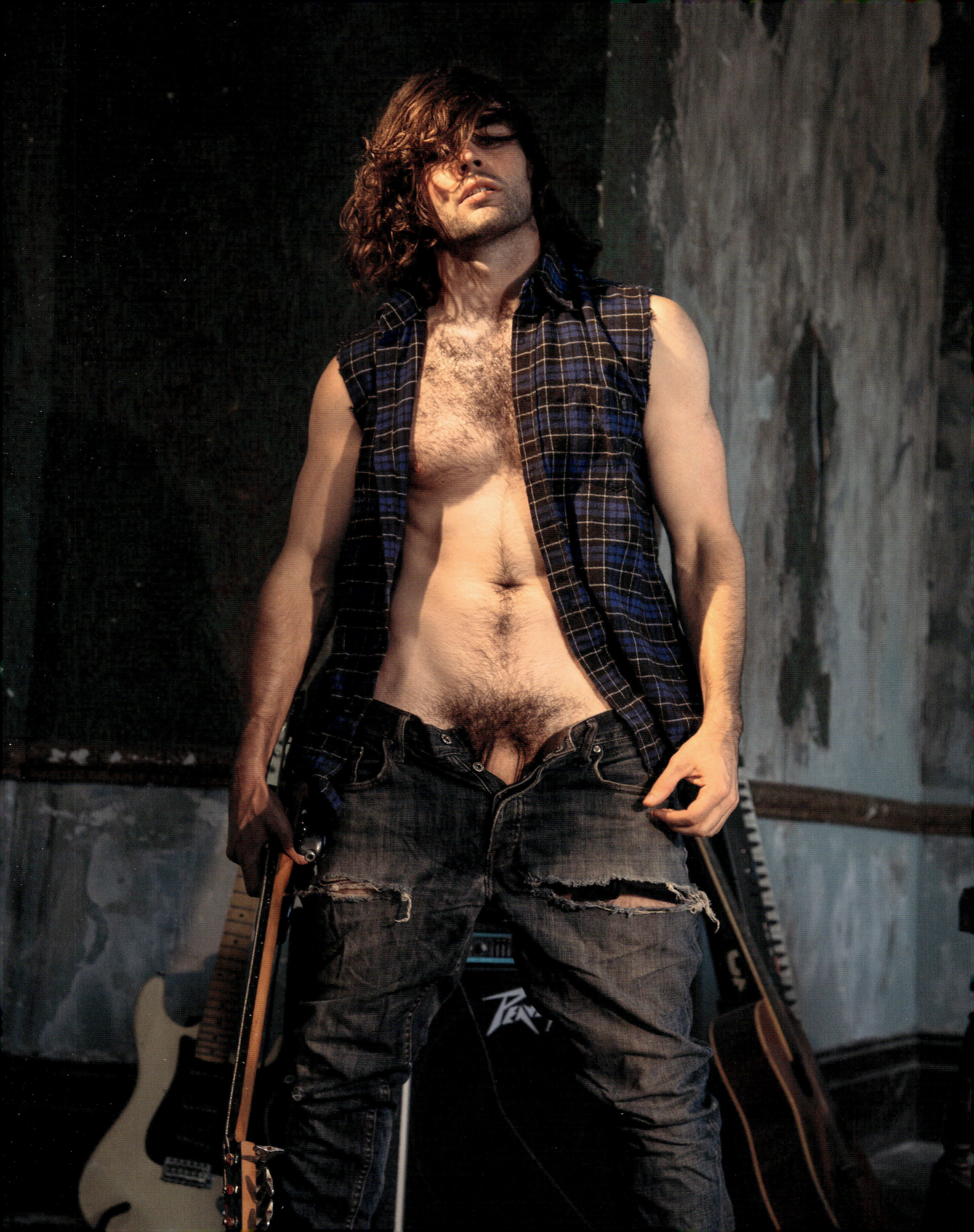

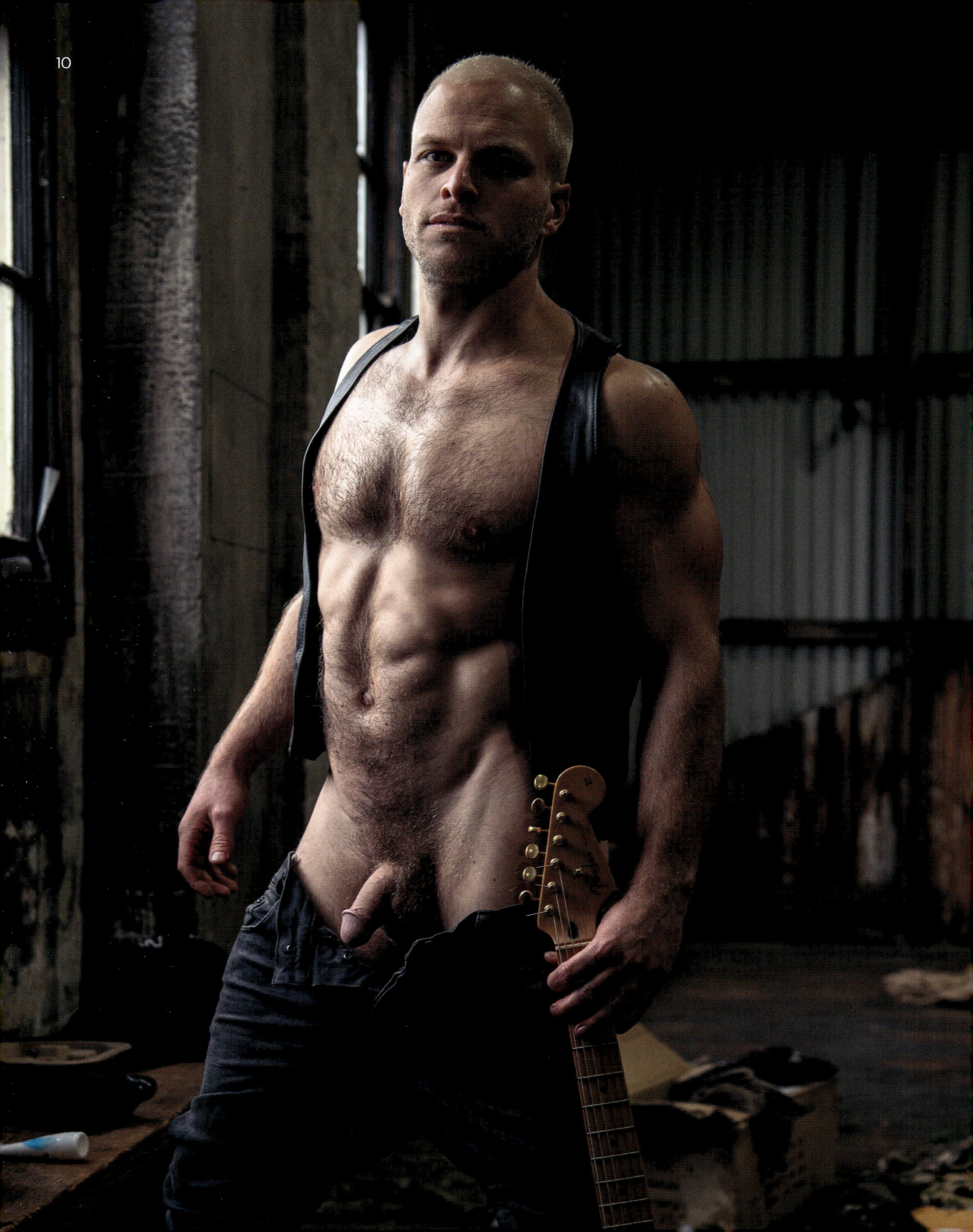

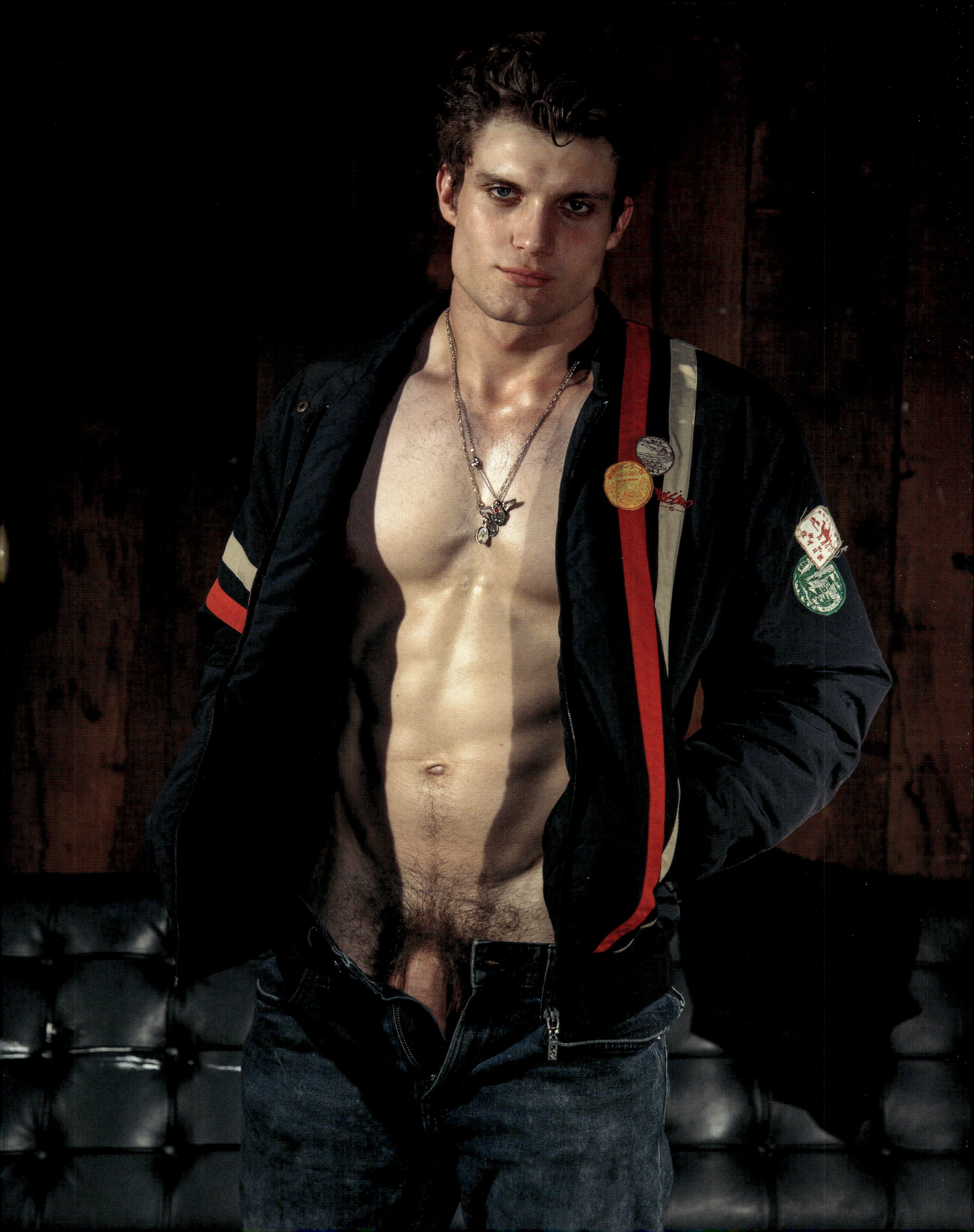

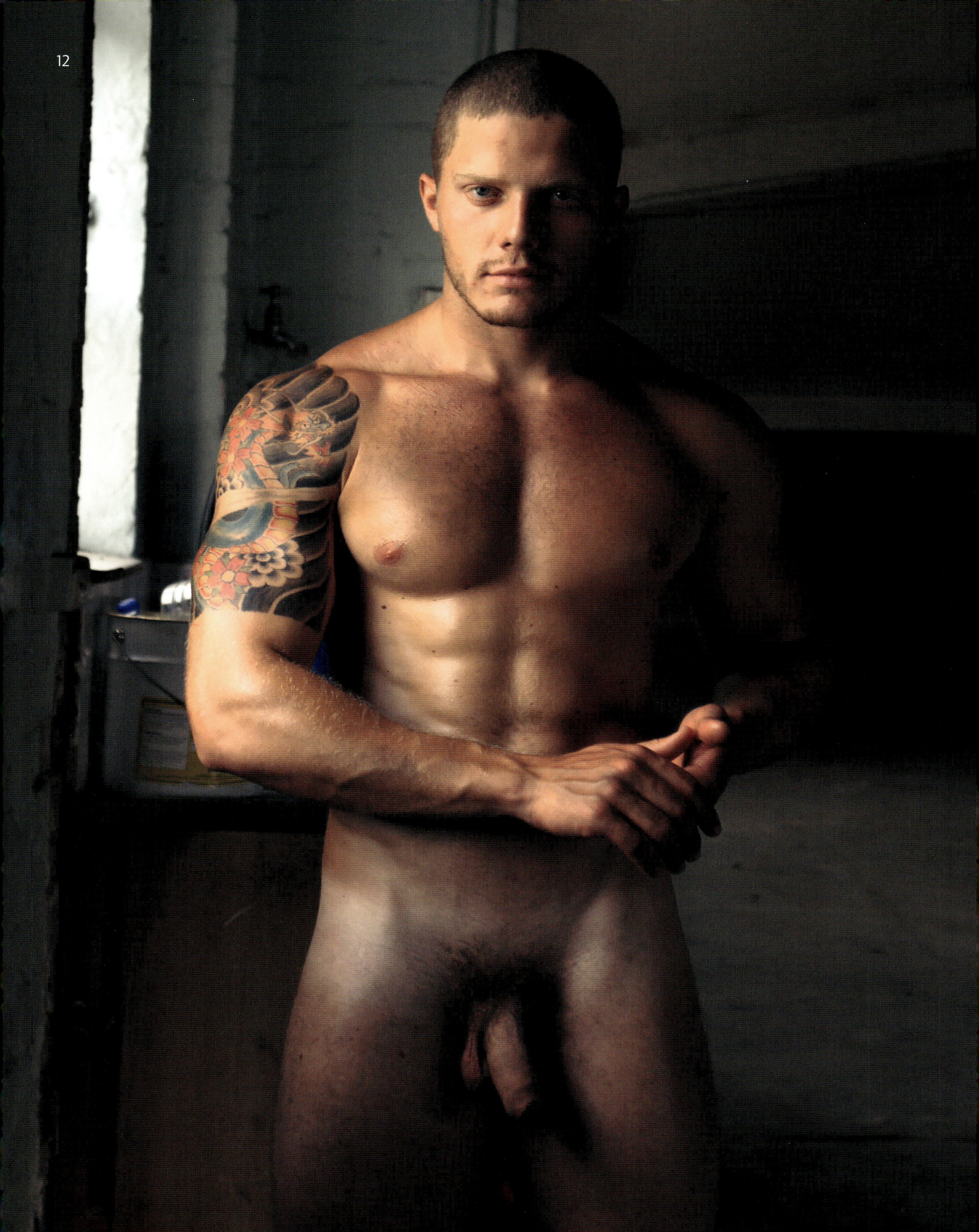

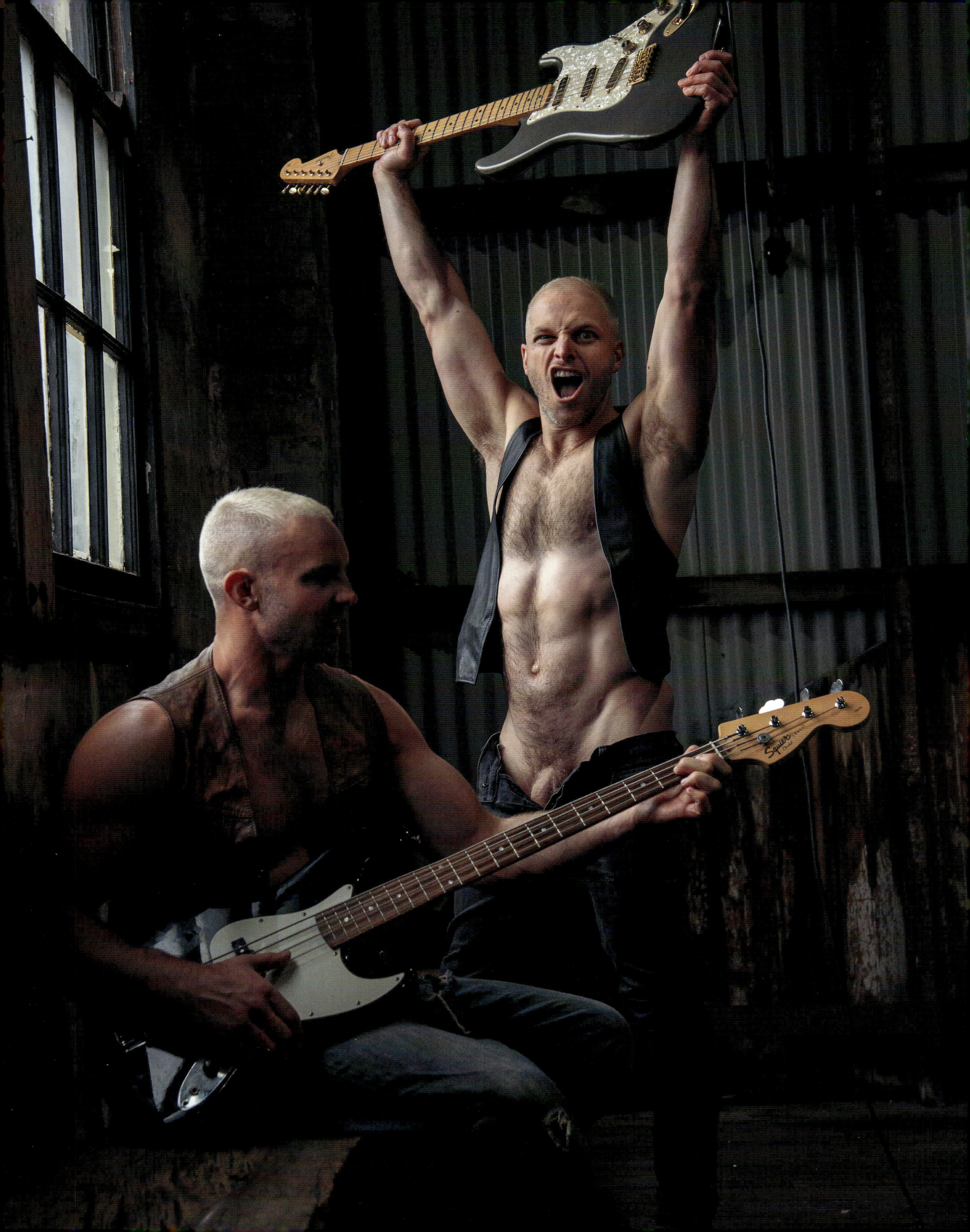
Squier

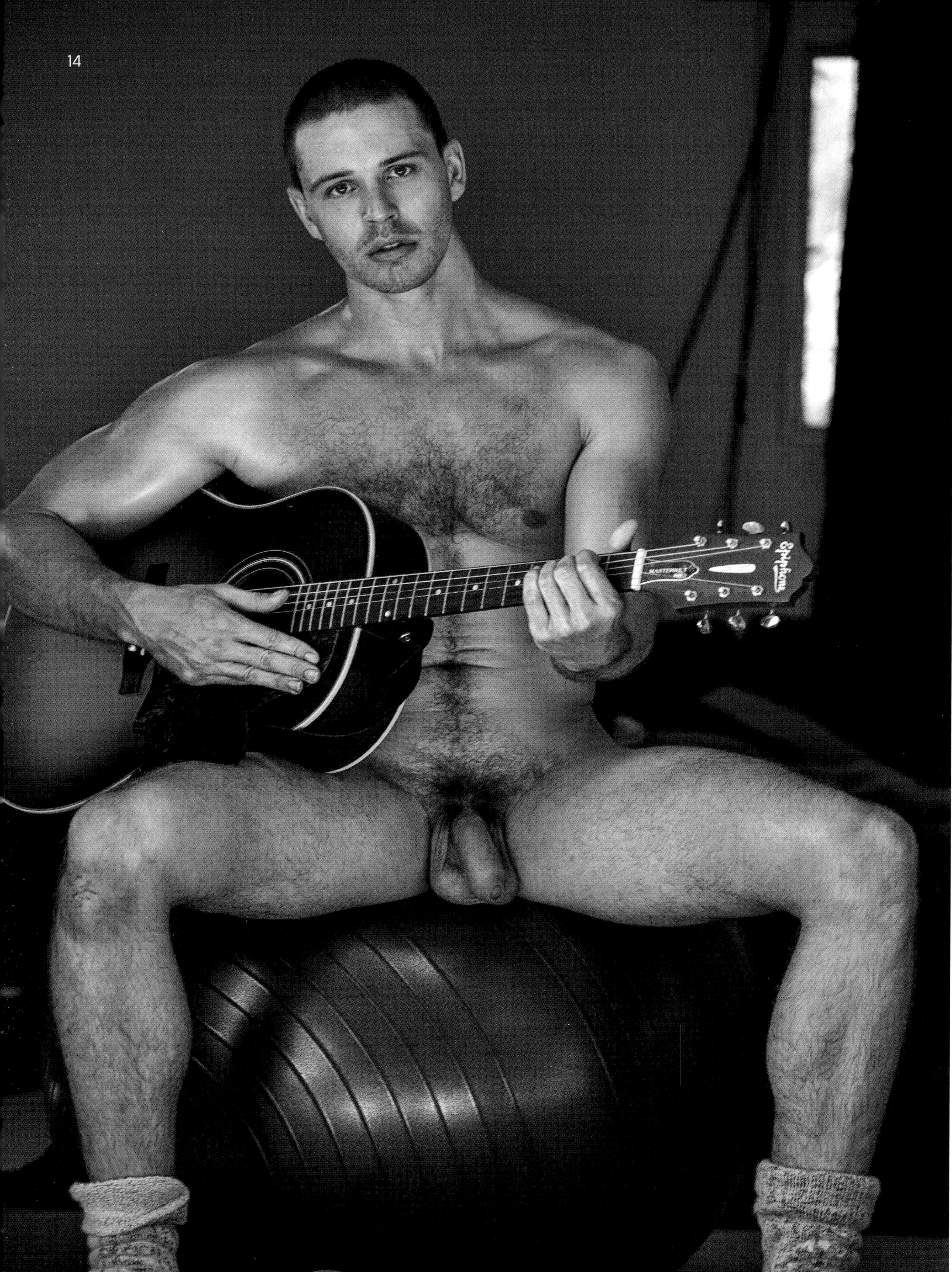
Epiphone
MASTERBILT

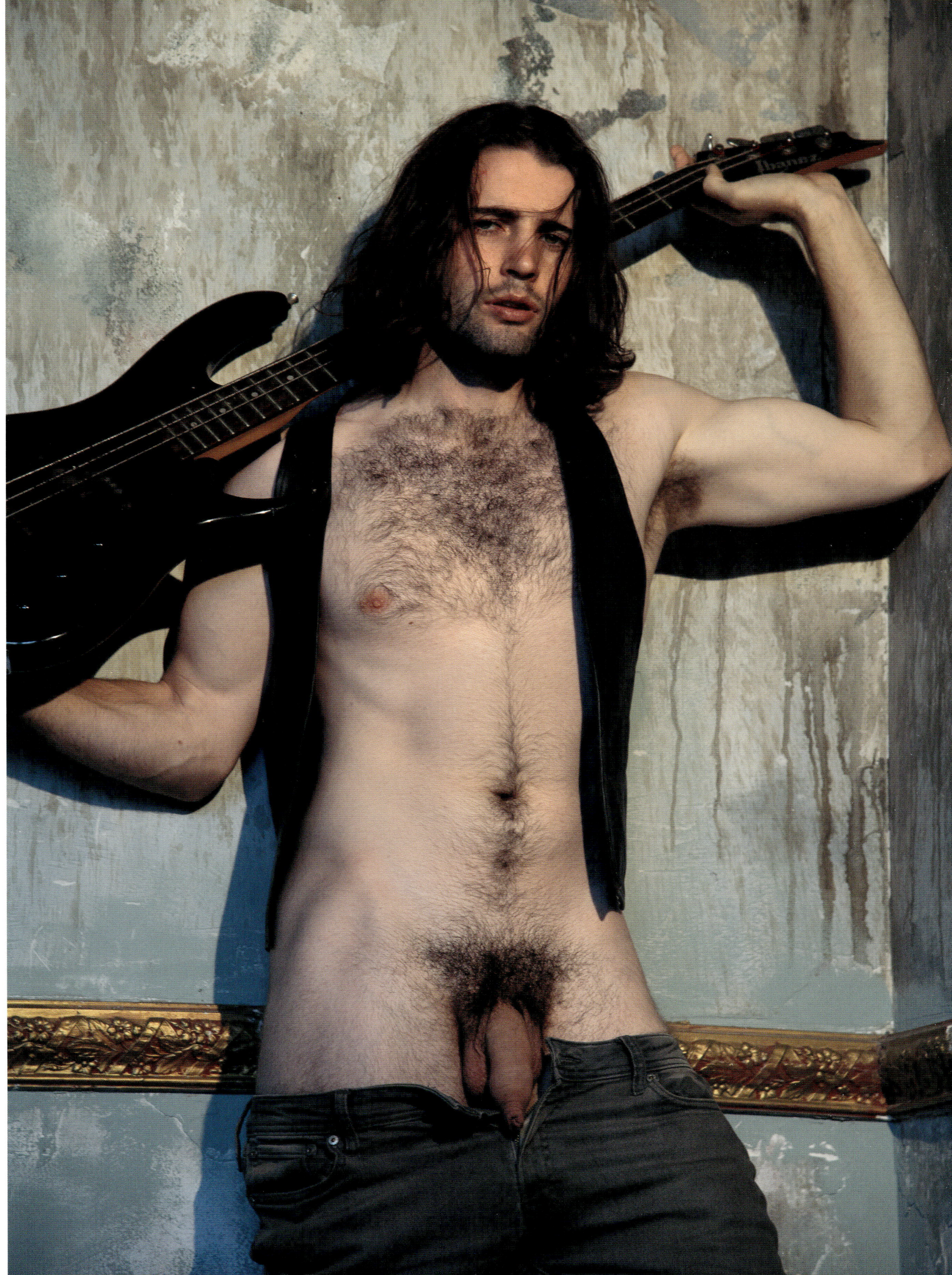

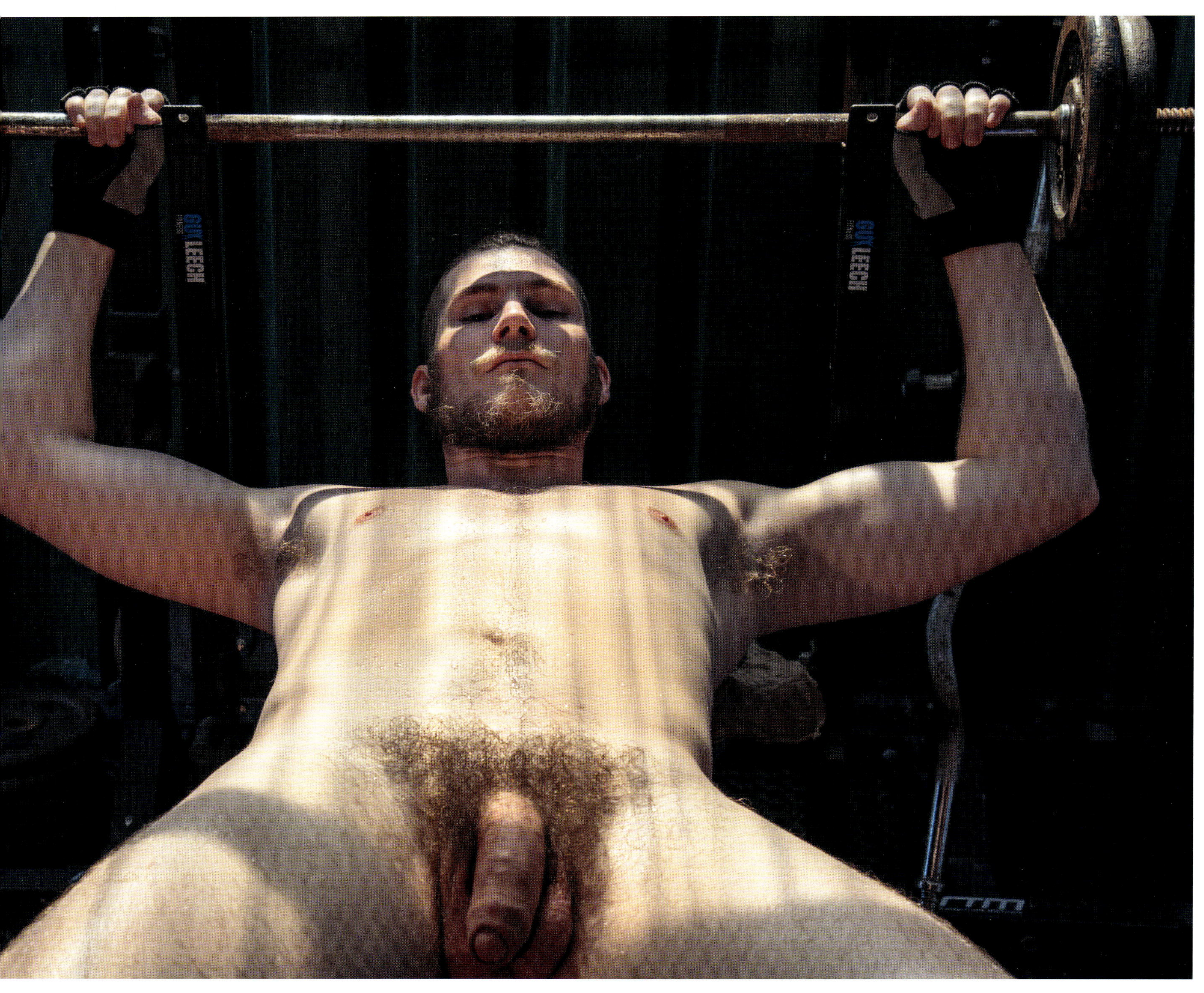
GUY LEECH
GUY LEECH

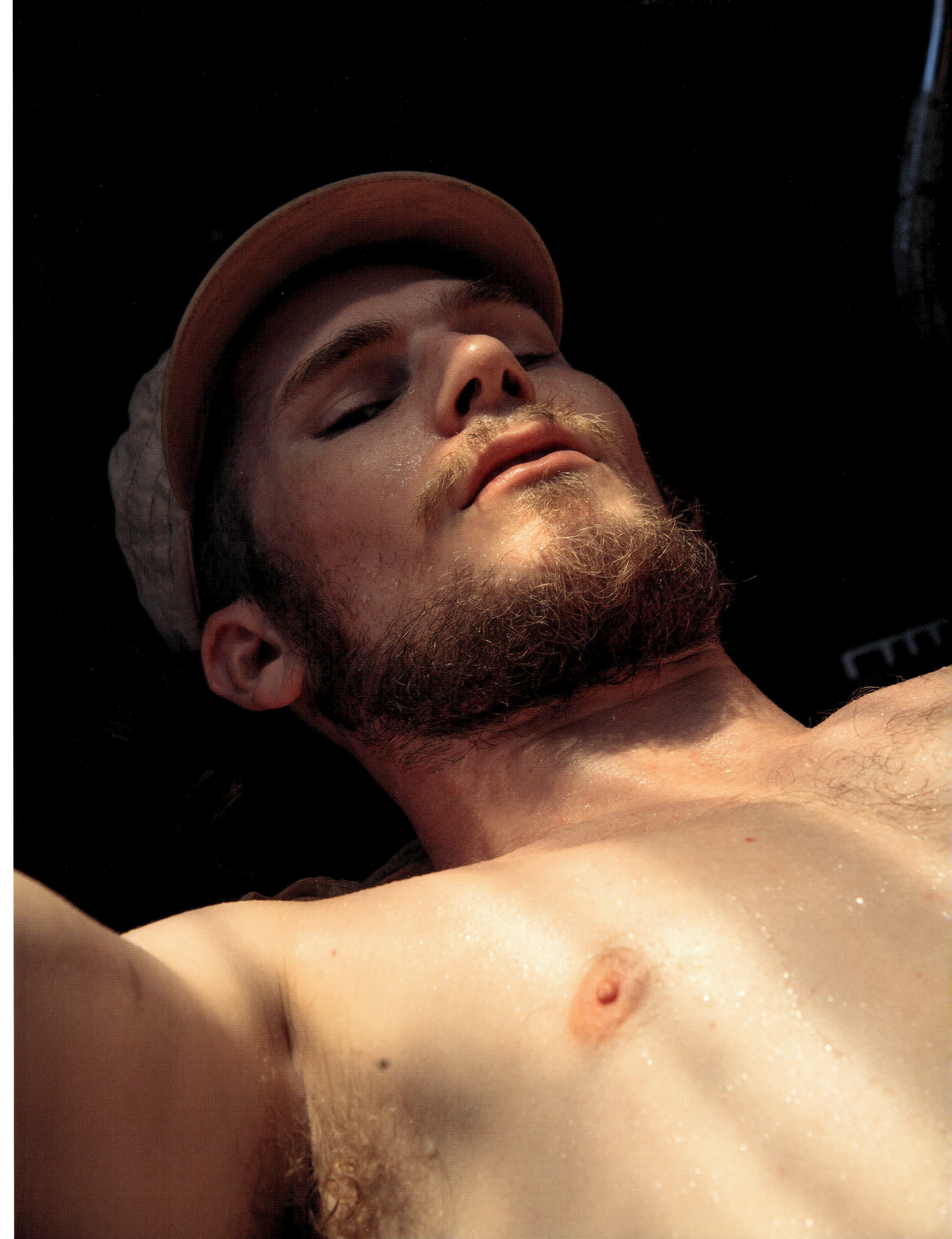

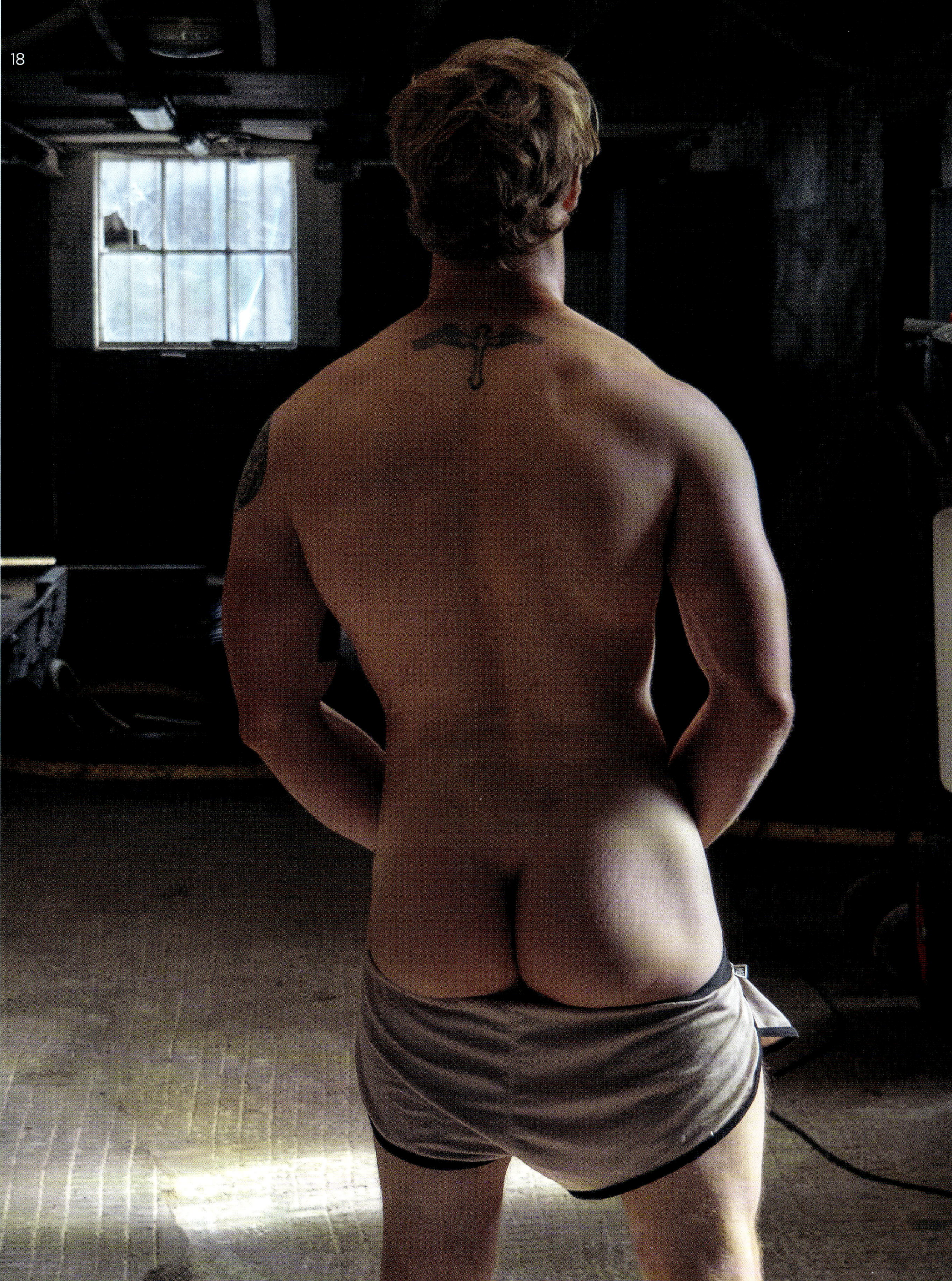

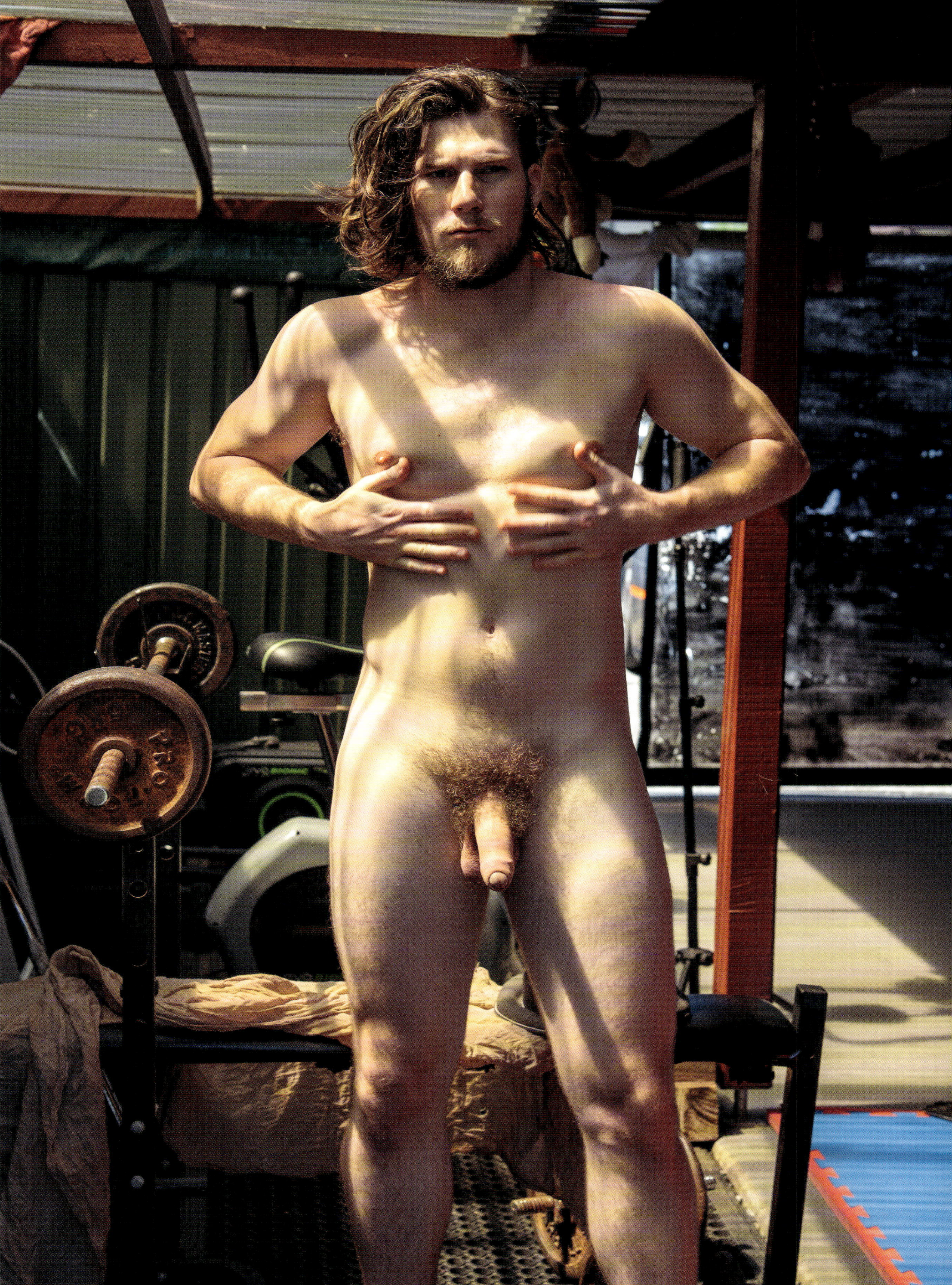
PRO

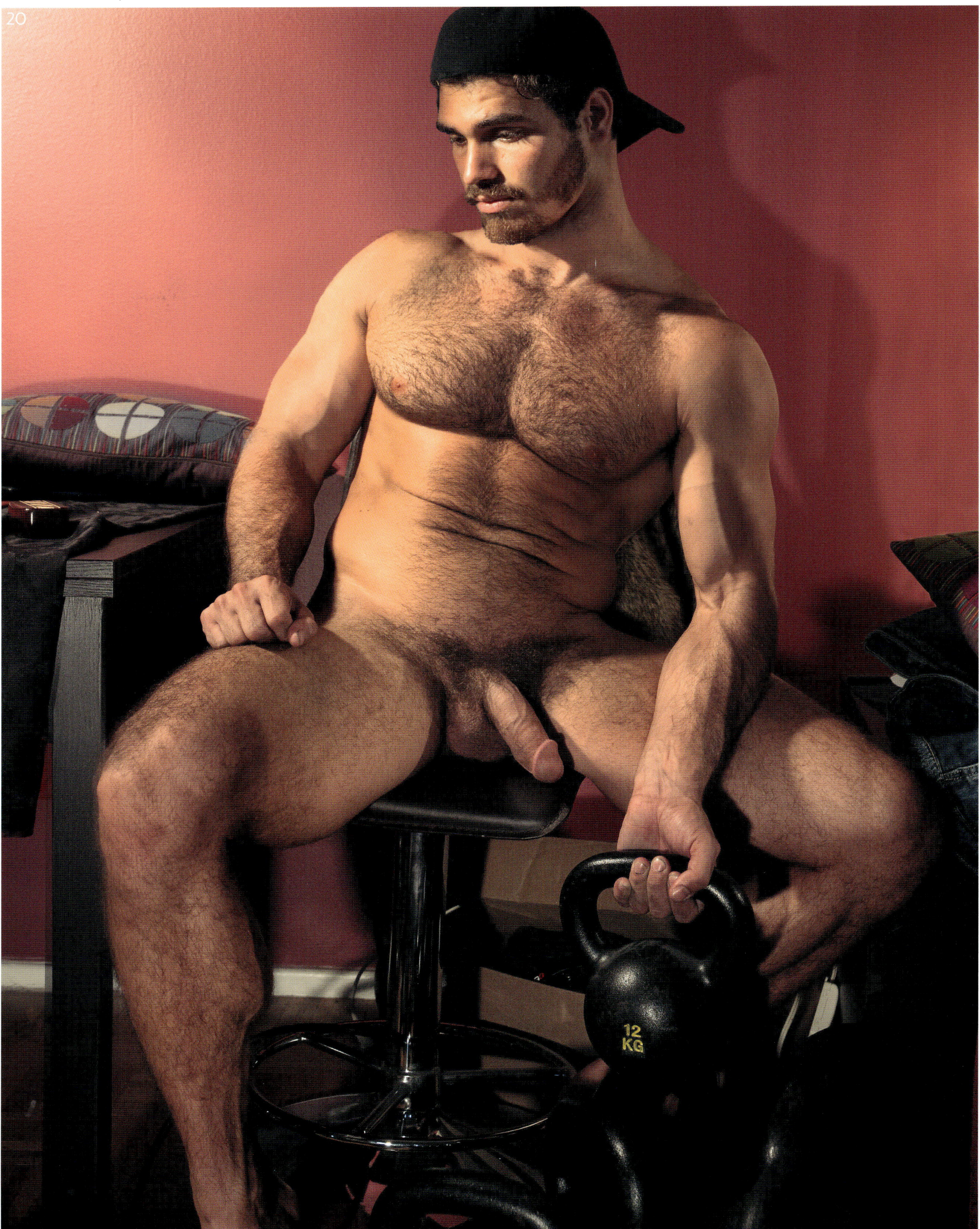
12
KG

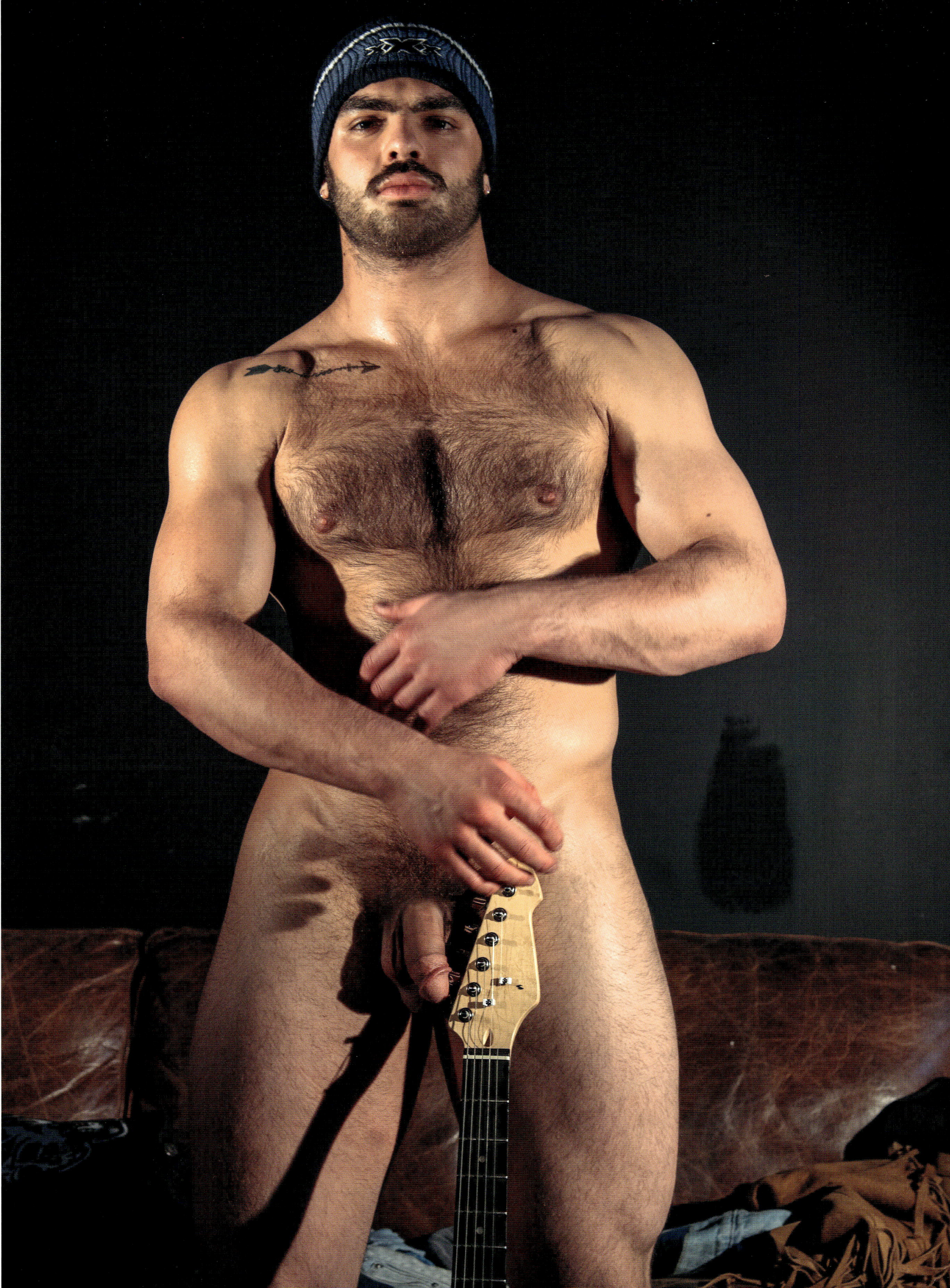

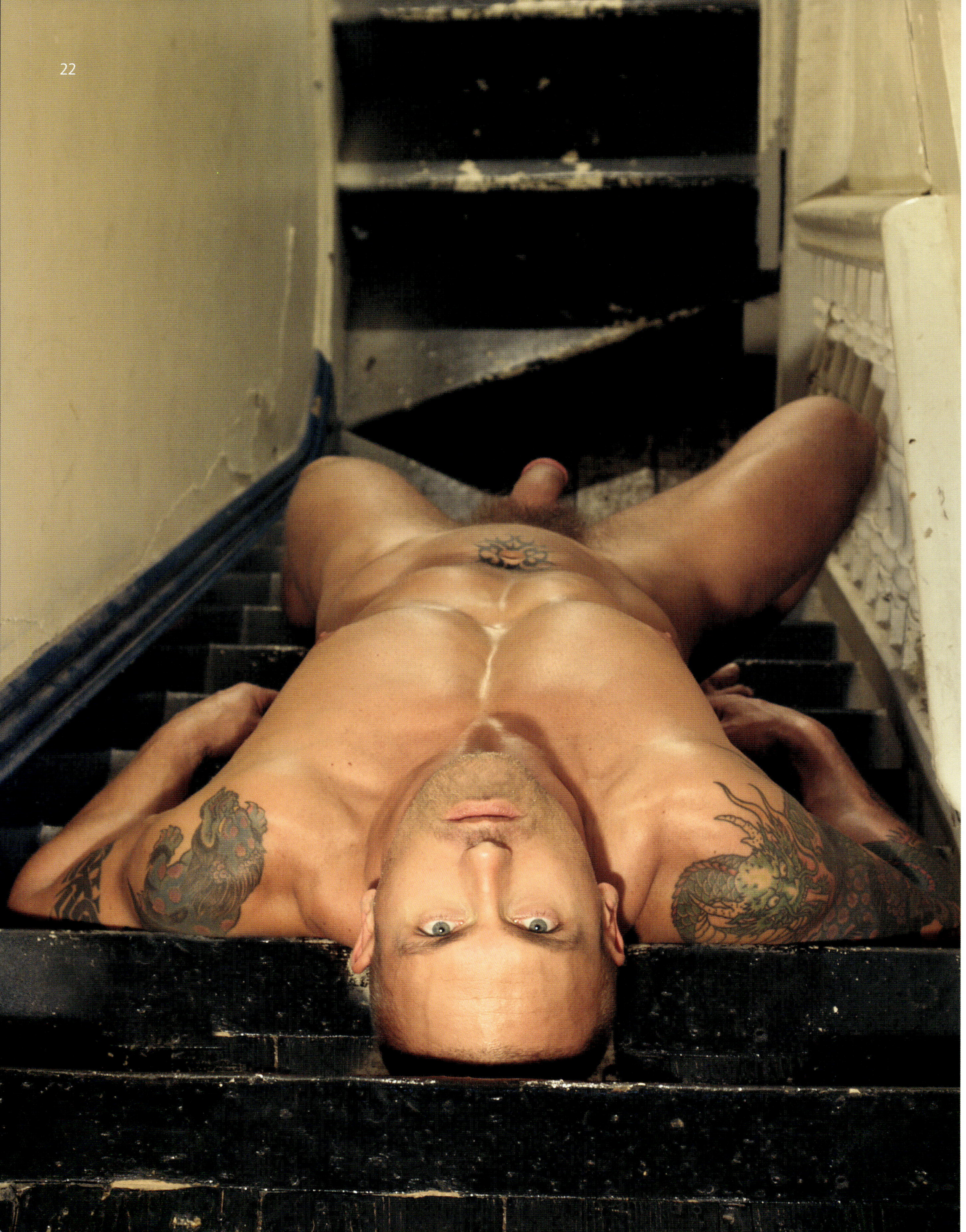

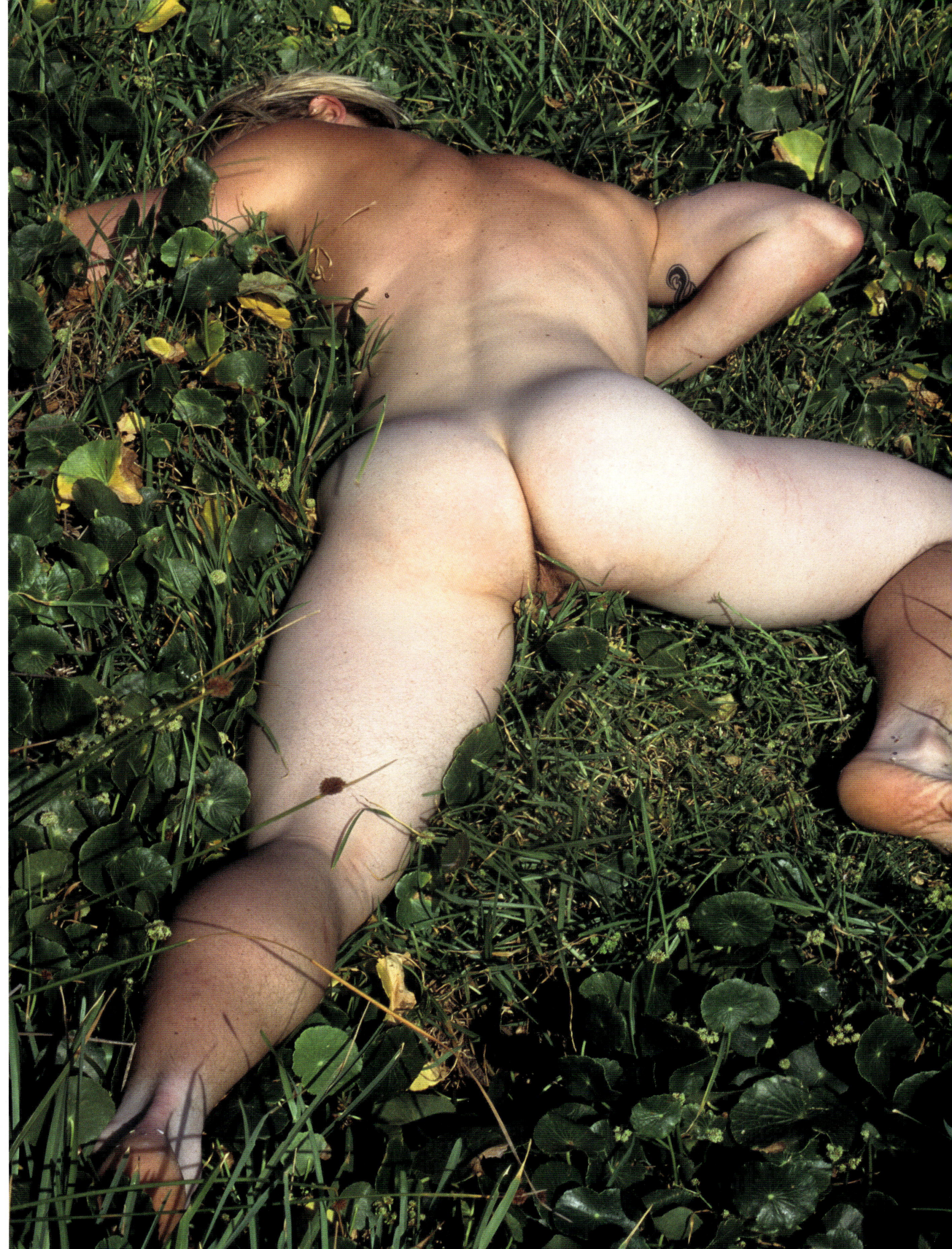

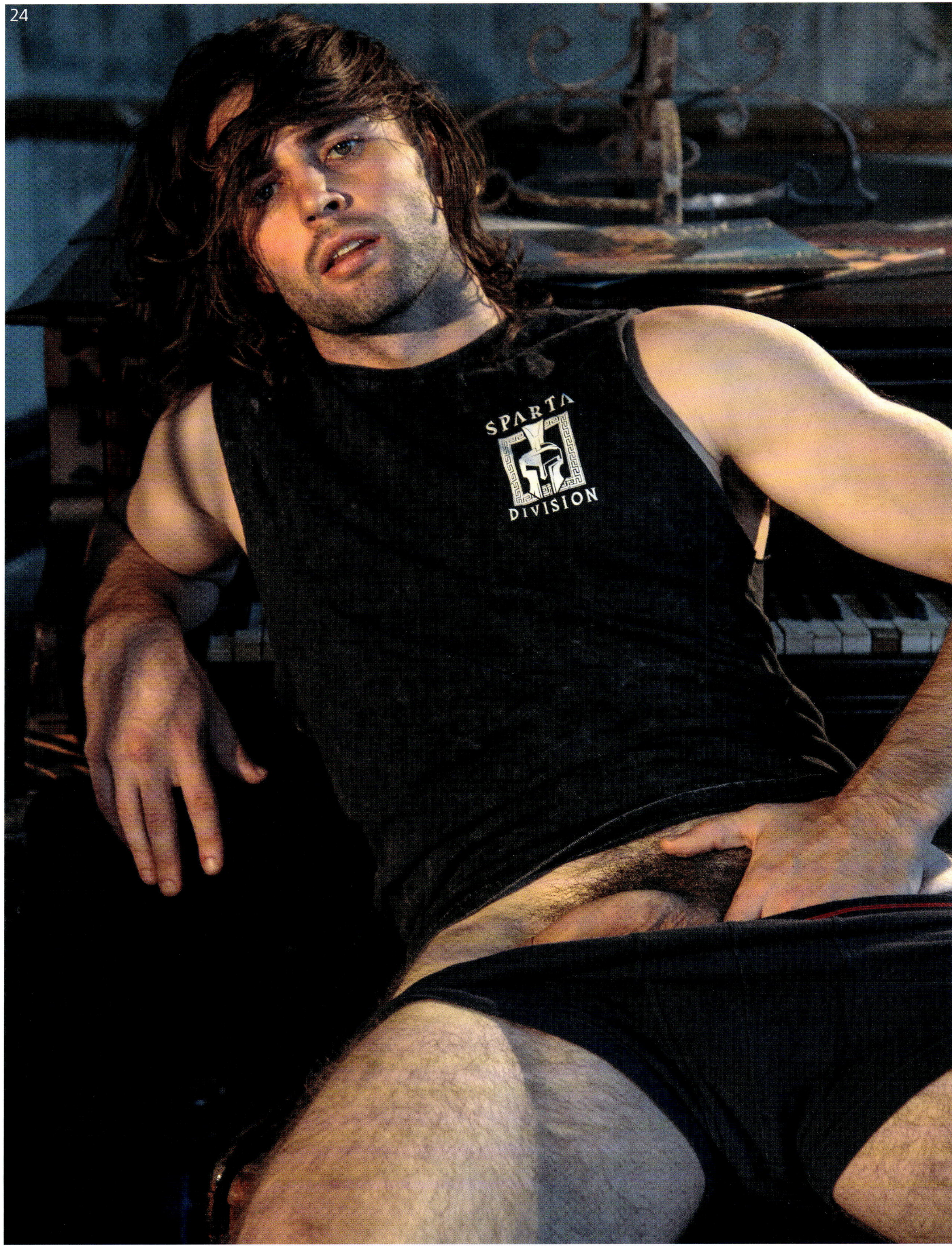
SPARTA
DIVISION

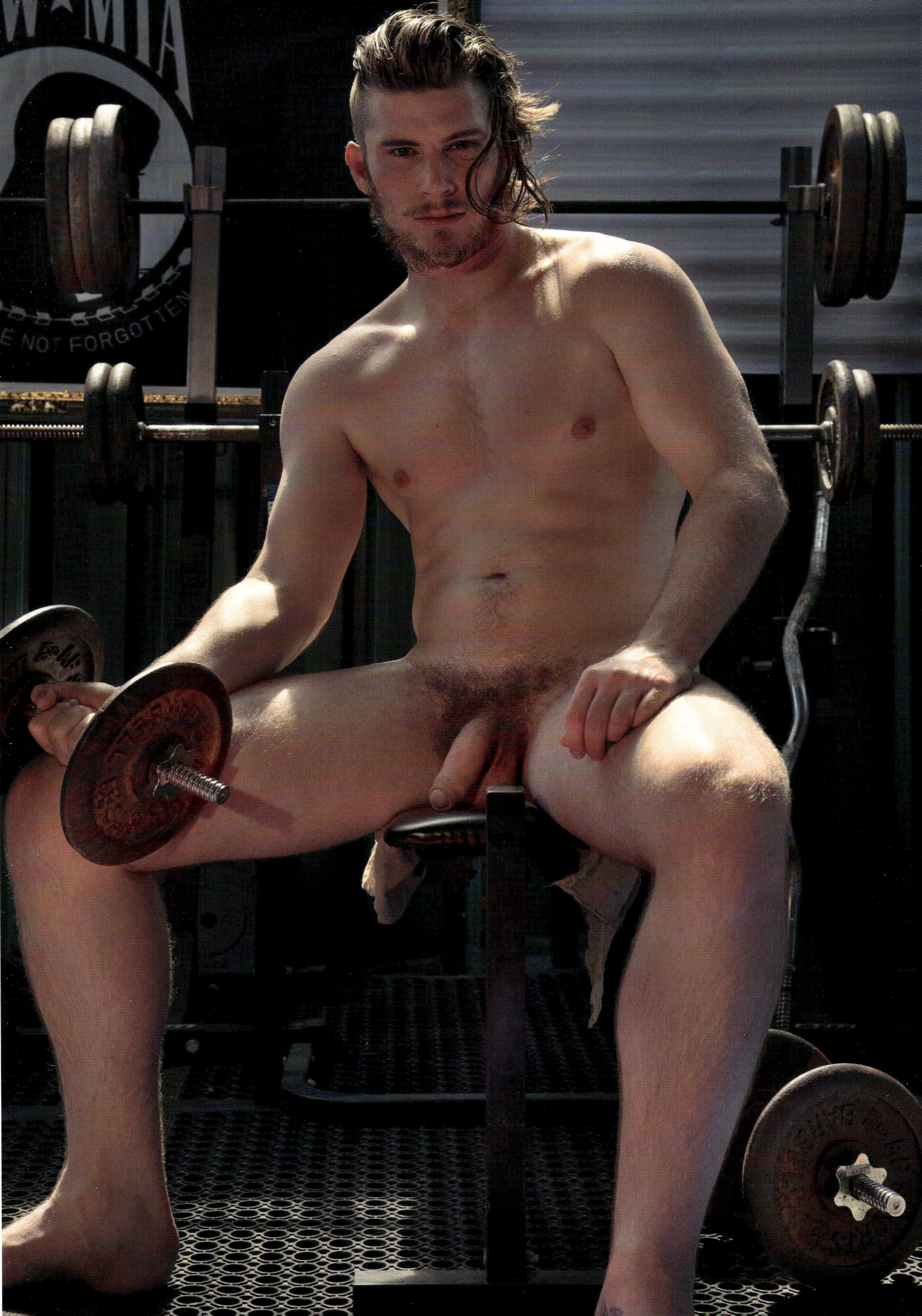

MIA
NOT FORGOTTEN

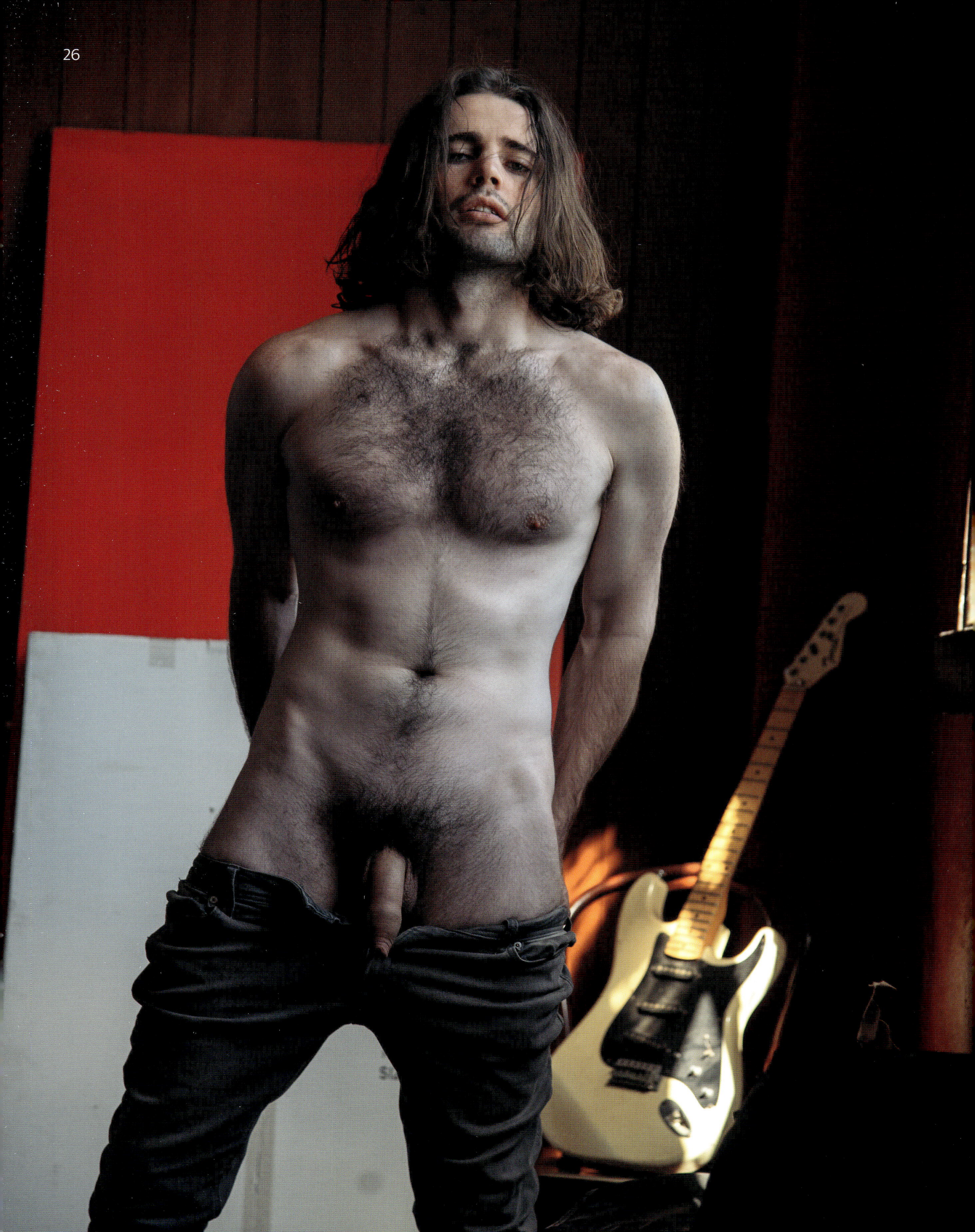

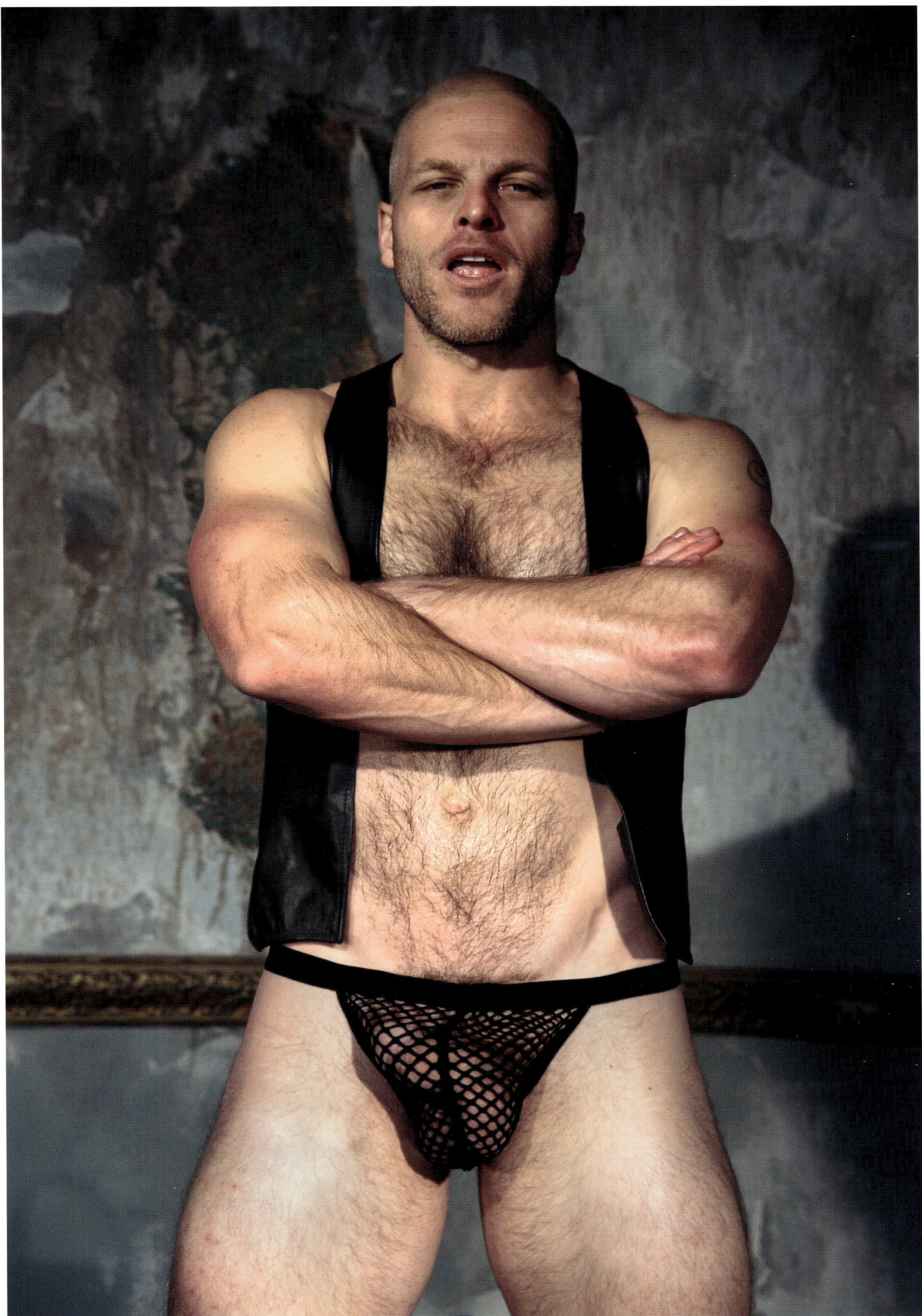

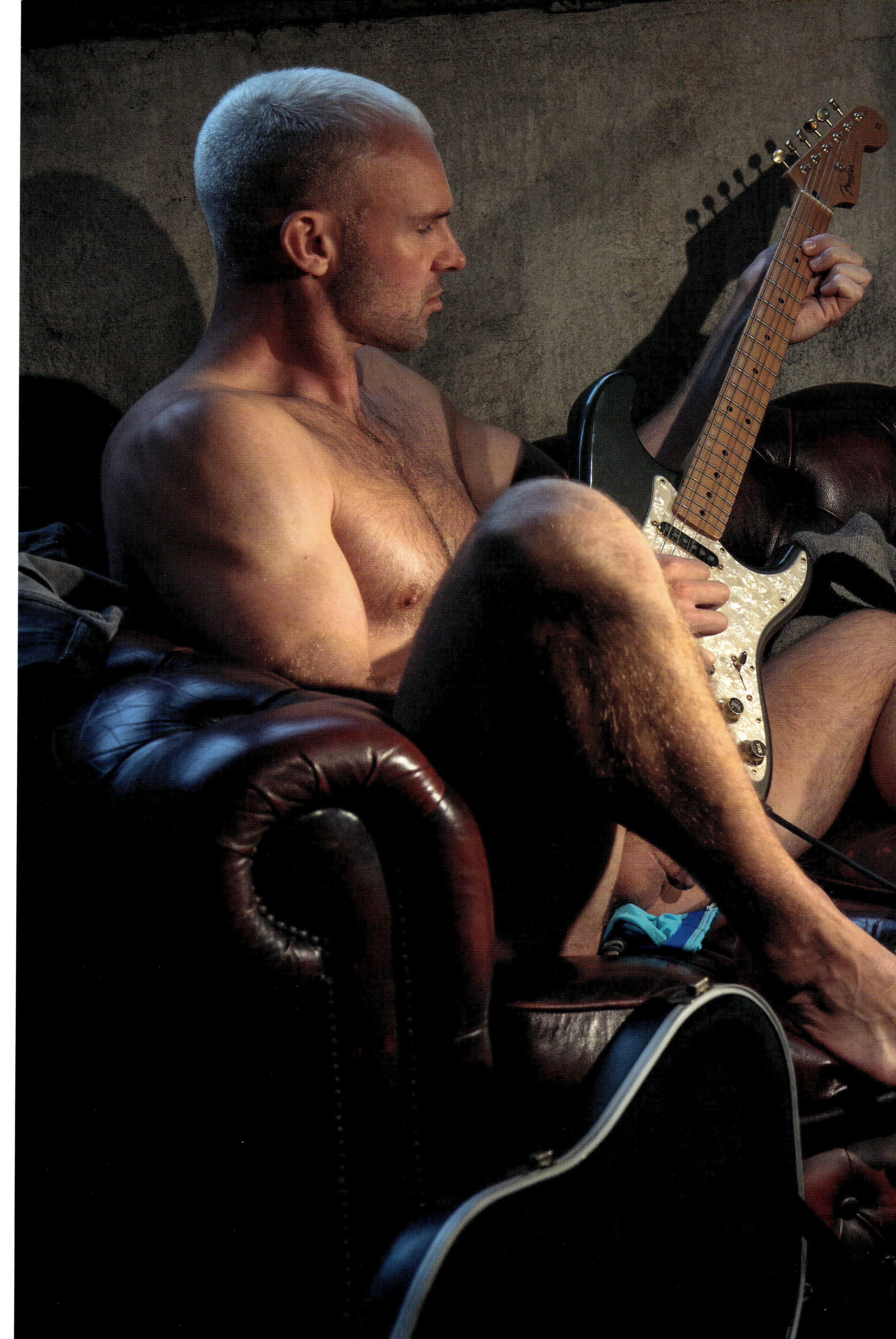

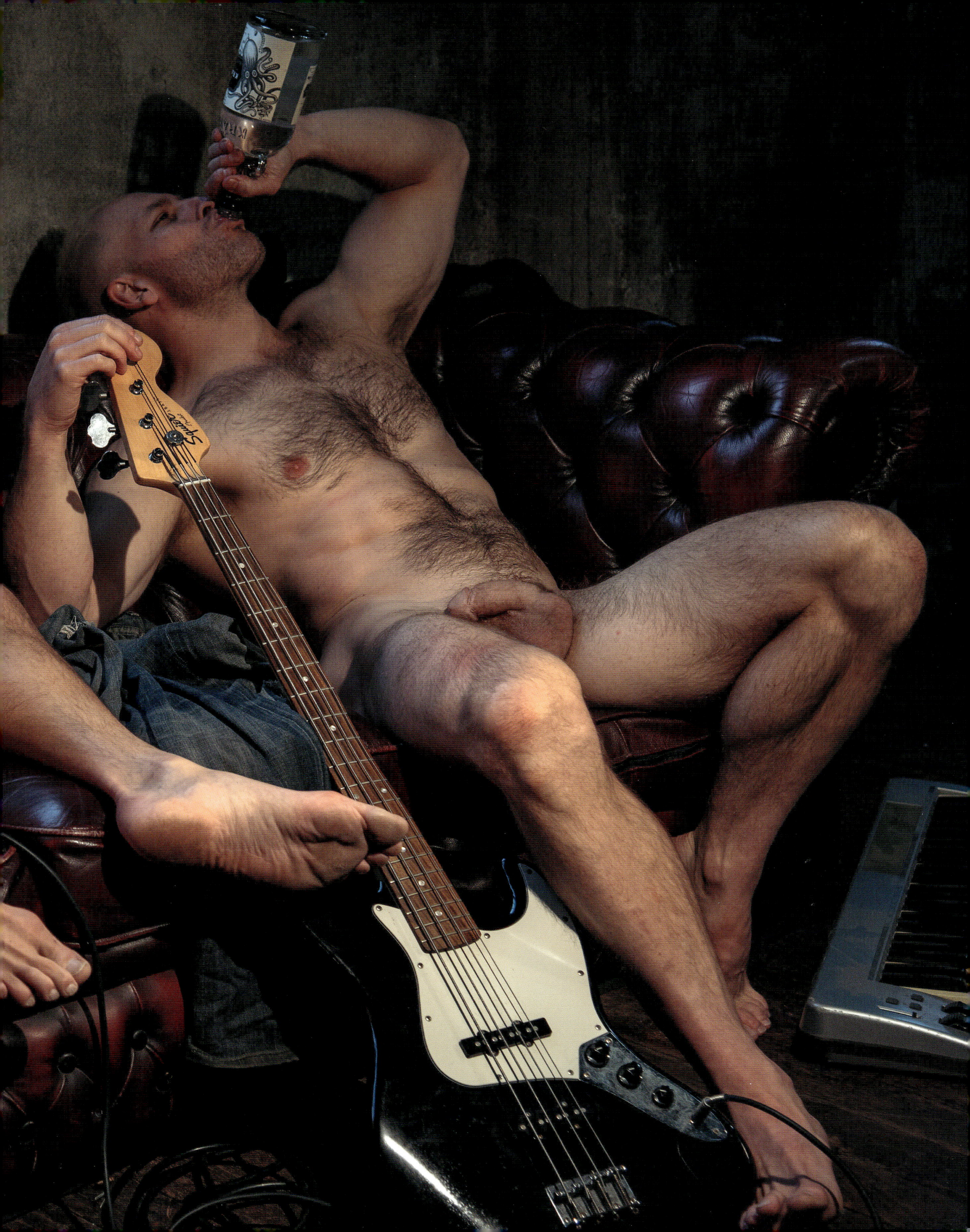

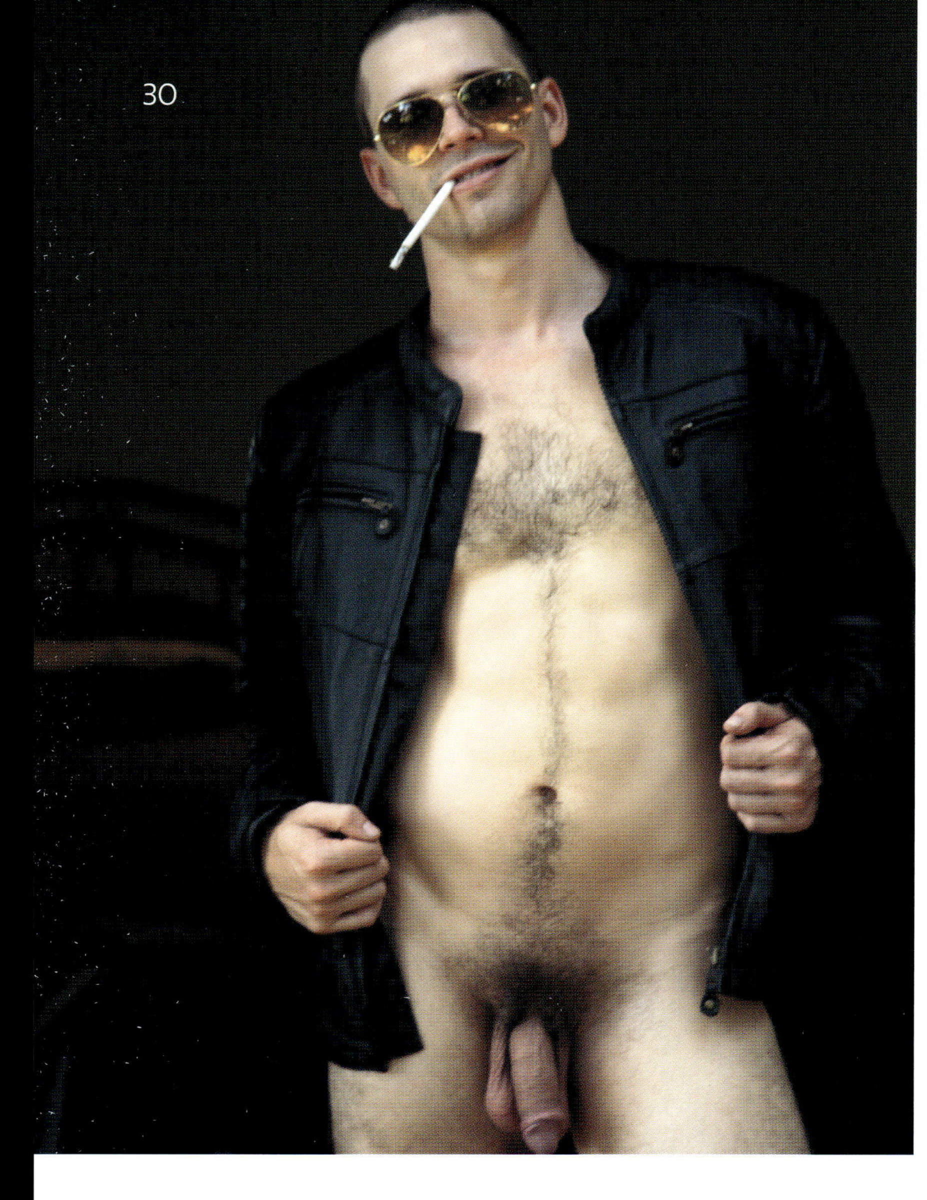

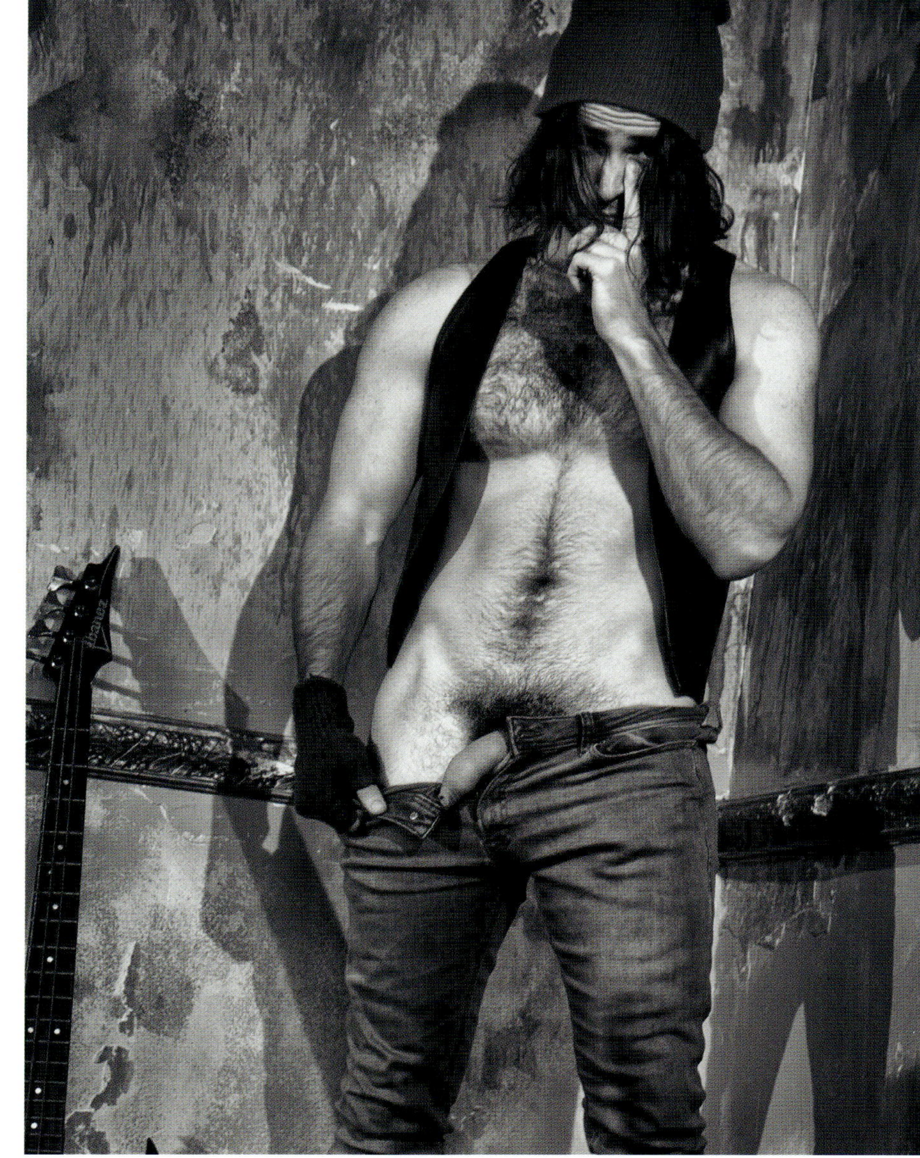

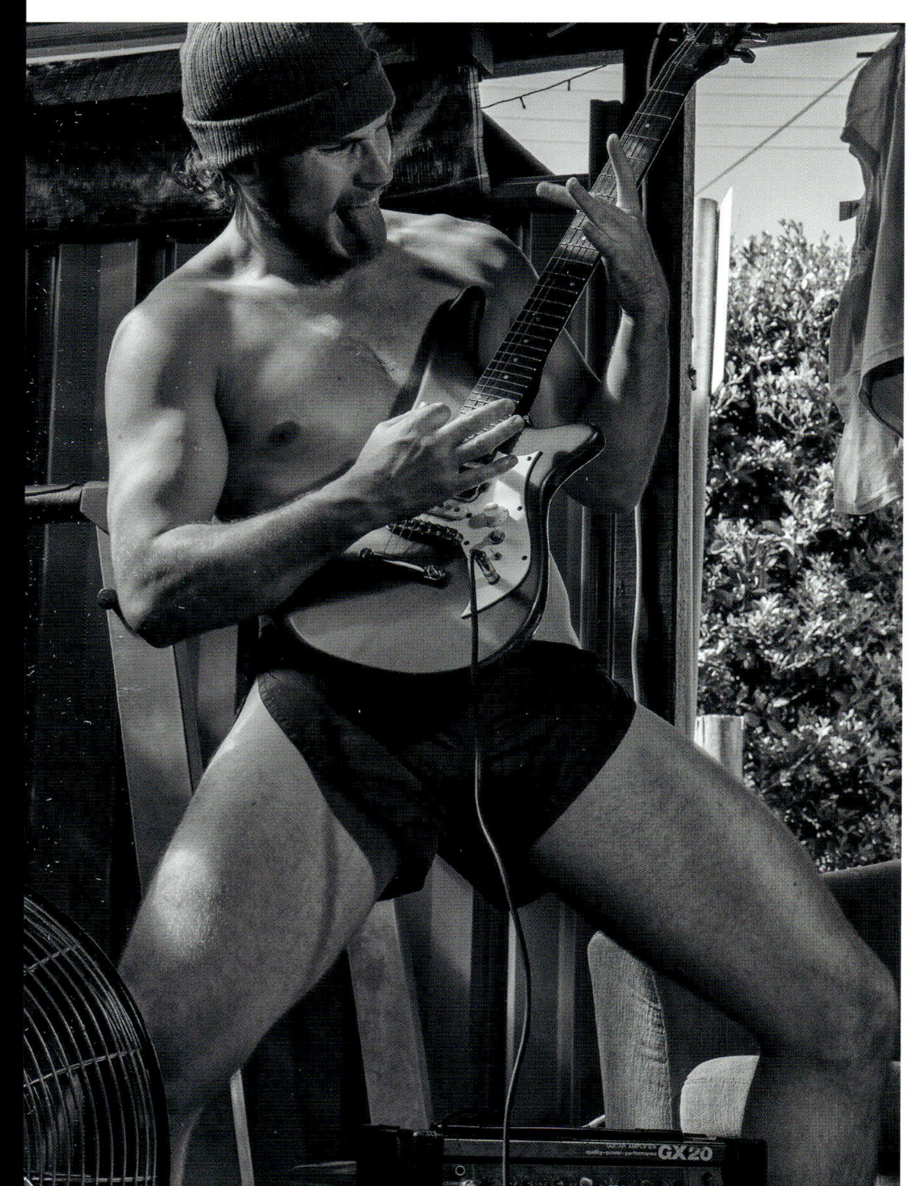
GX20

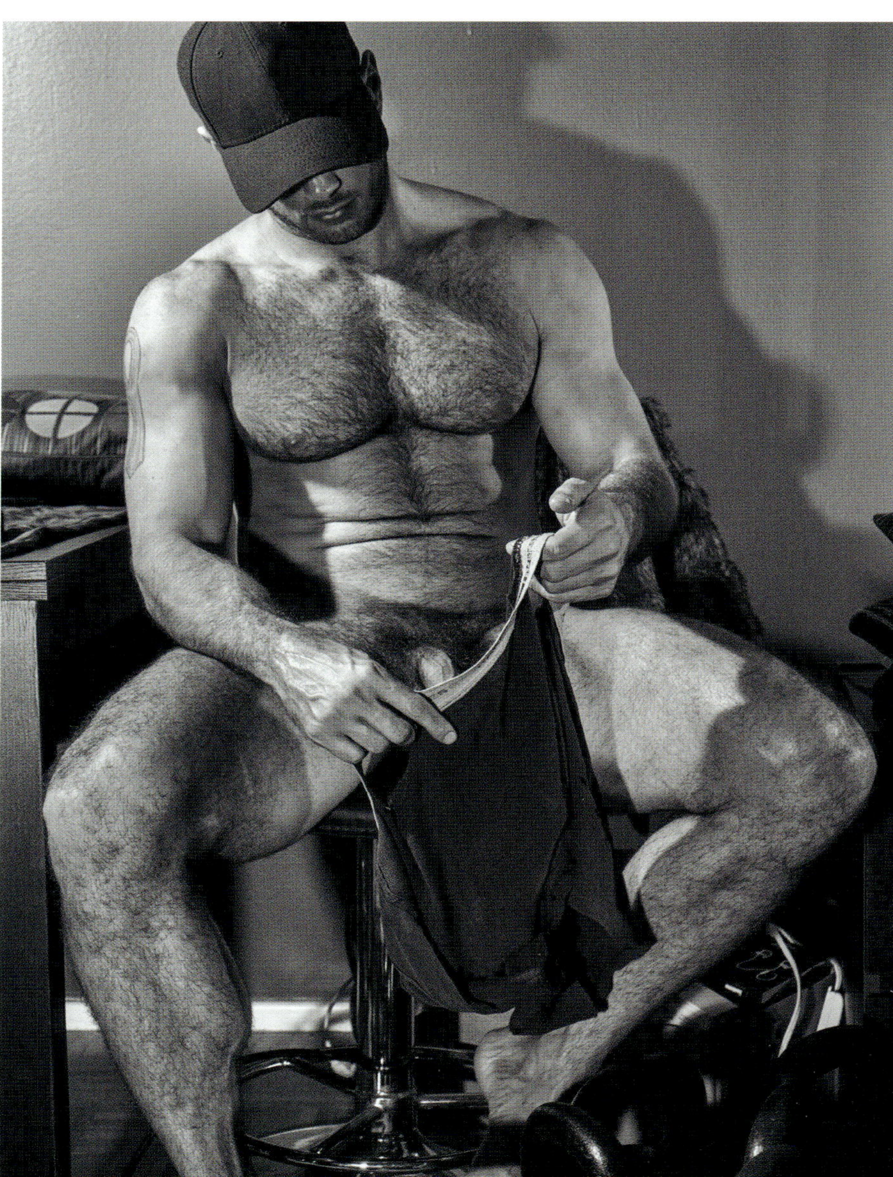

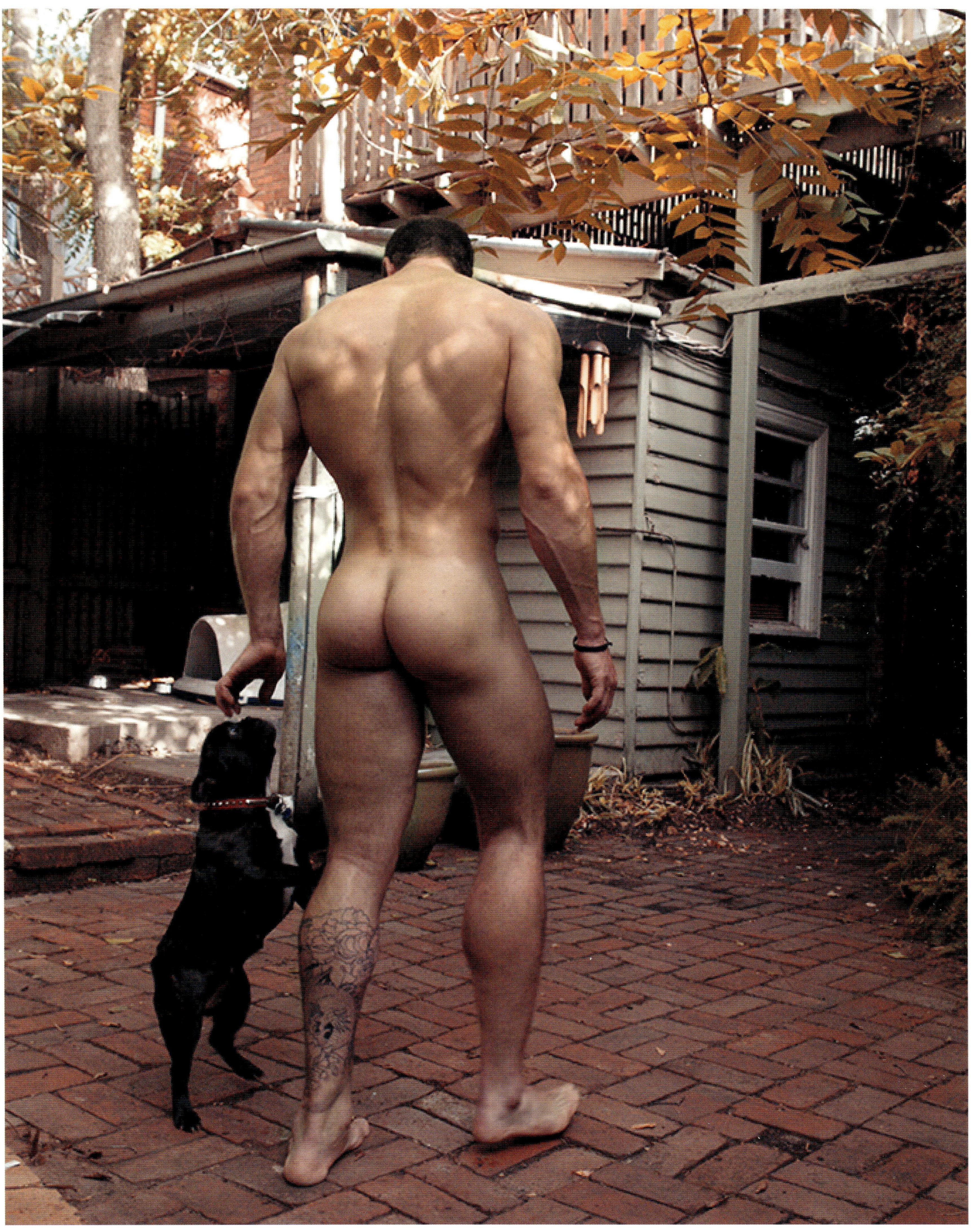

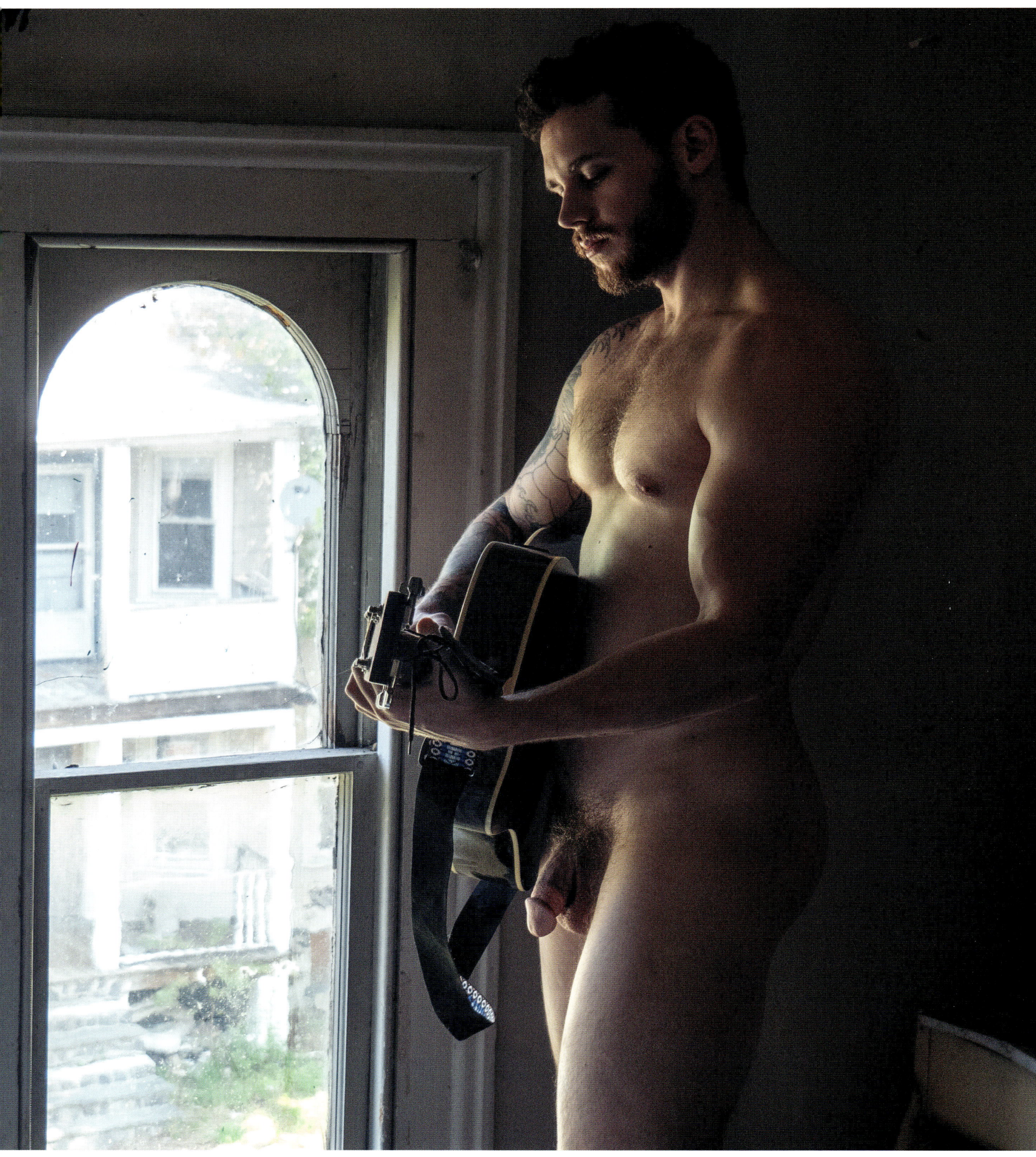

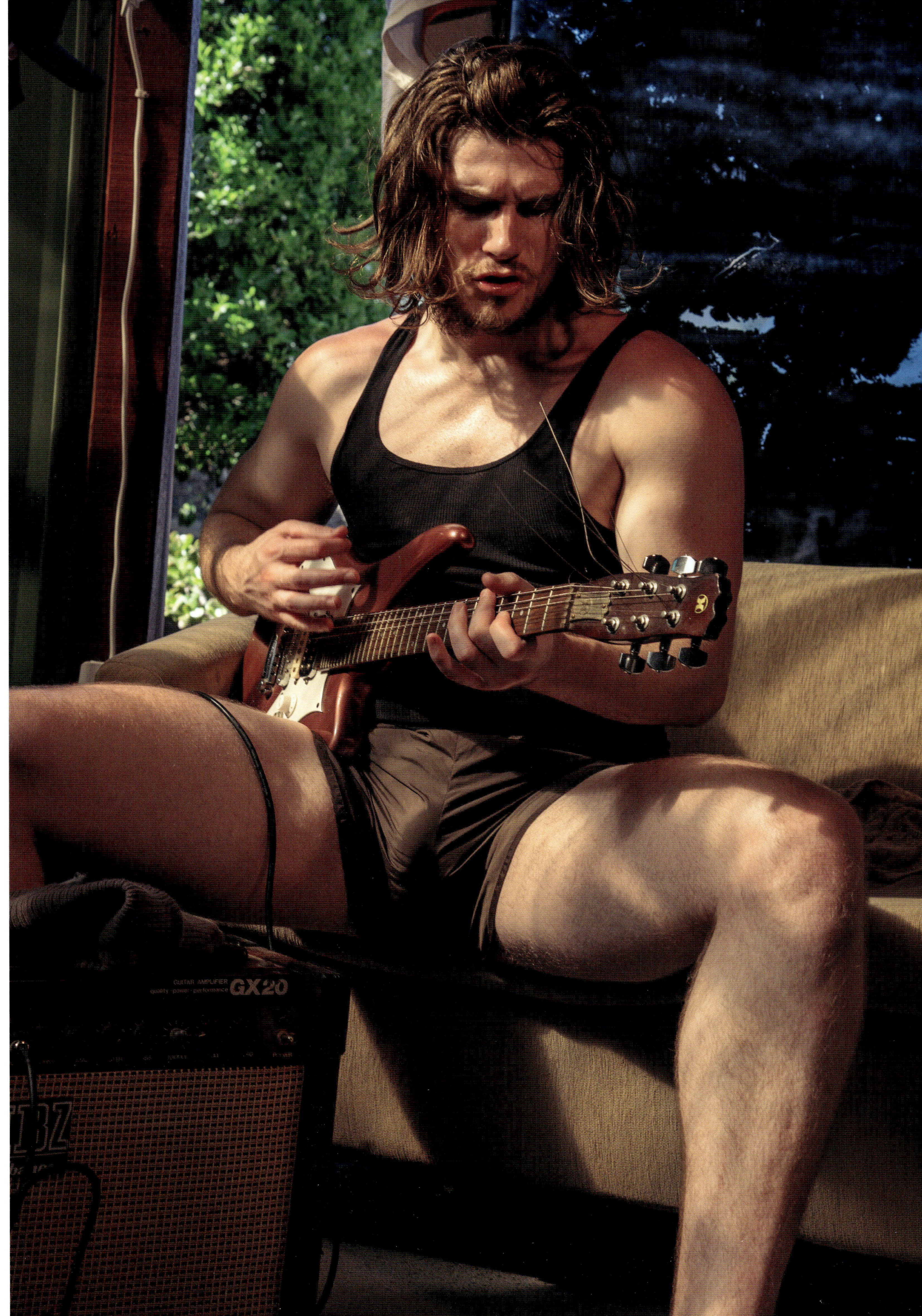
GUITAR AMPLIFIER
quality · power · performance
GX20

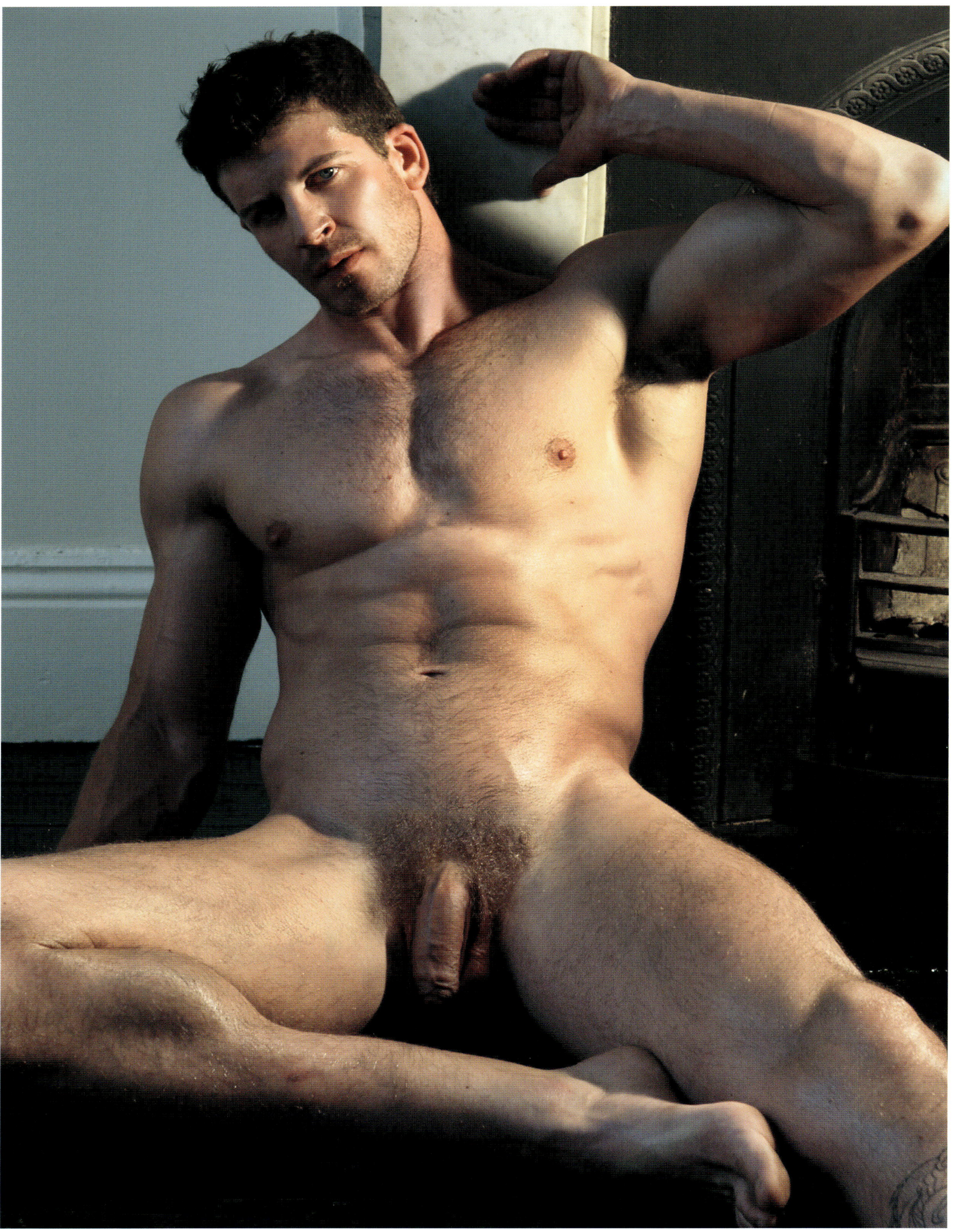

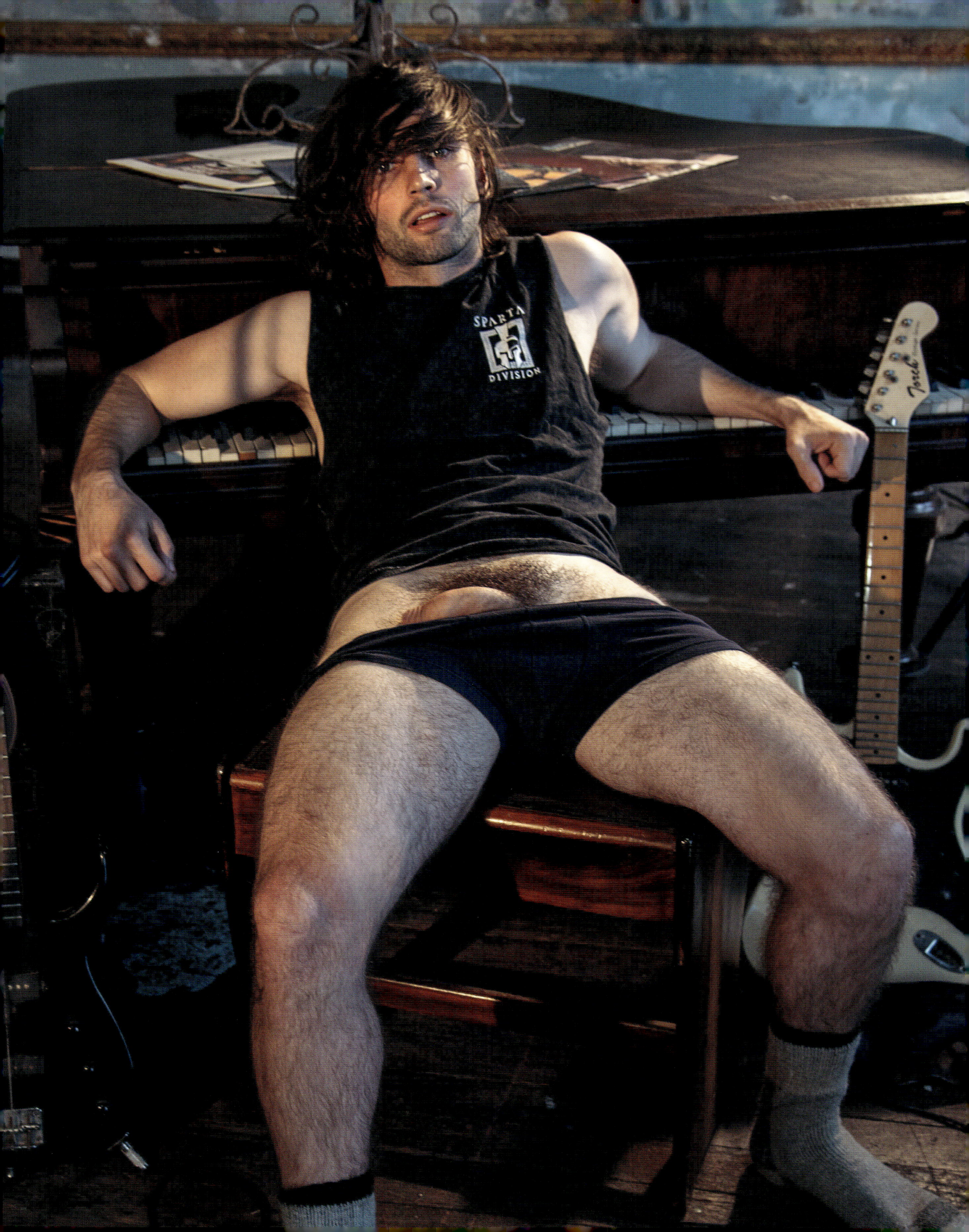
SPARTA
DIVISION

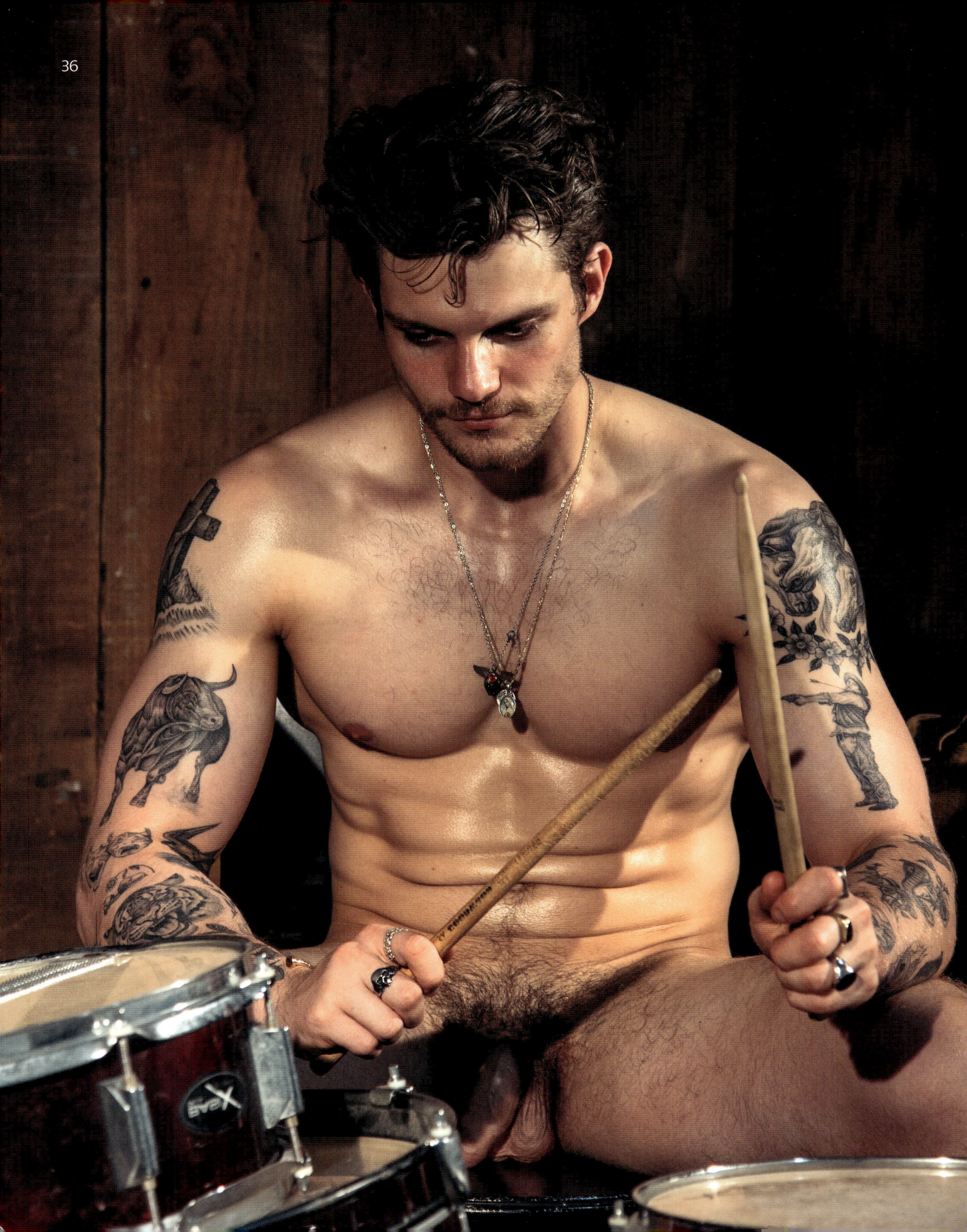

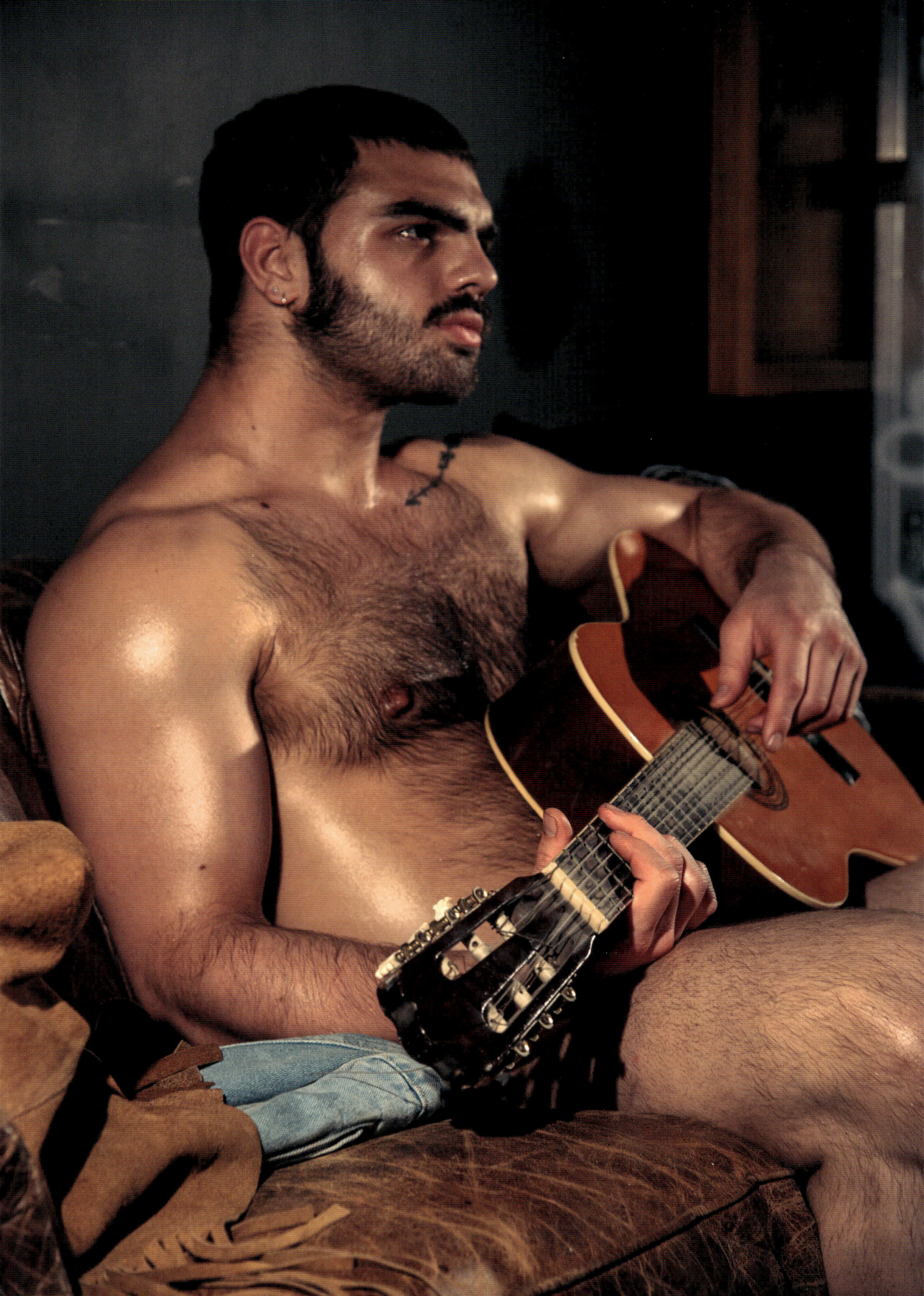

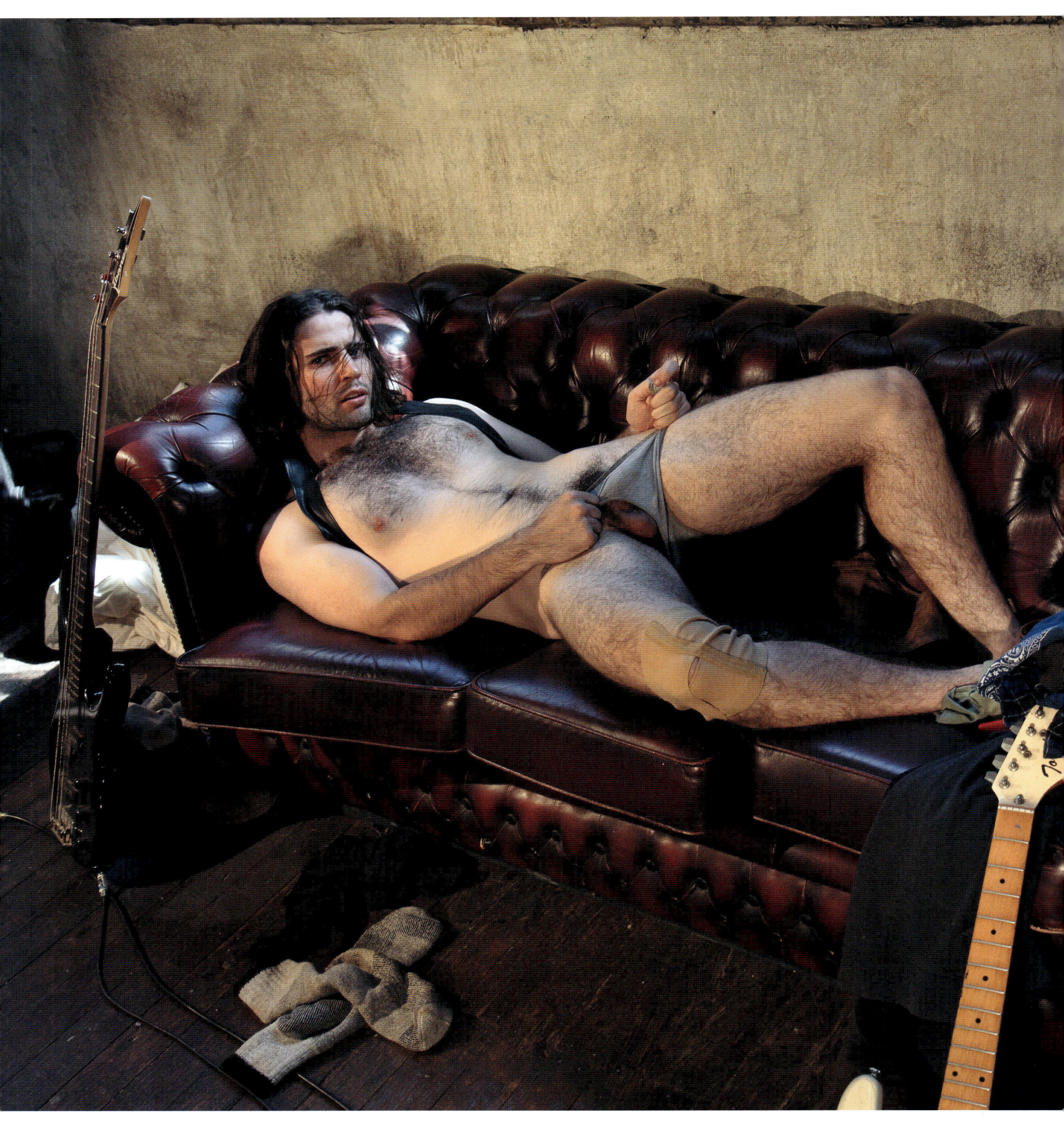

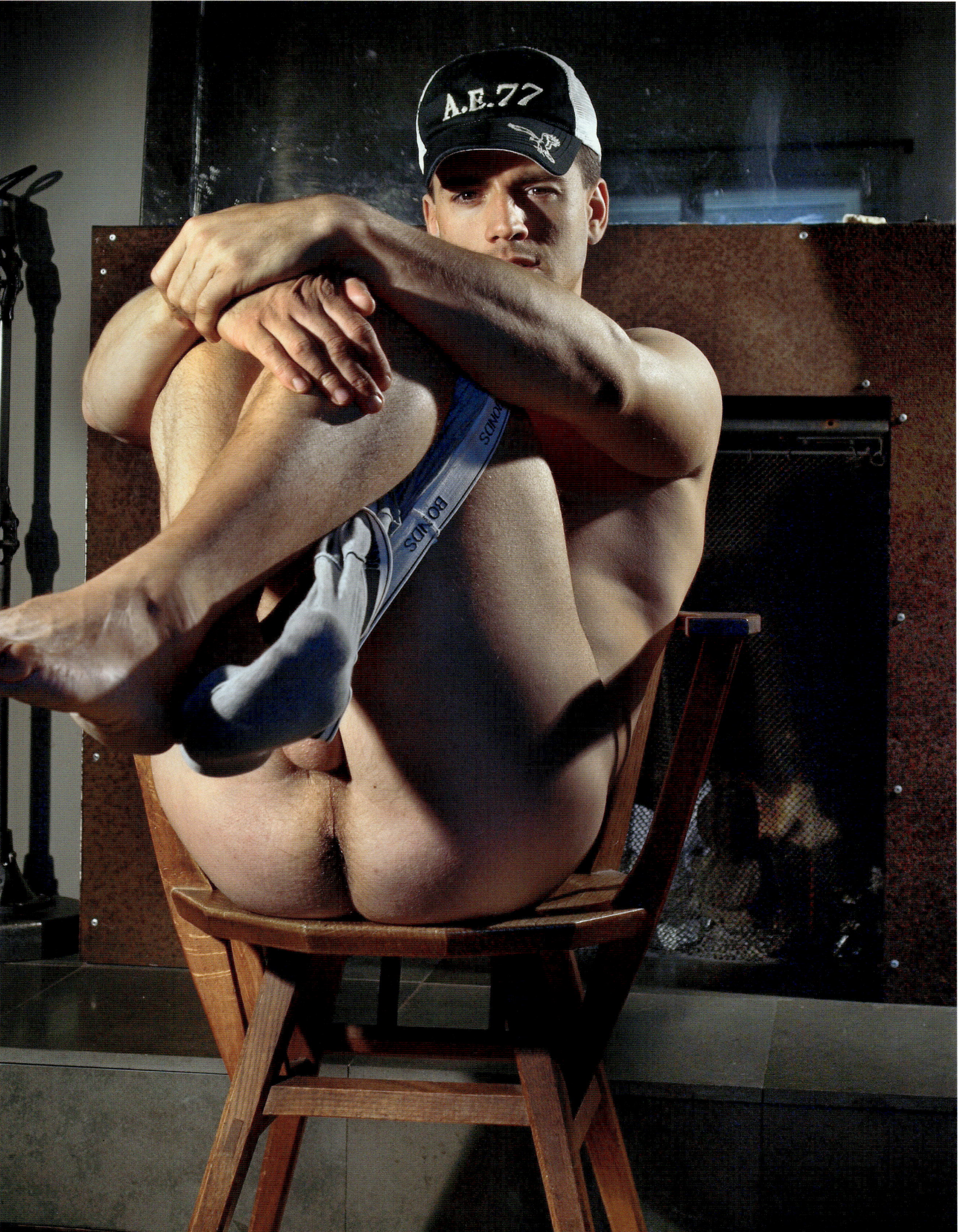
A.E.77
BONDS

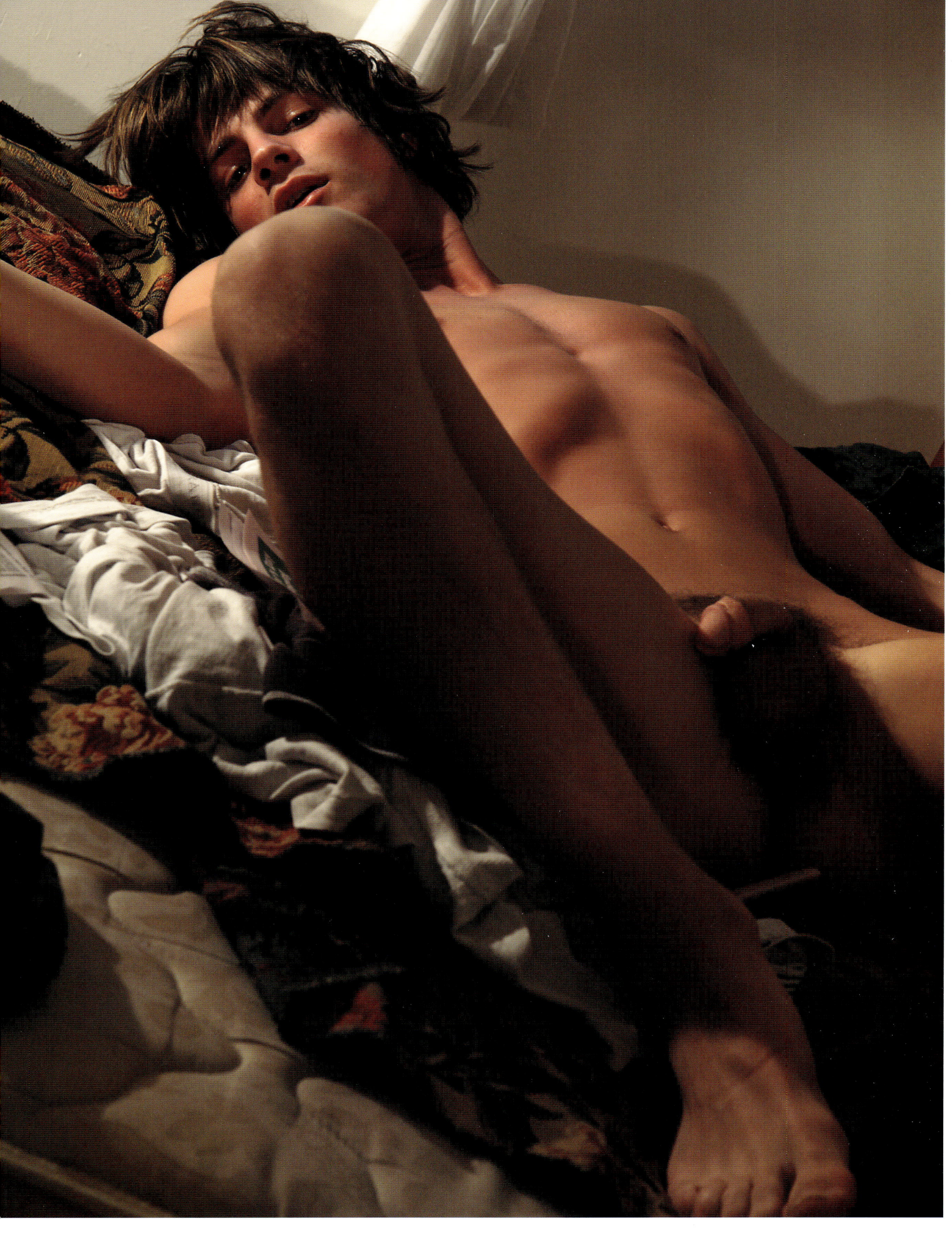

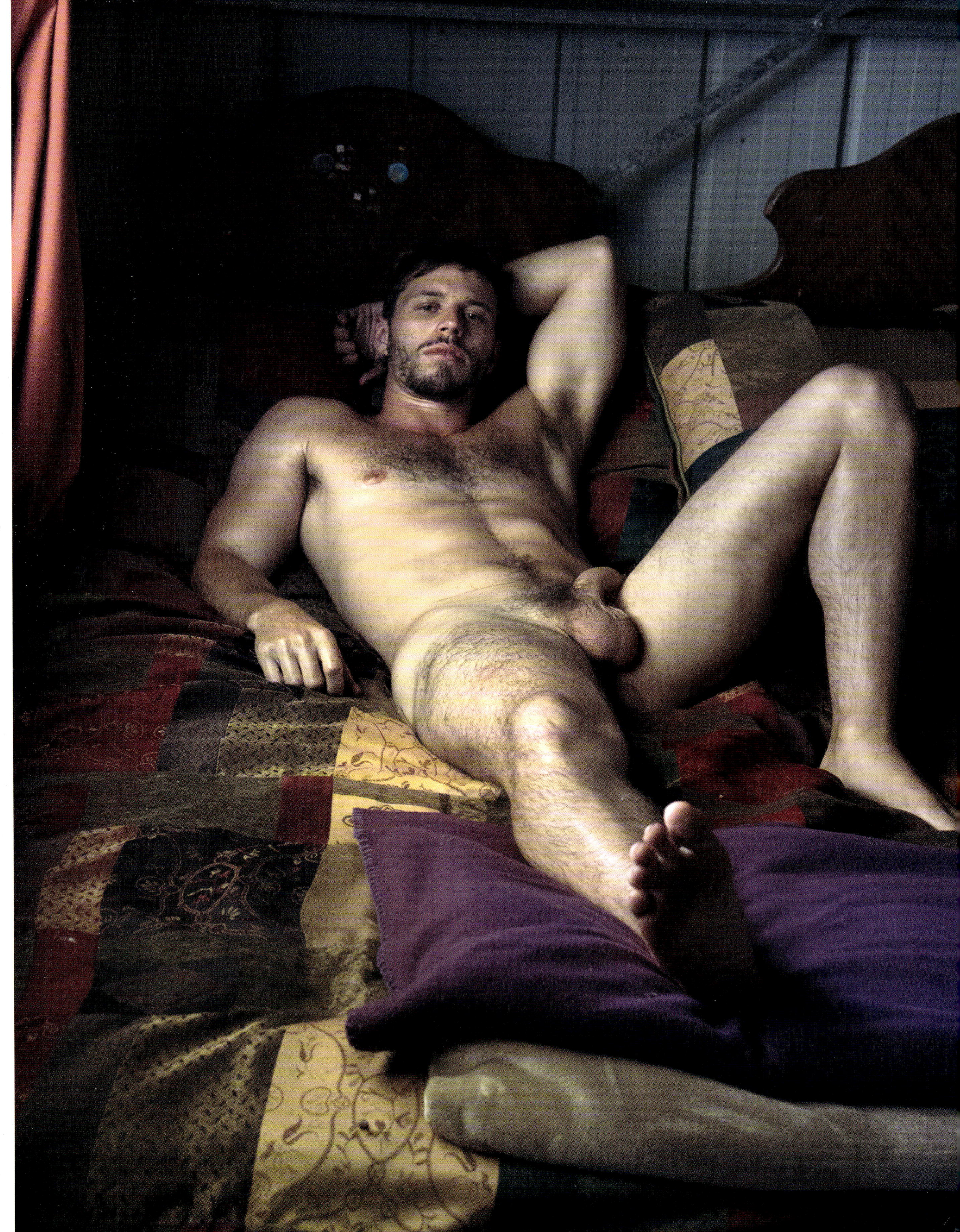

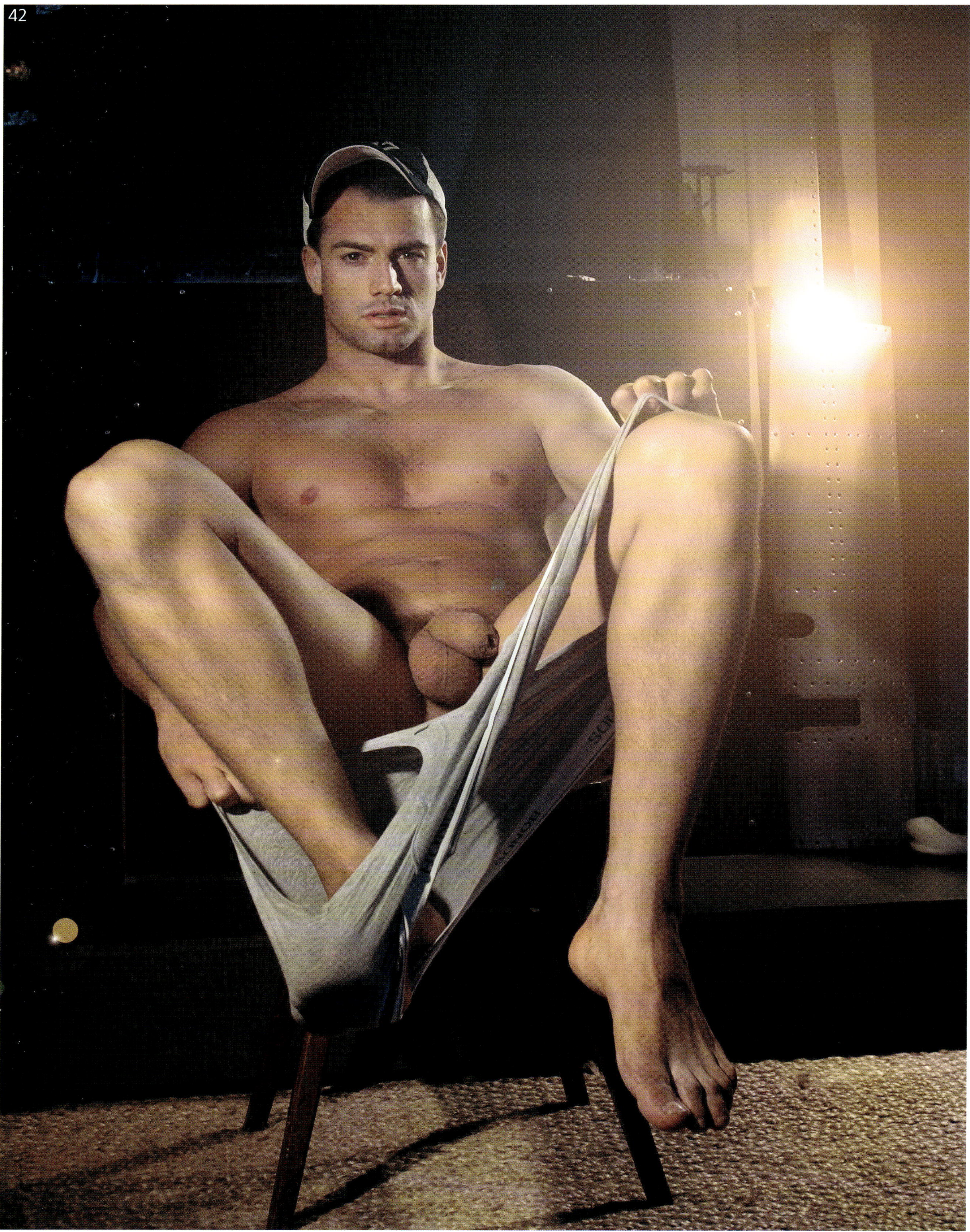

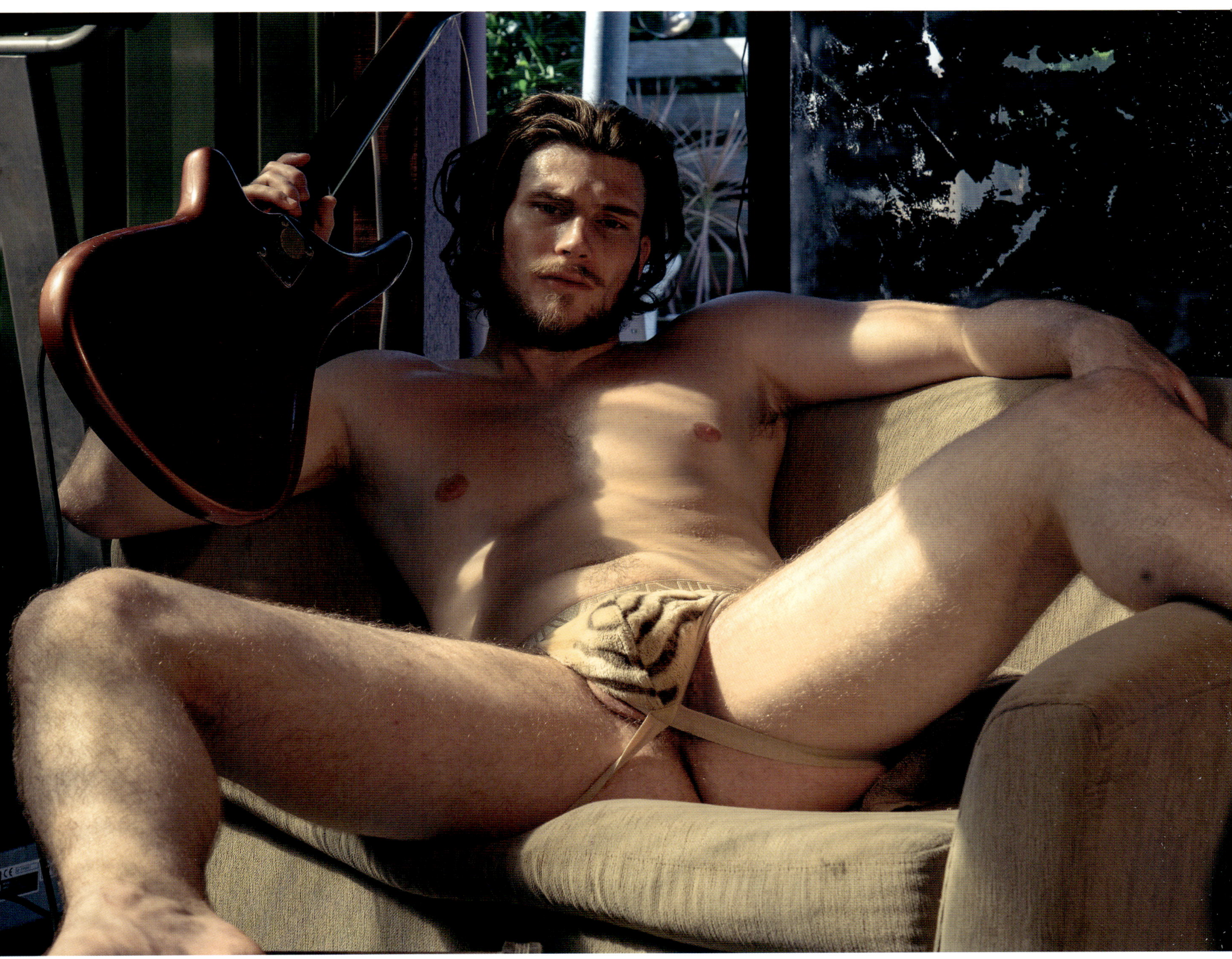

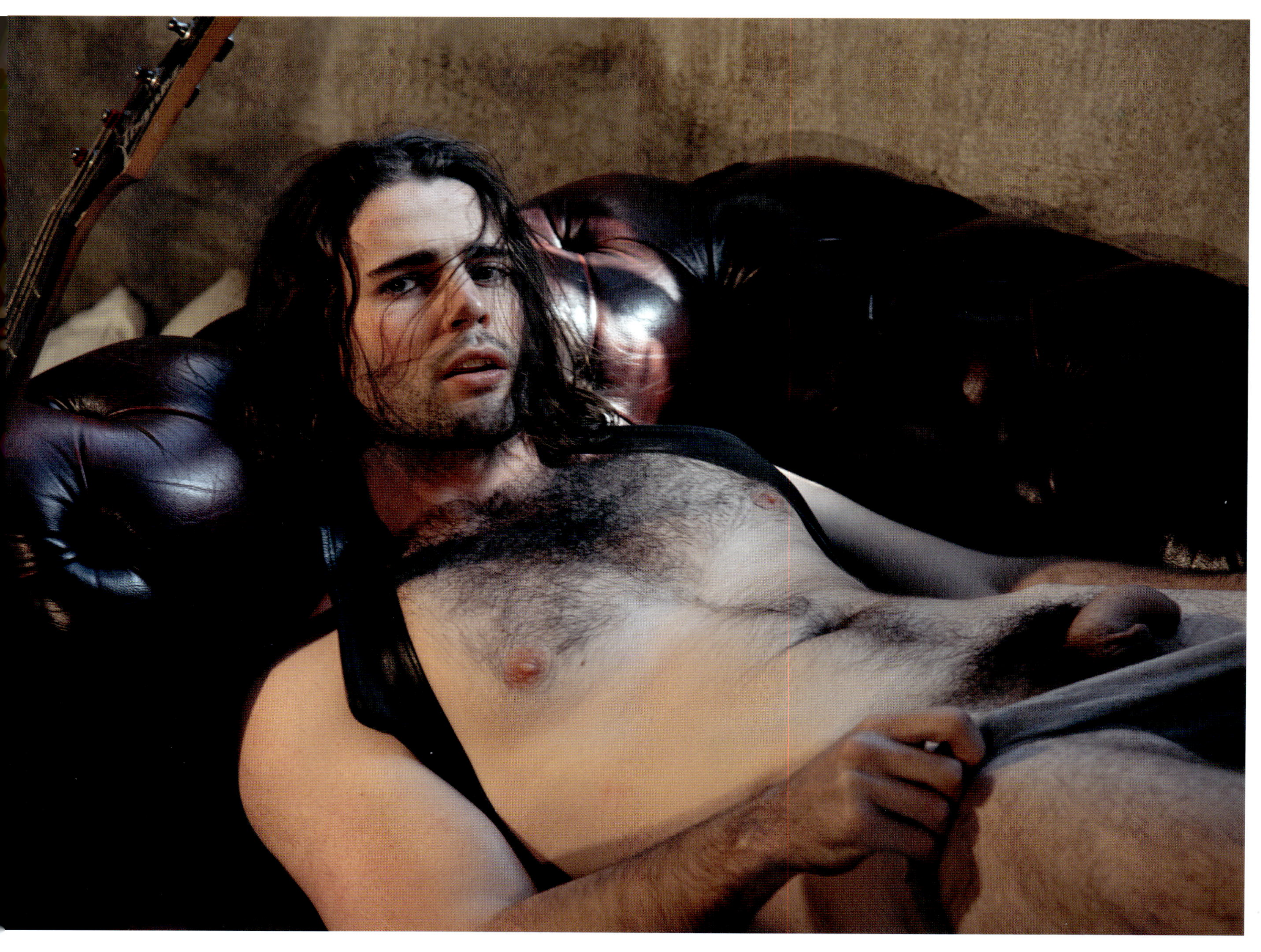

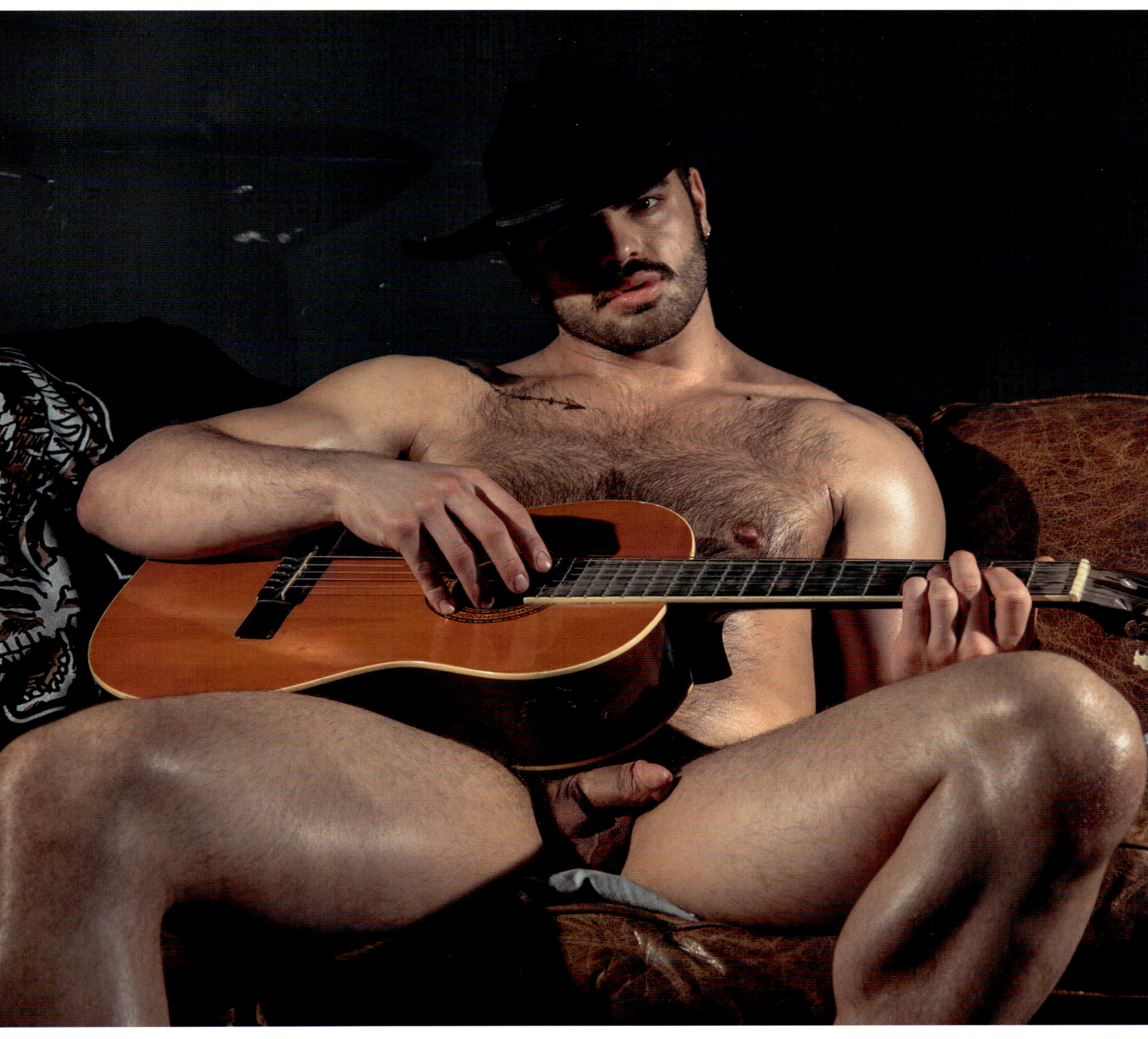

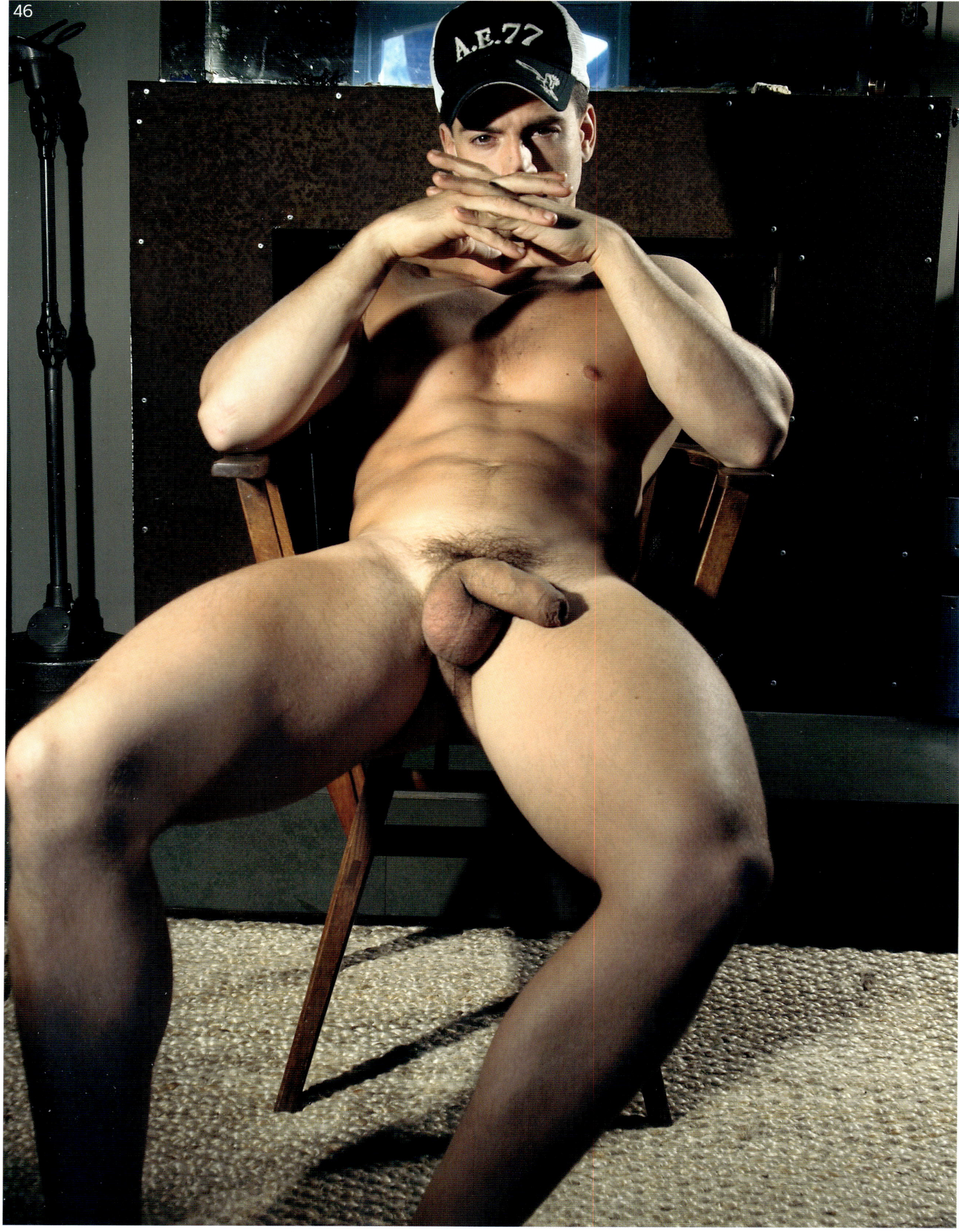
A.E.77

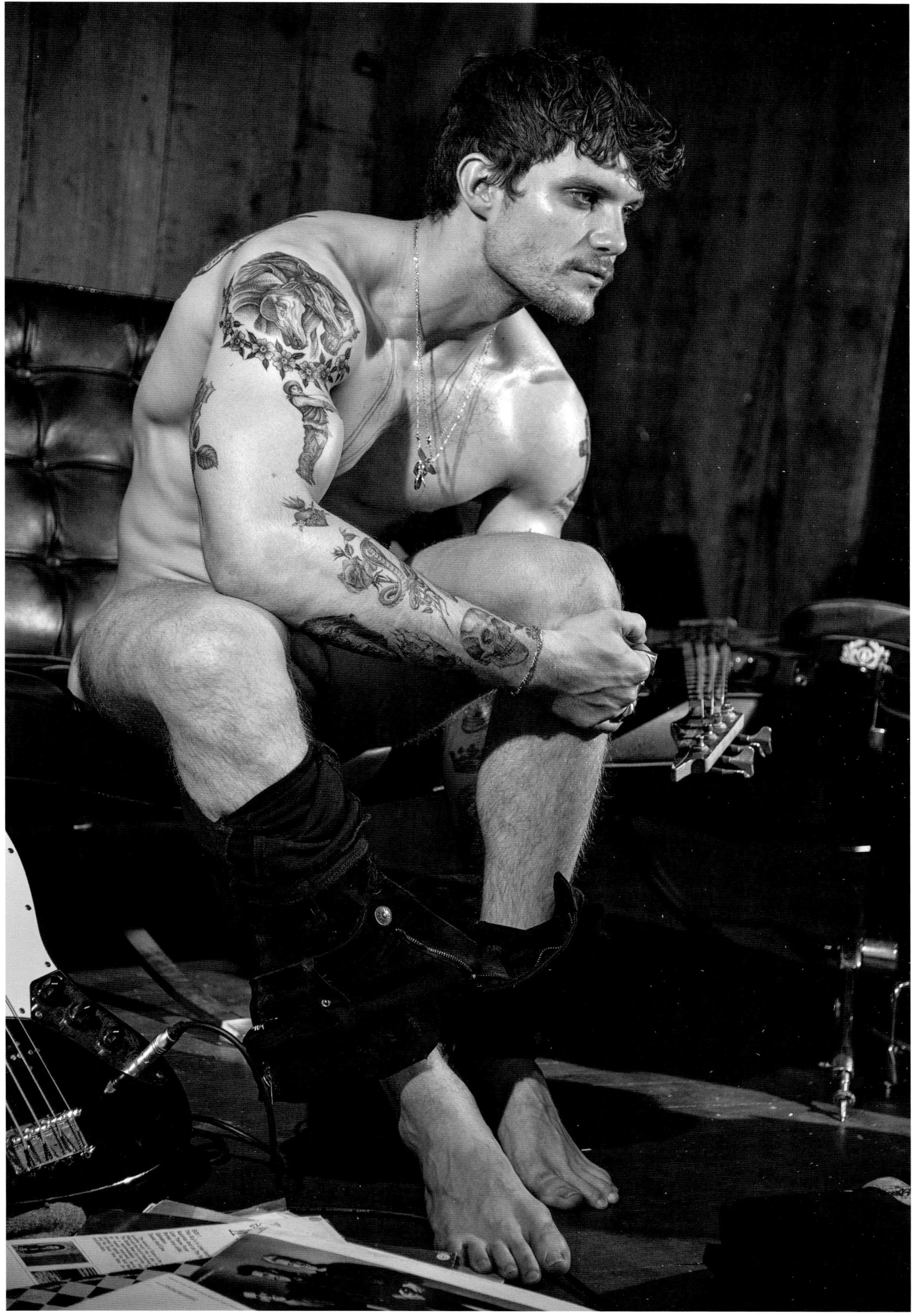

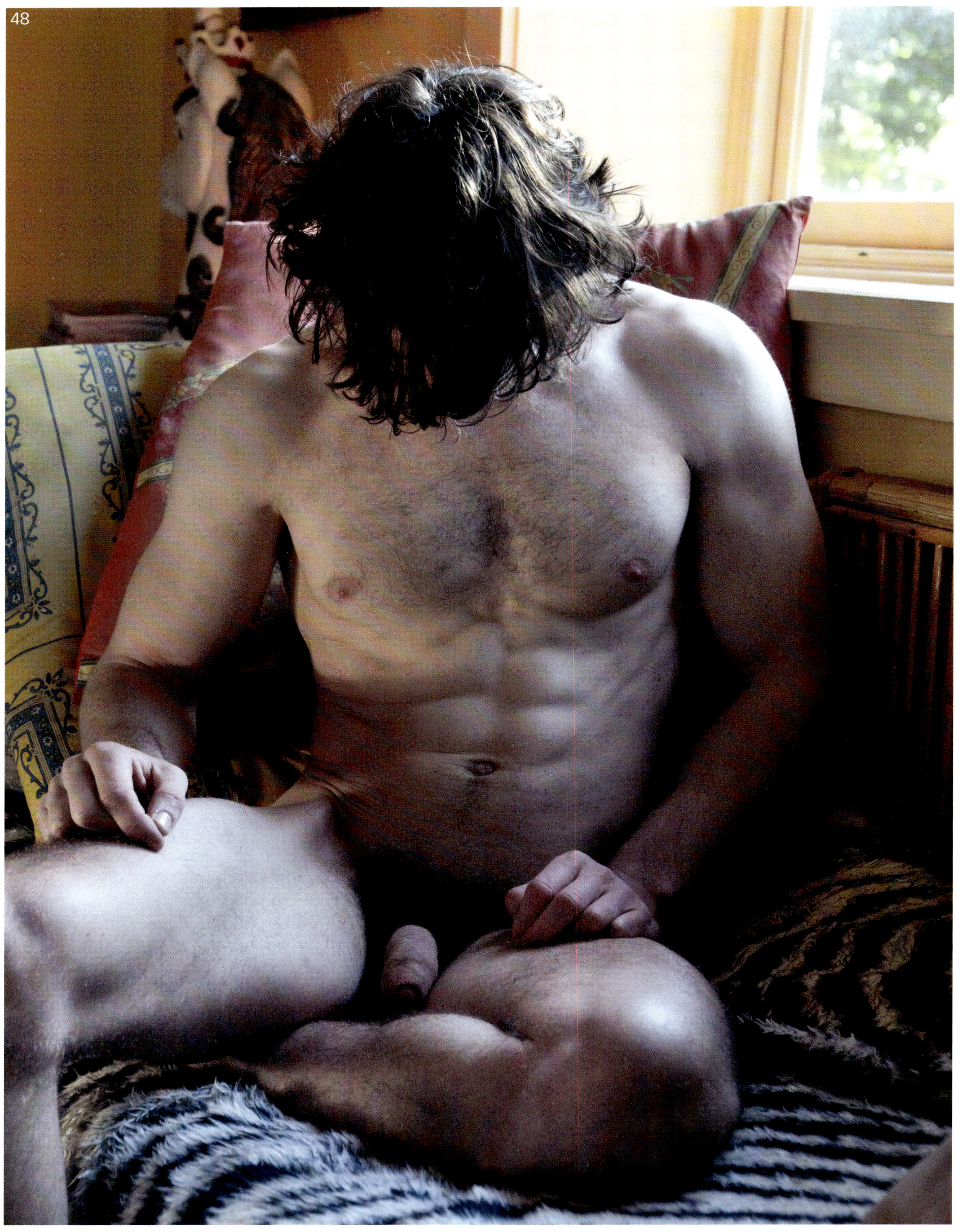

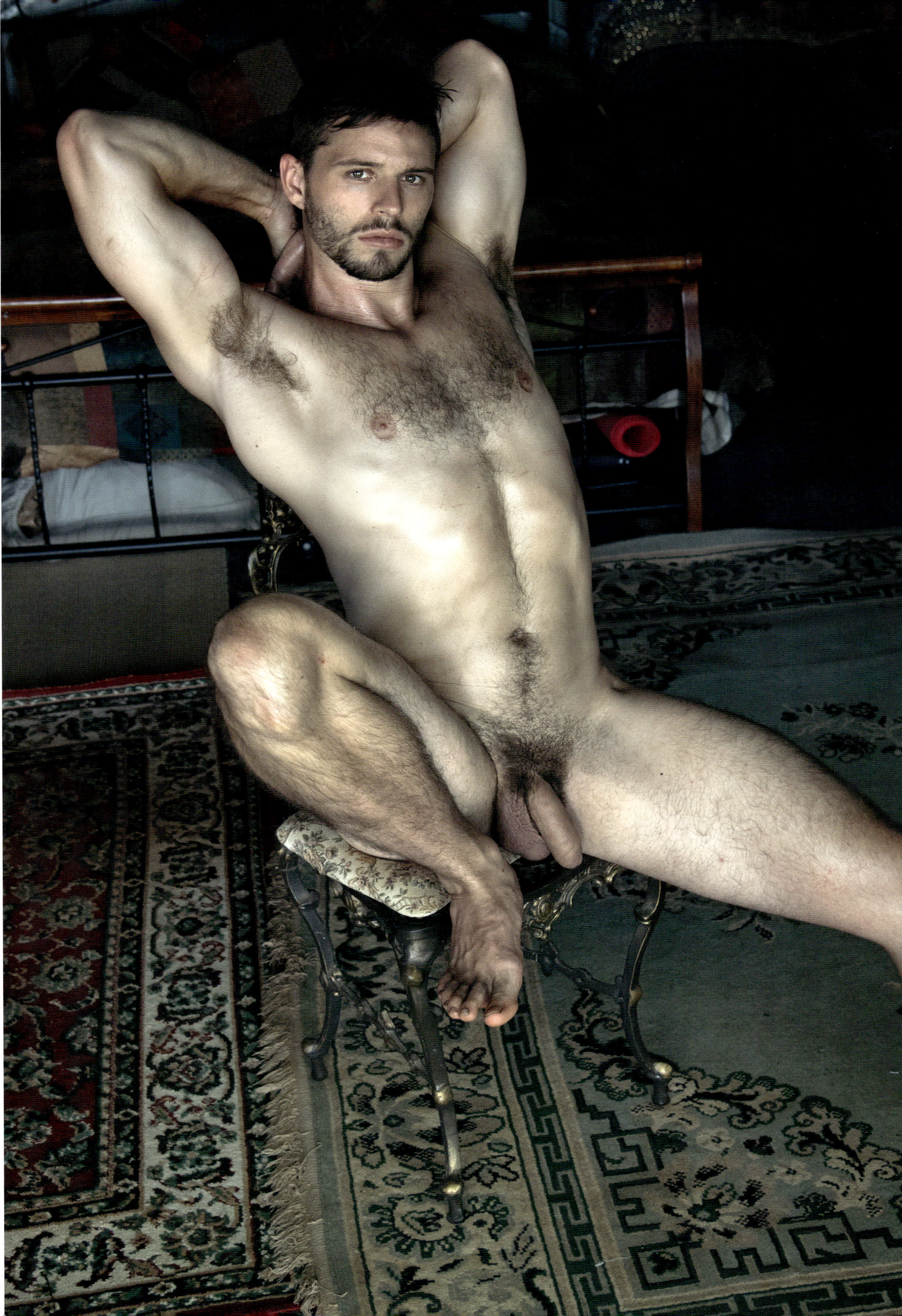

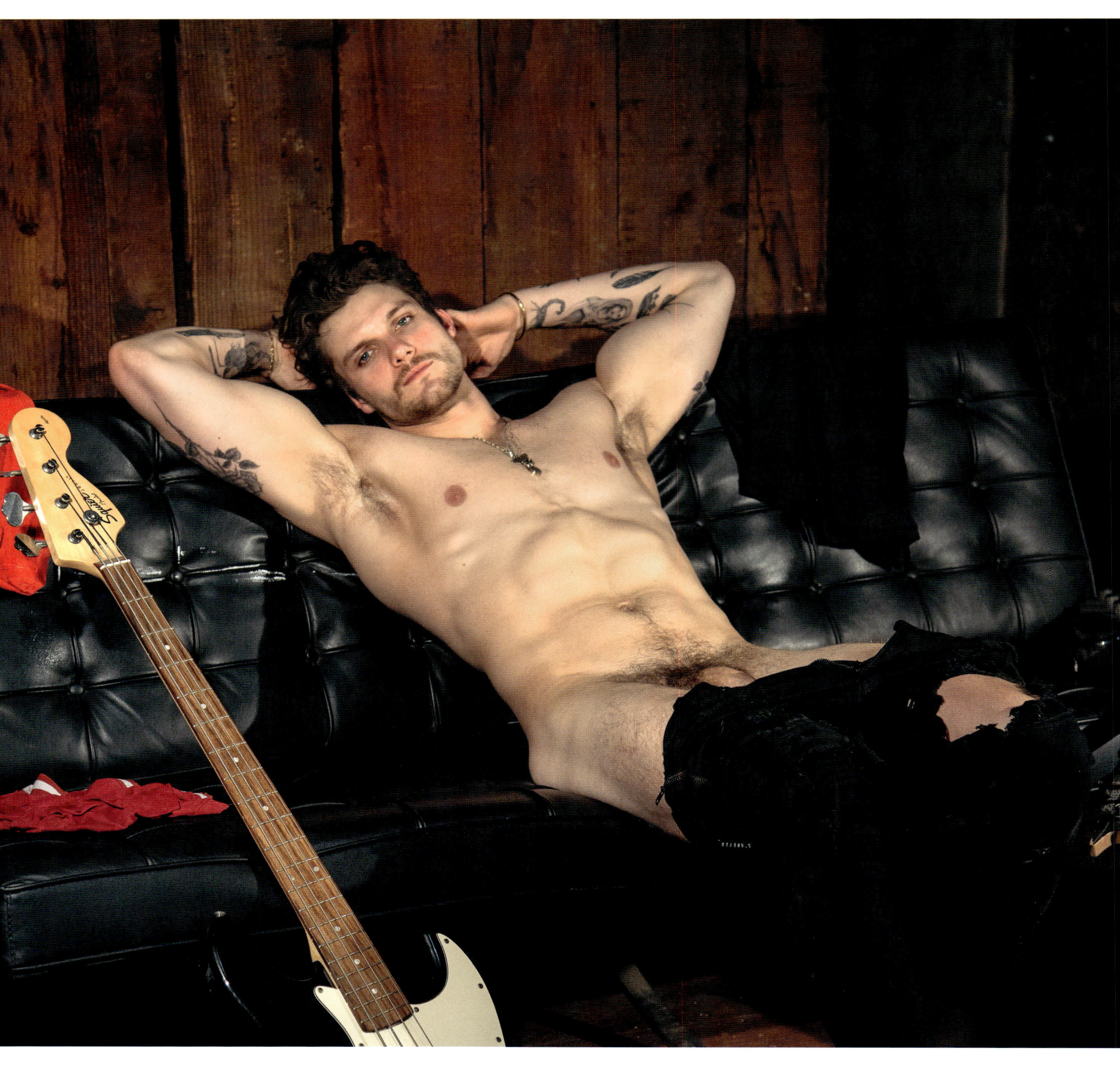

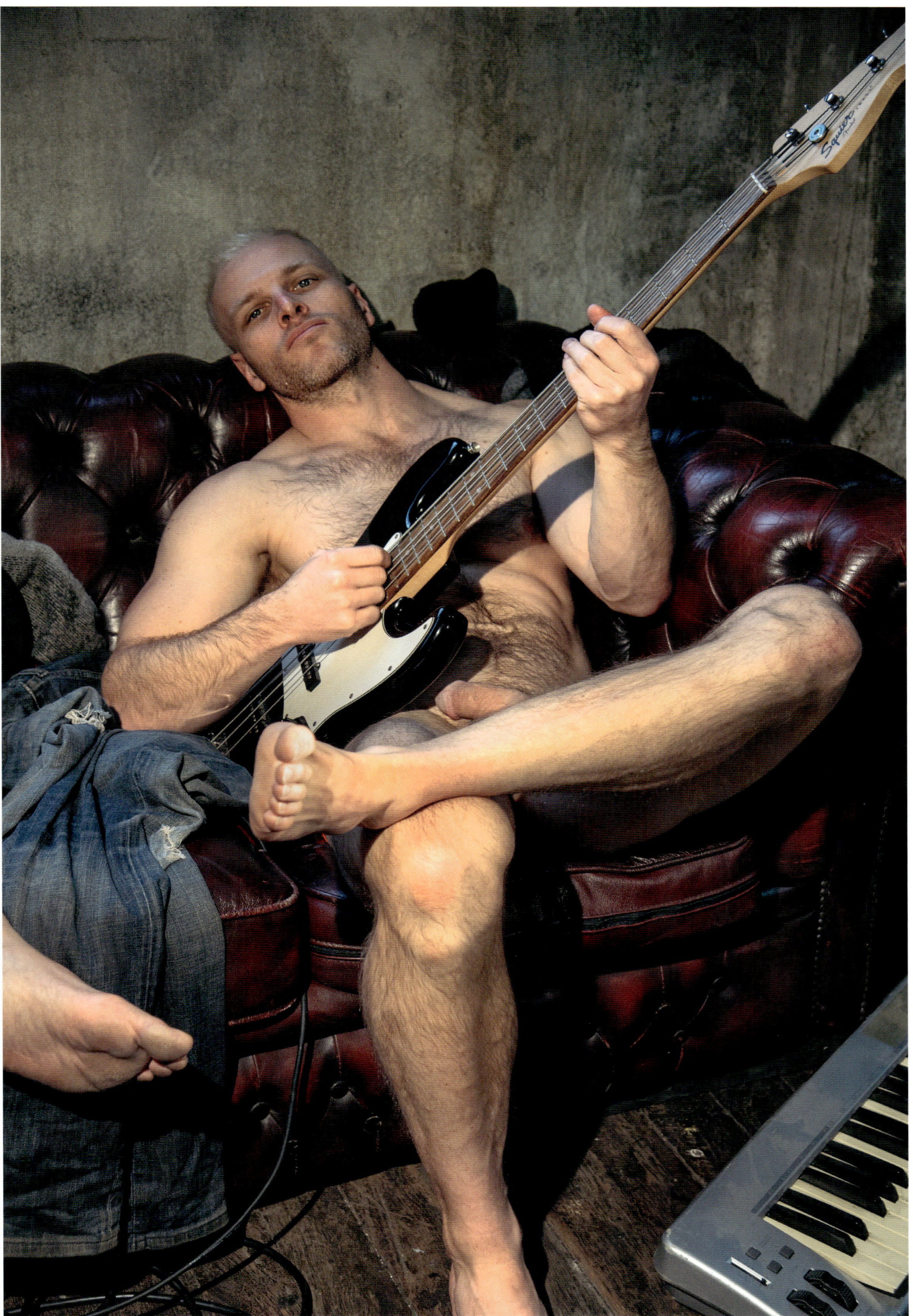
Squier

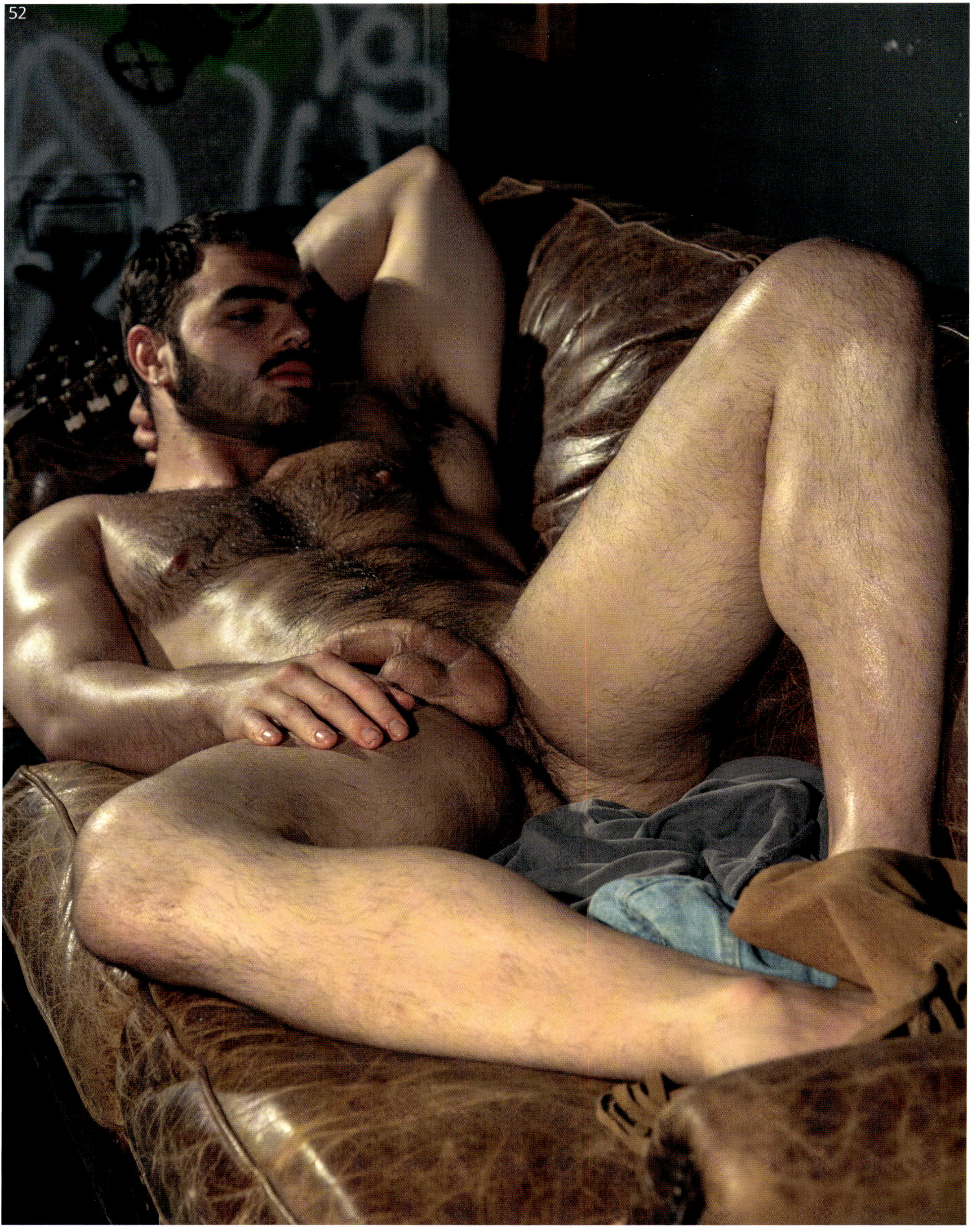

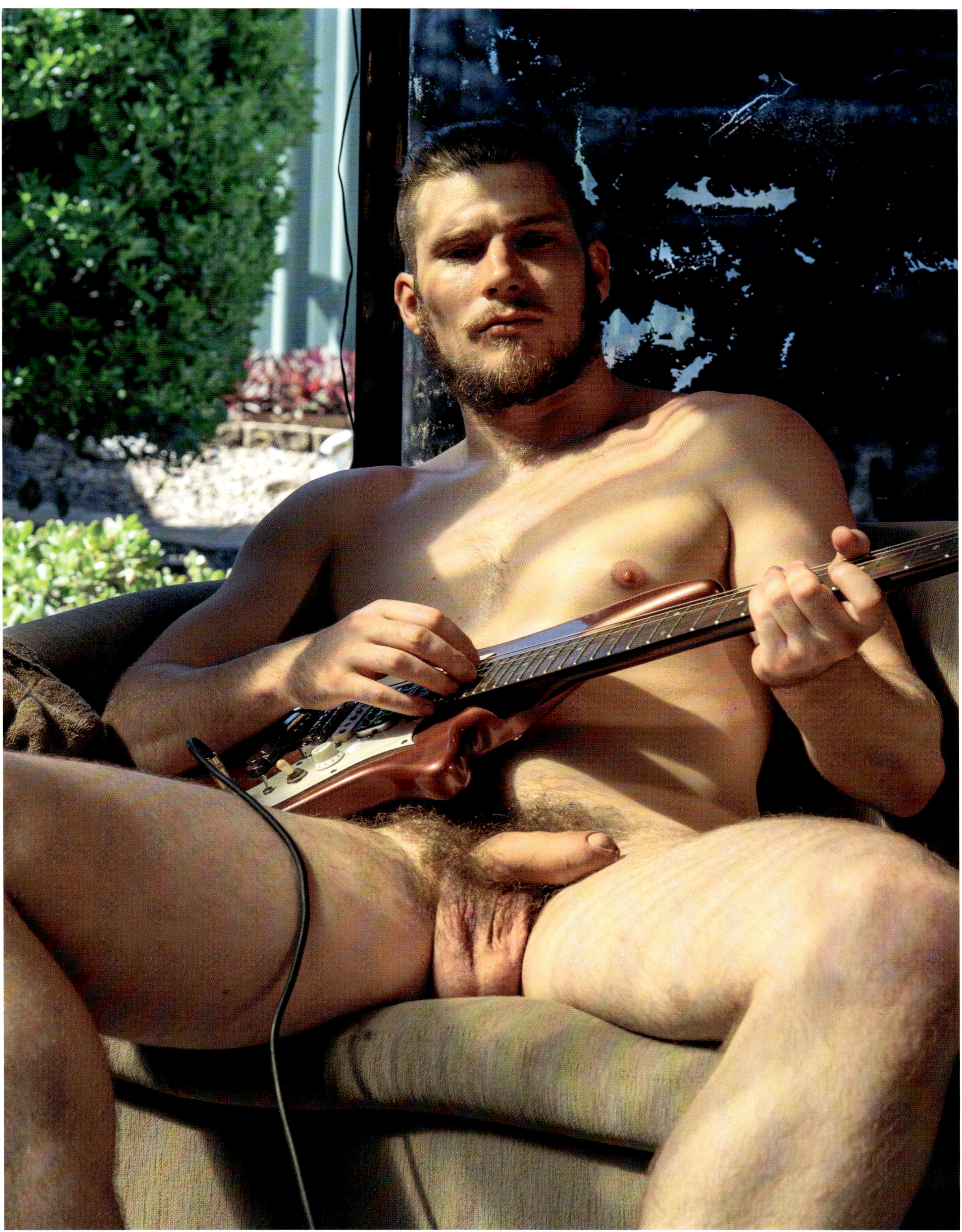

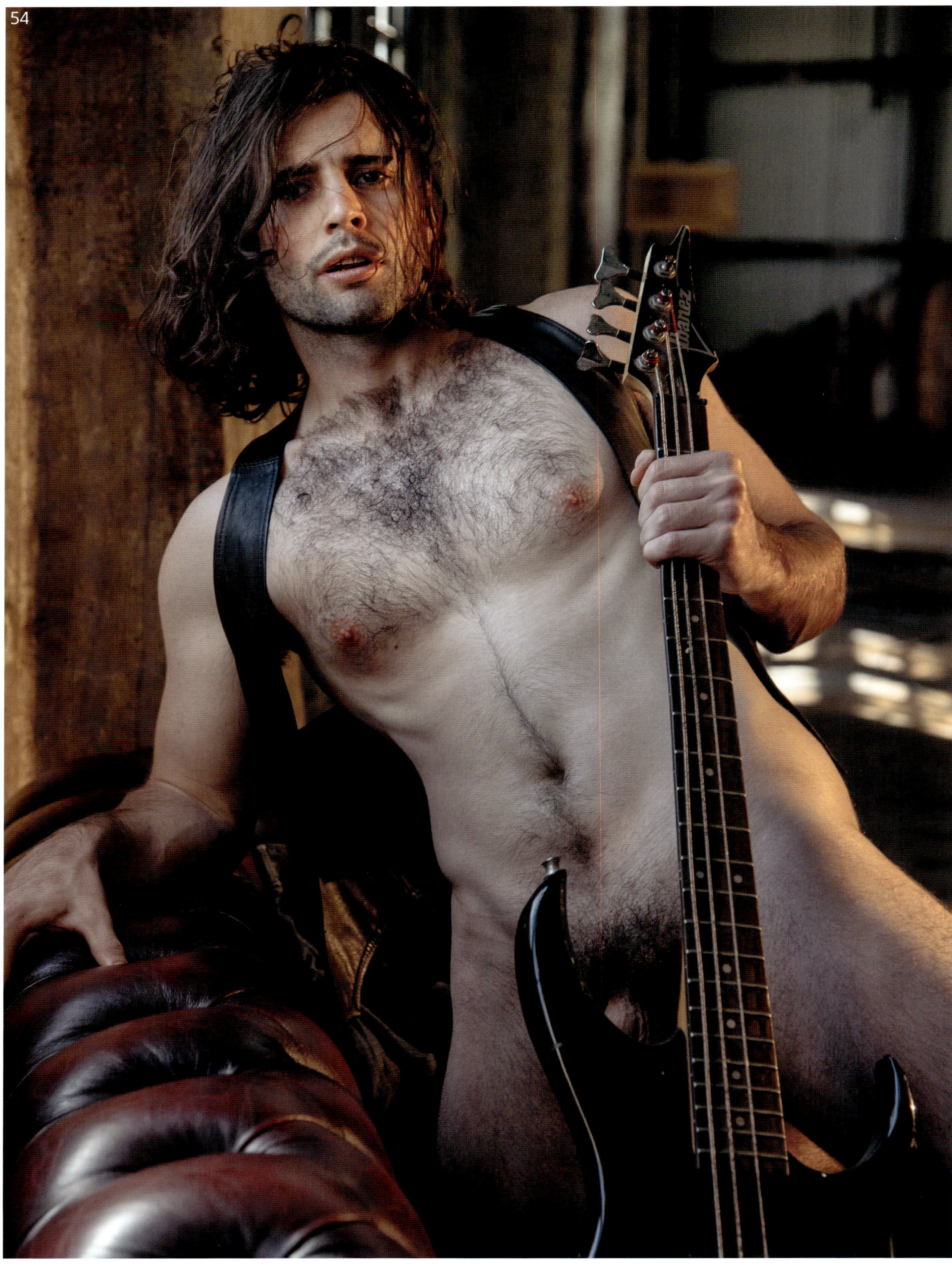
Ibanez

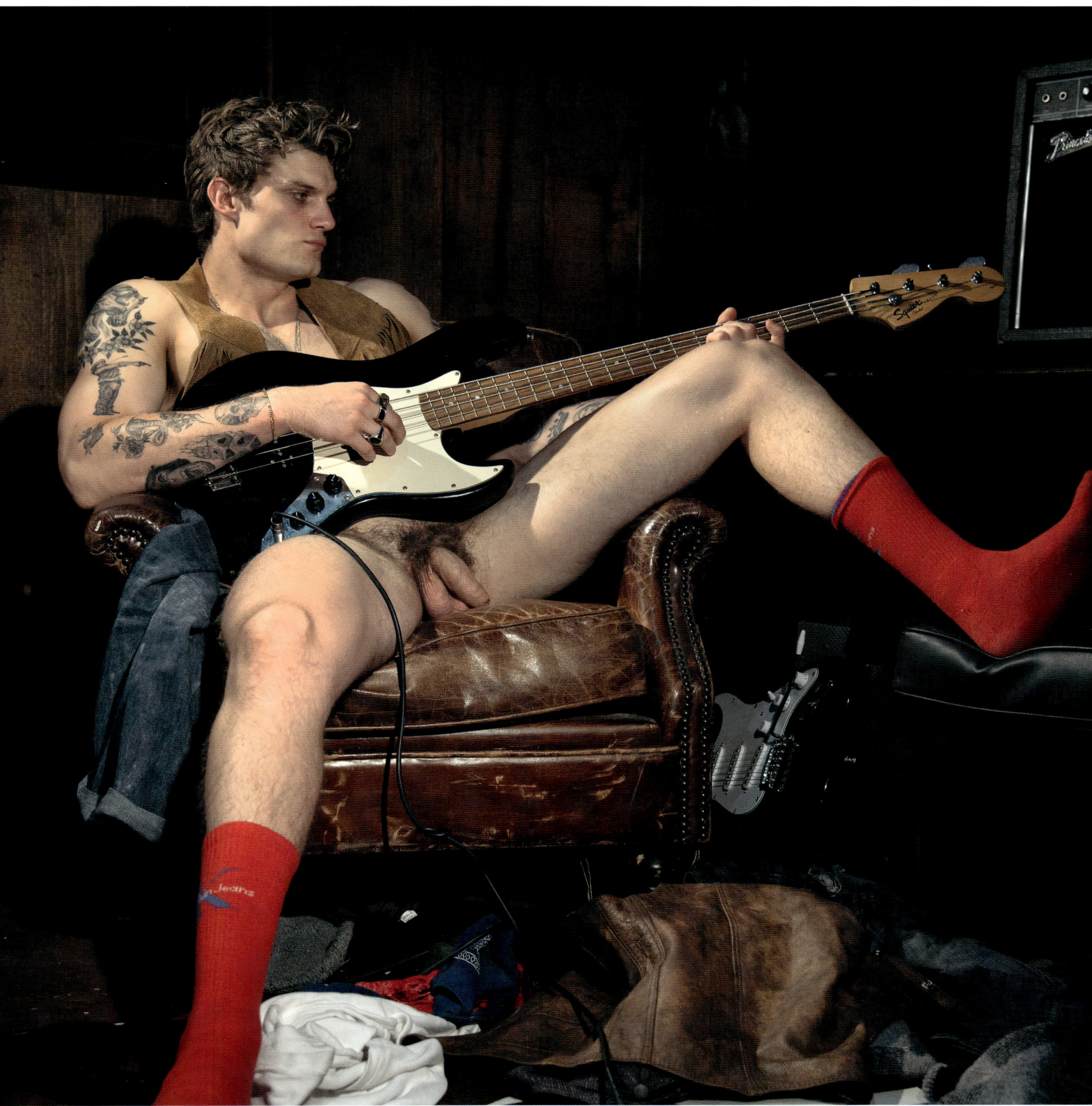
Squier
Jeans

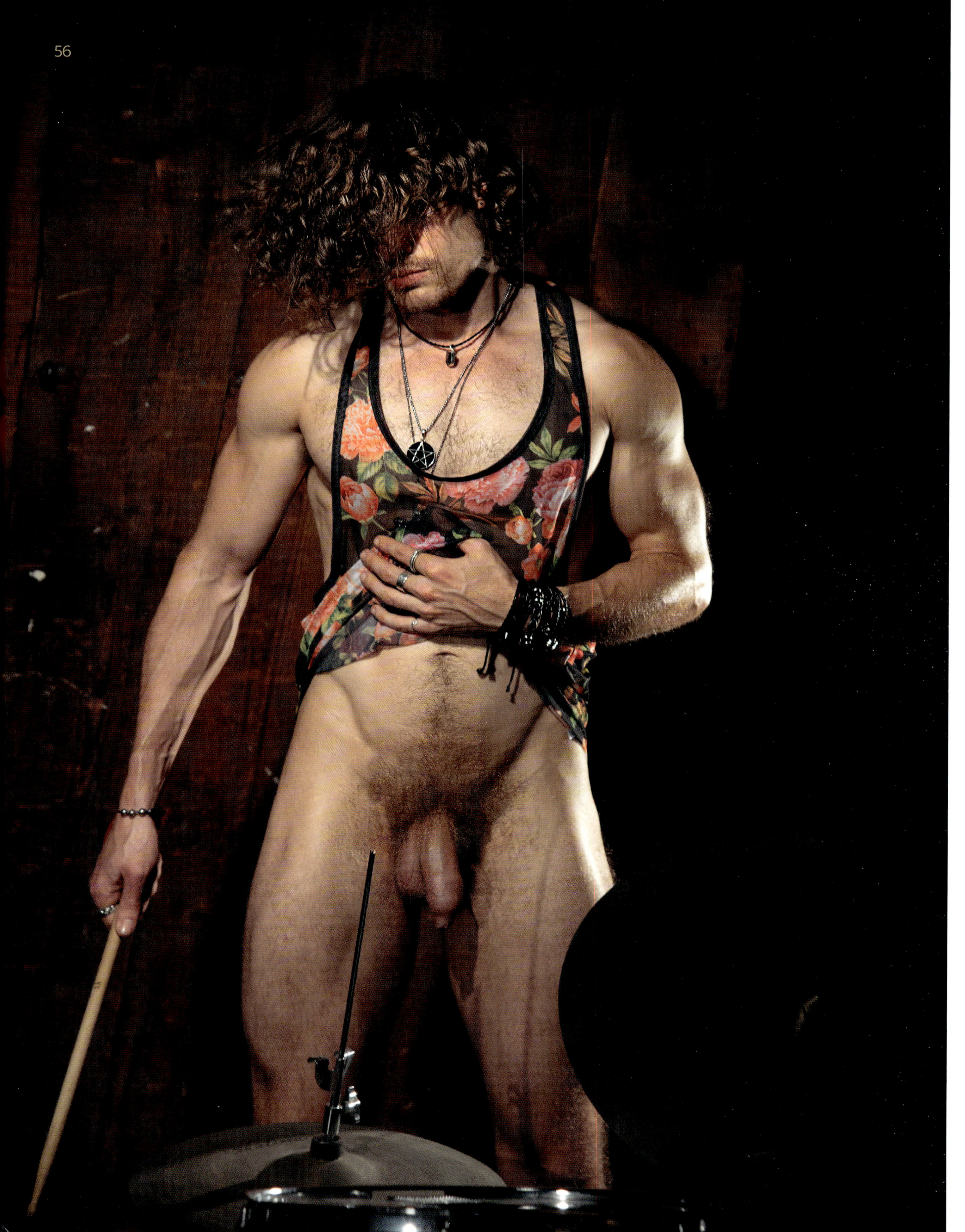

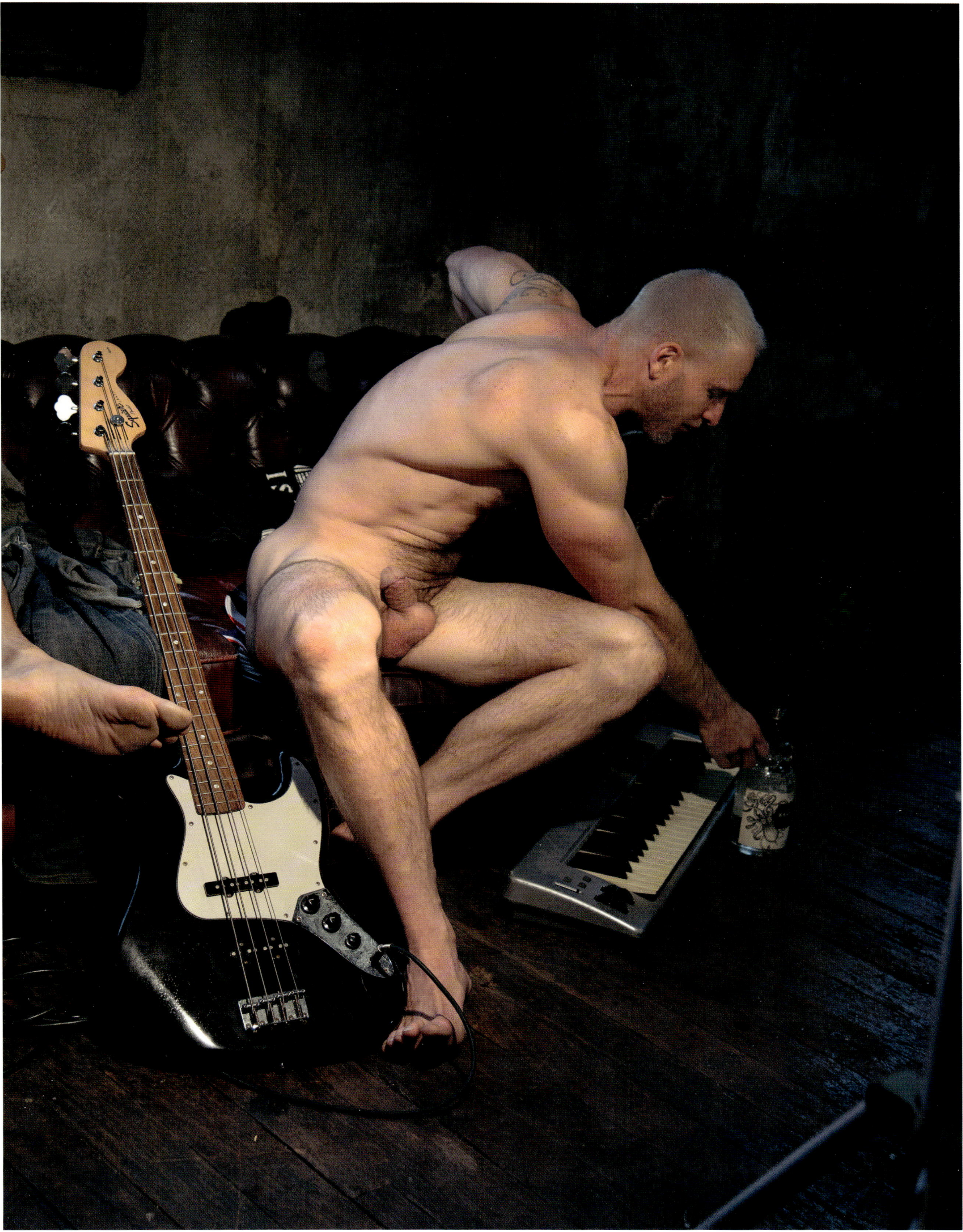

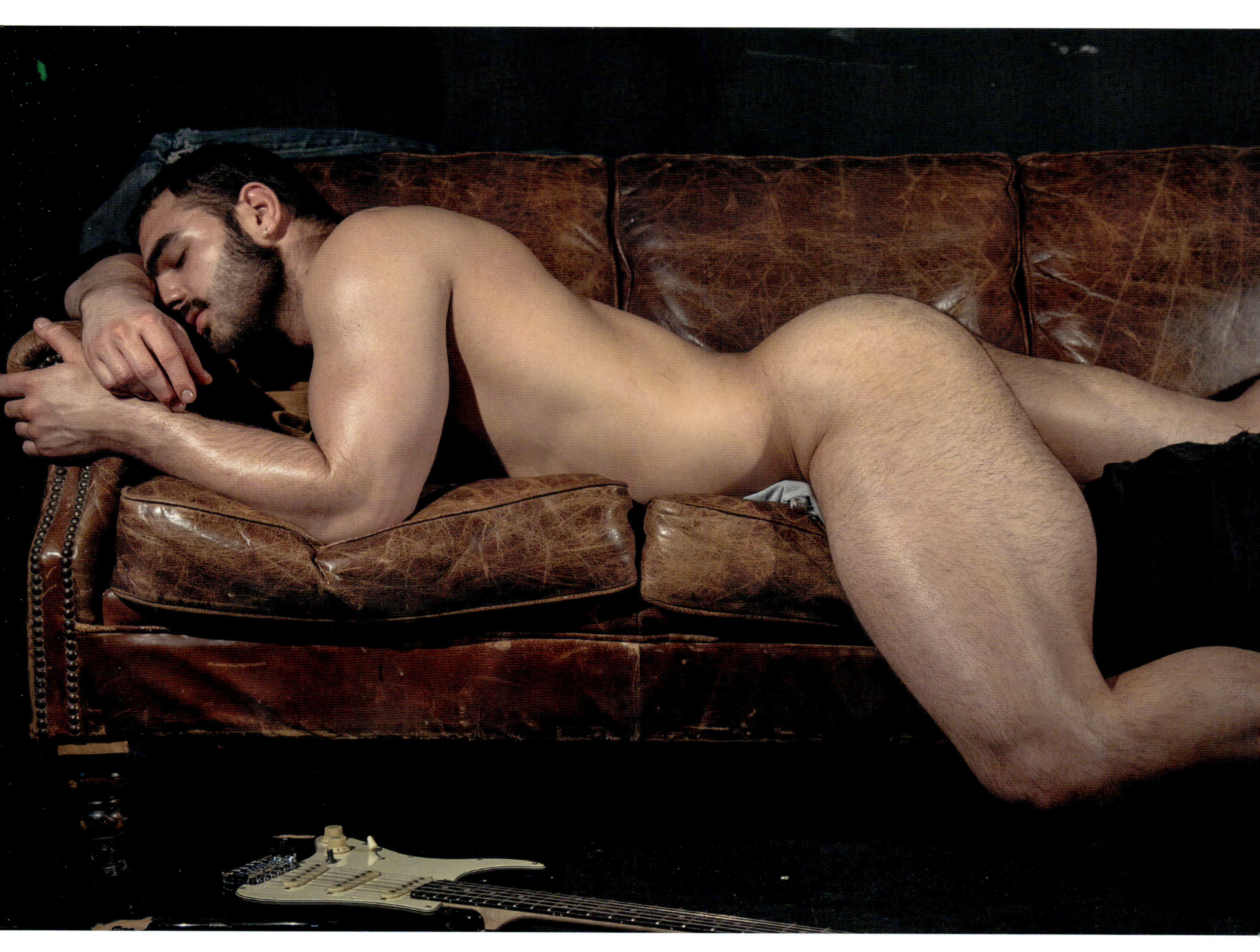

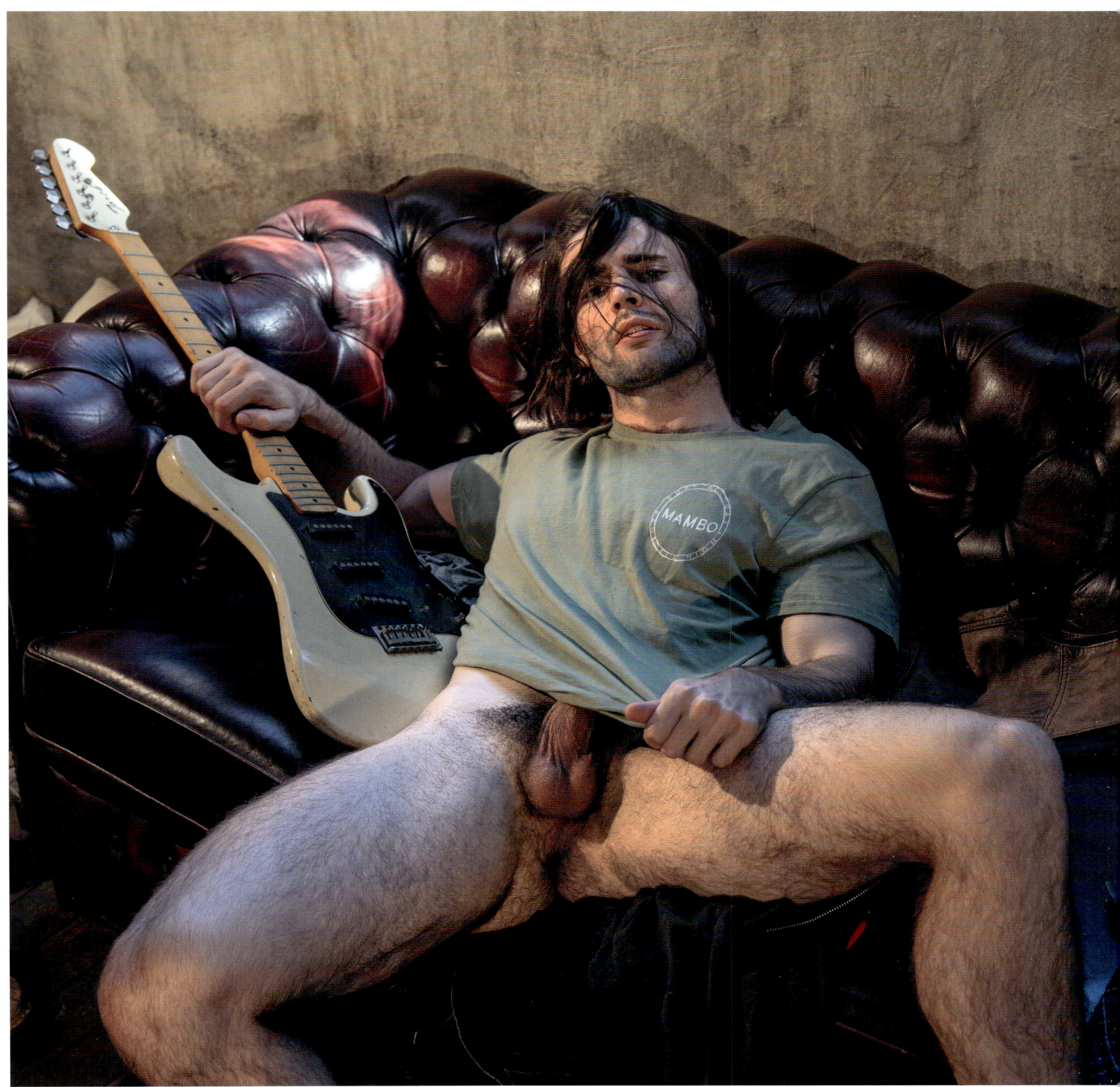
MAMBO

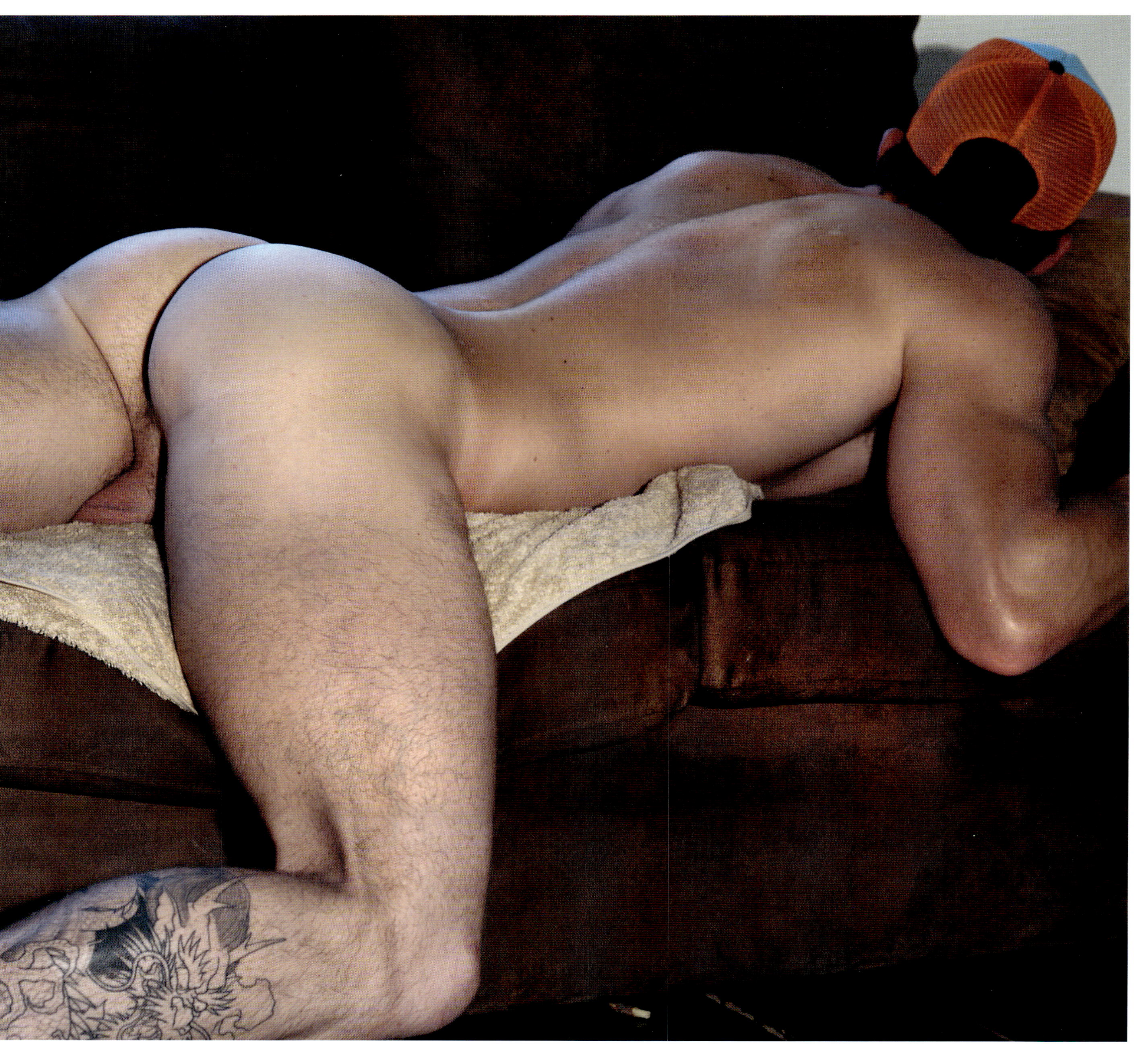

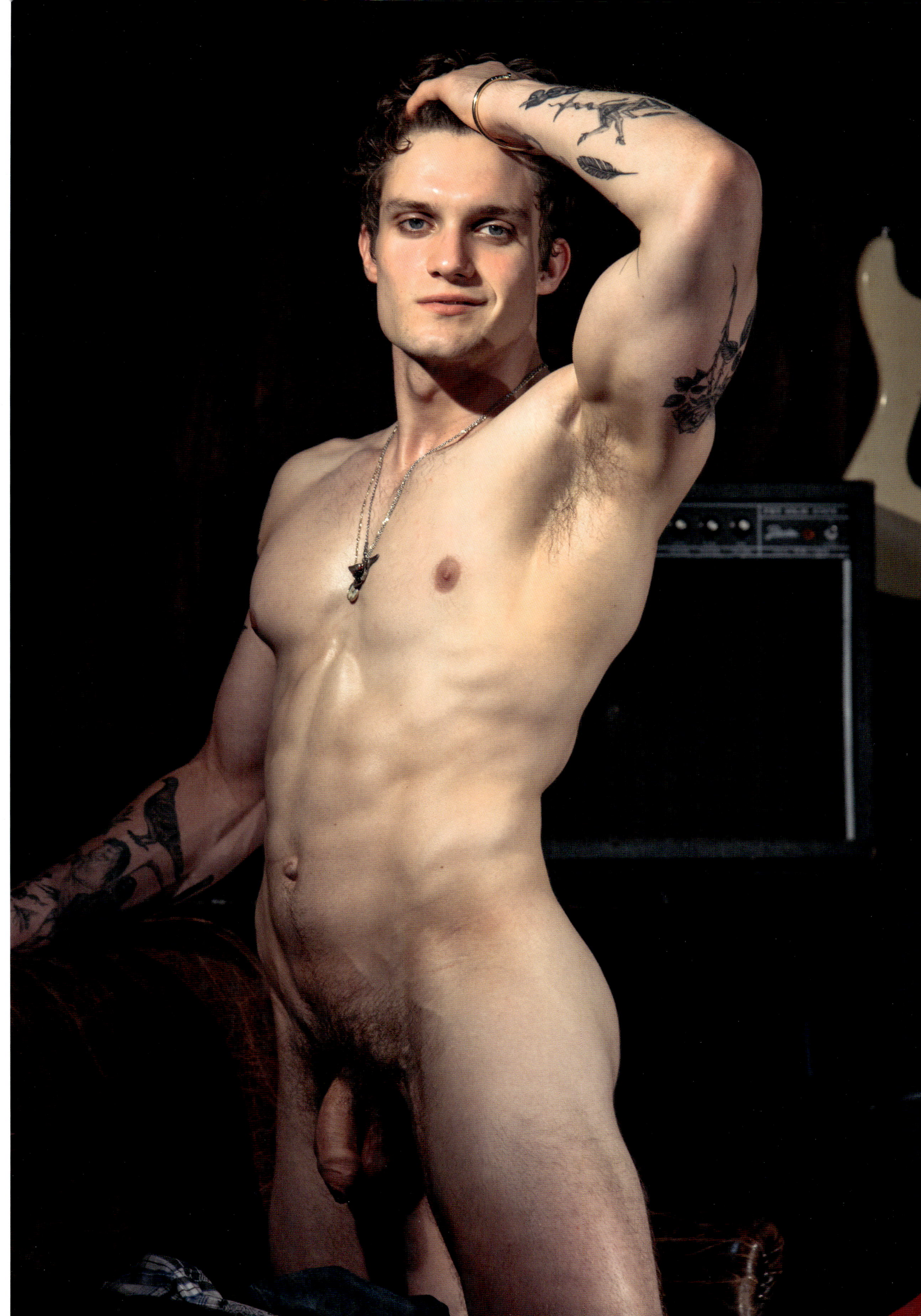

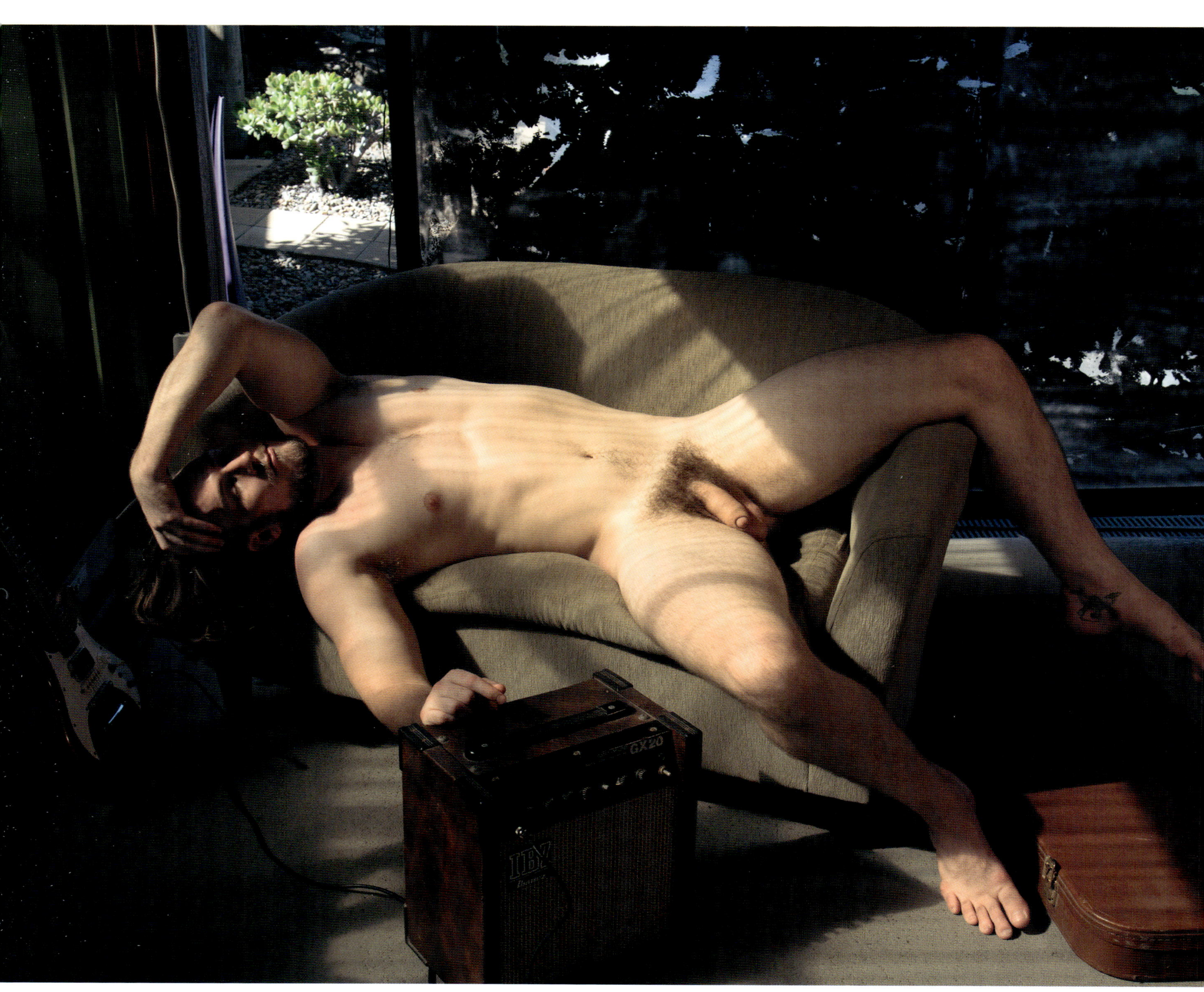
GX20

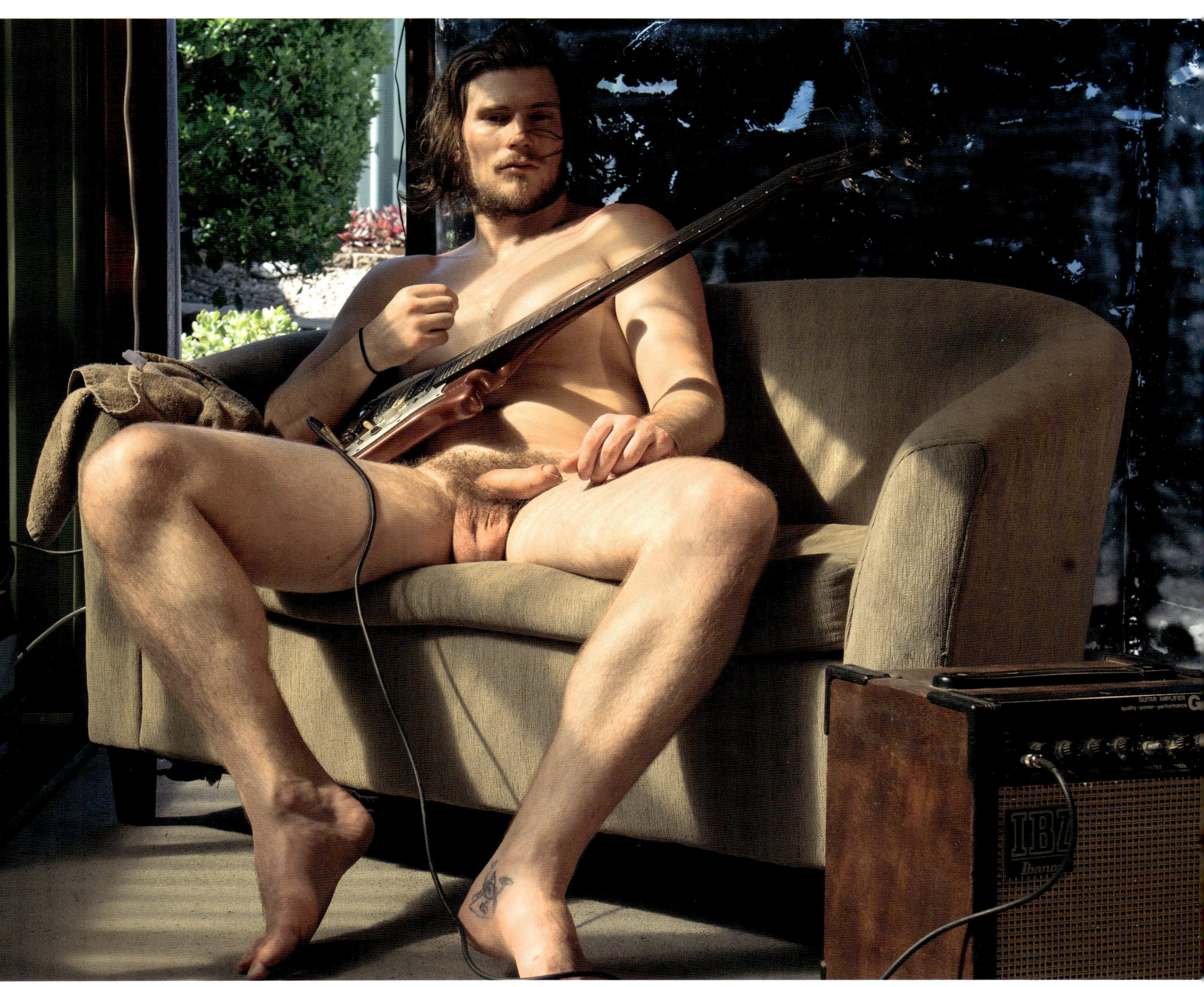
GUITAR AMPLIFIER
quality-power-performance
IBZ

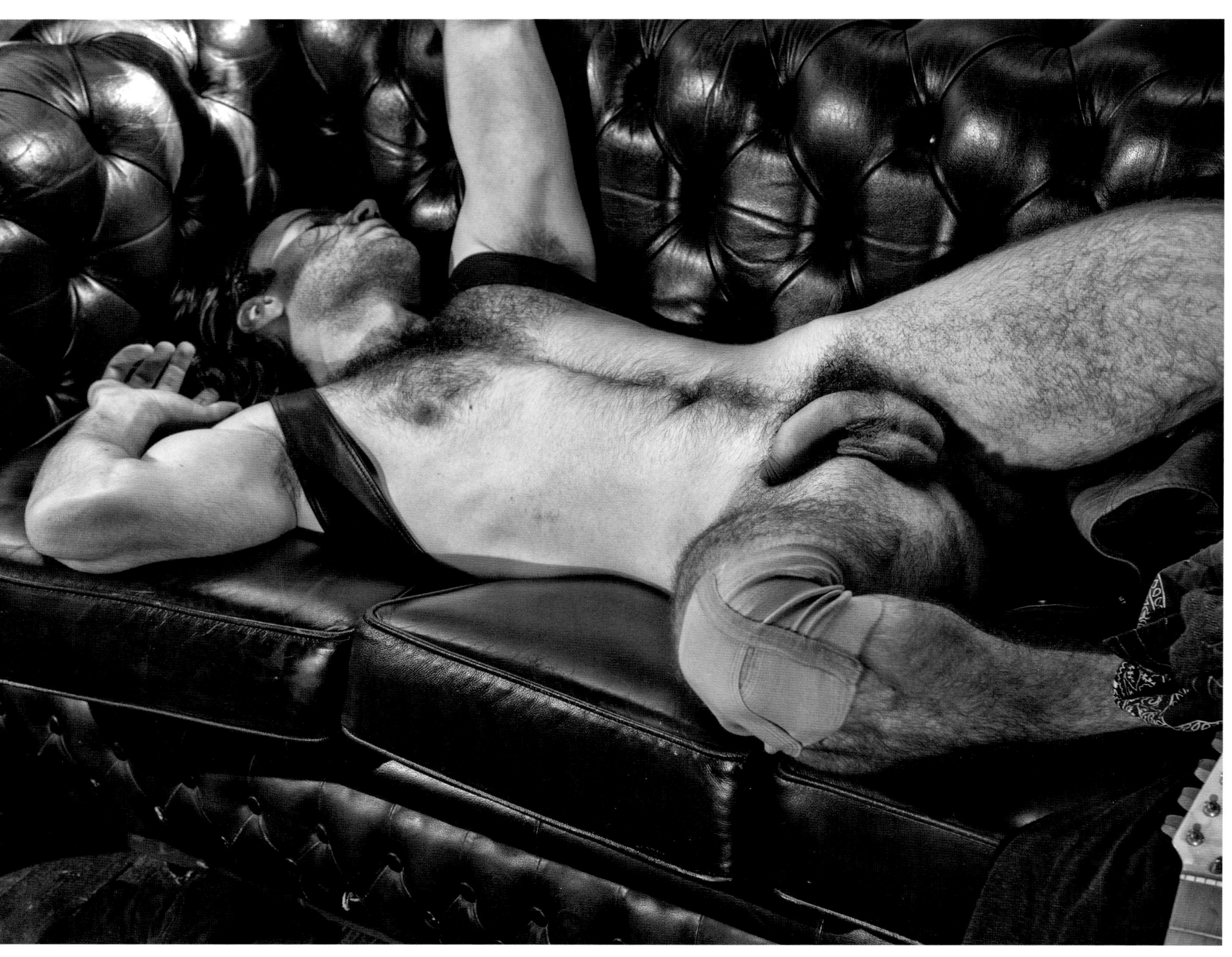

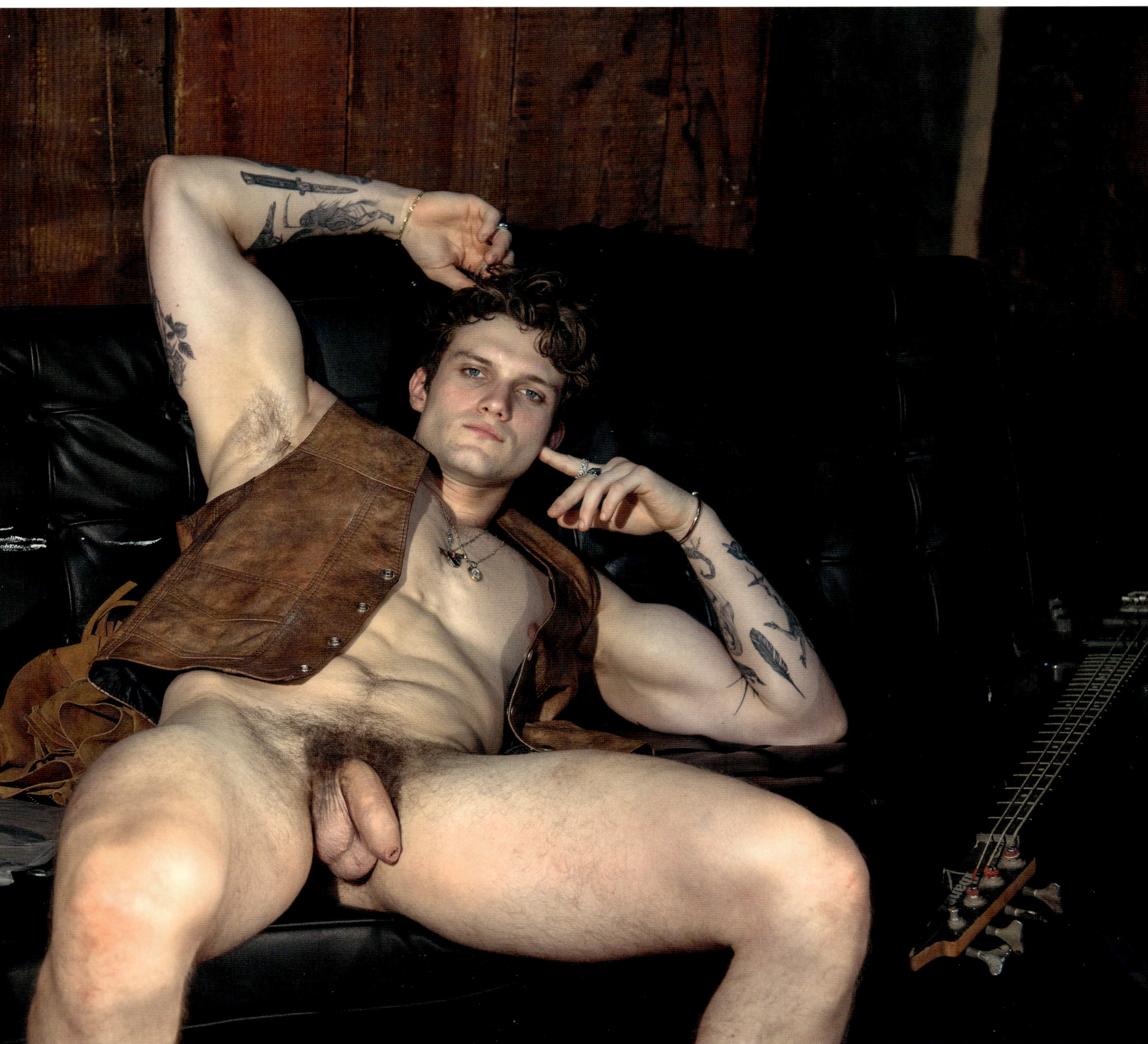

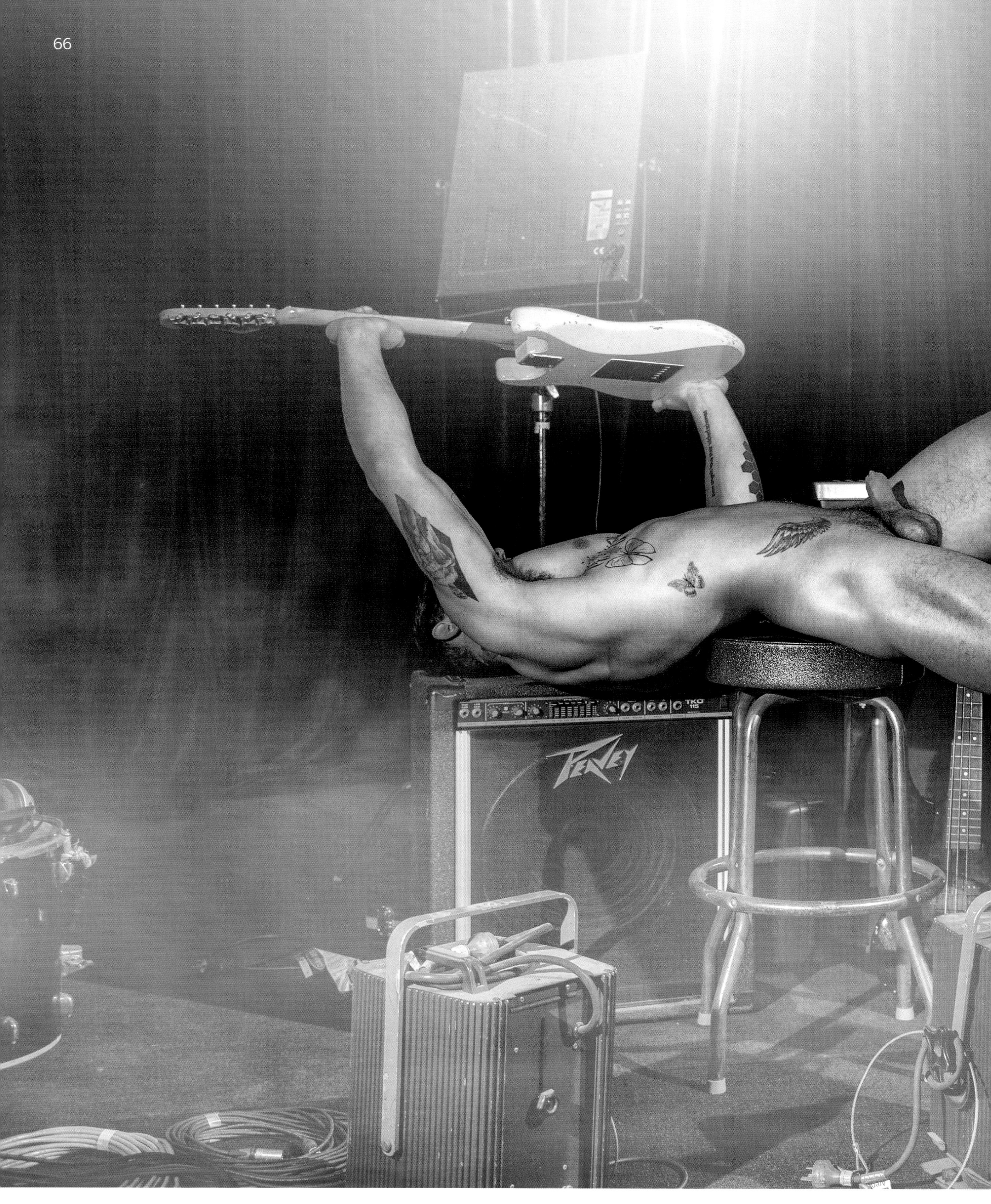
TKO
115
PEAVEY

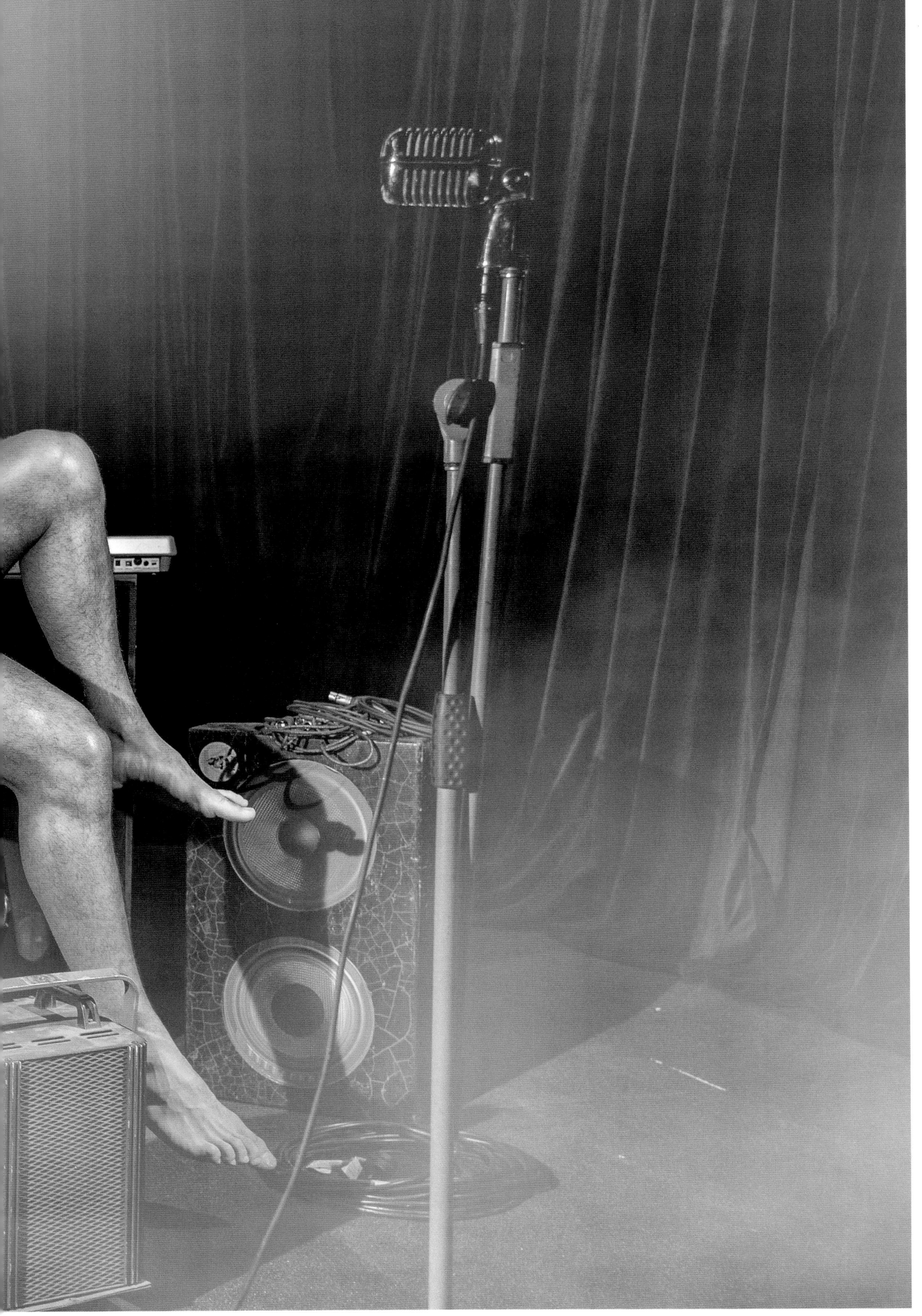

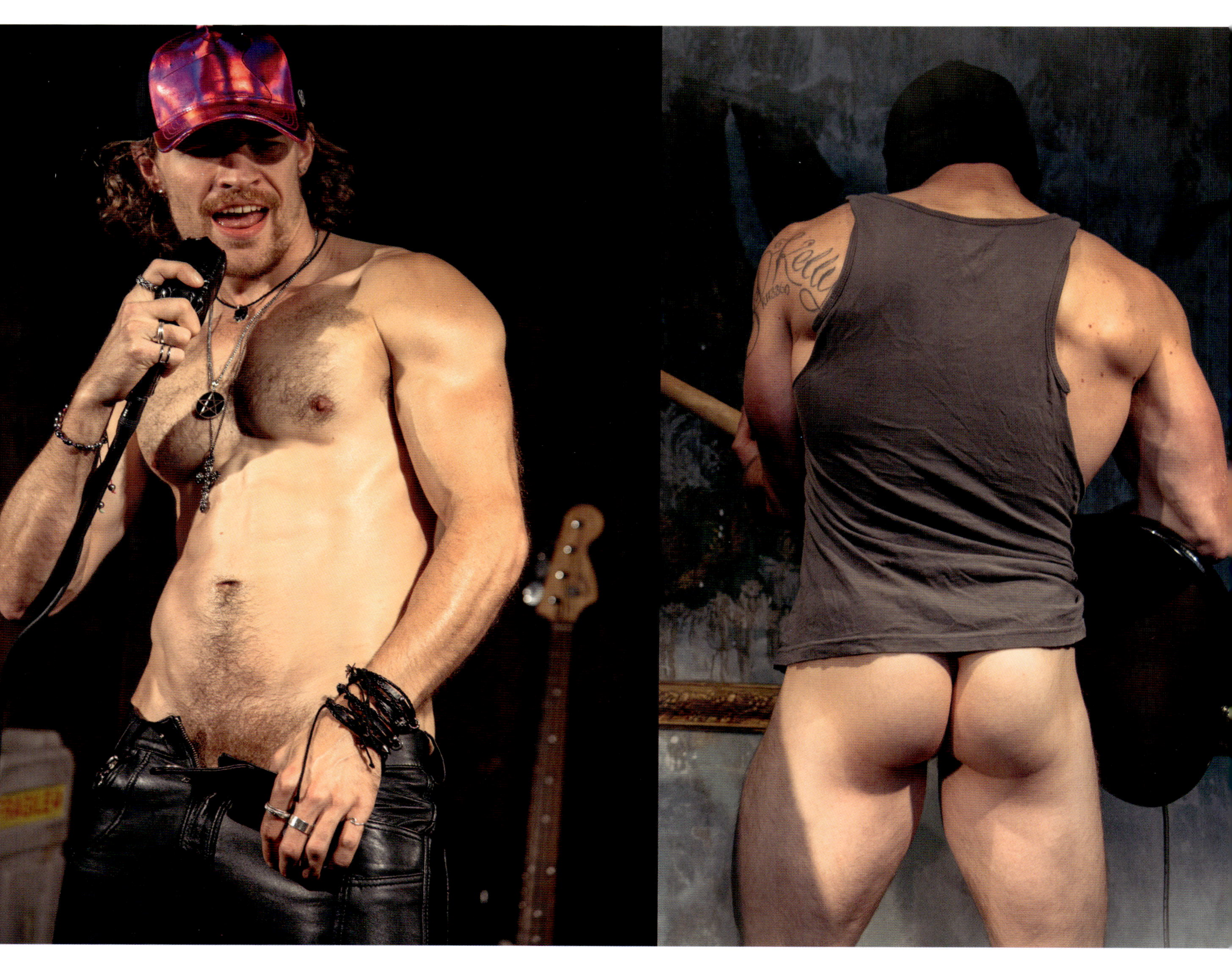

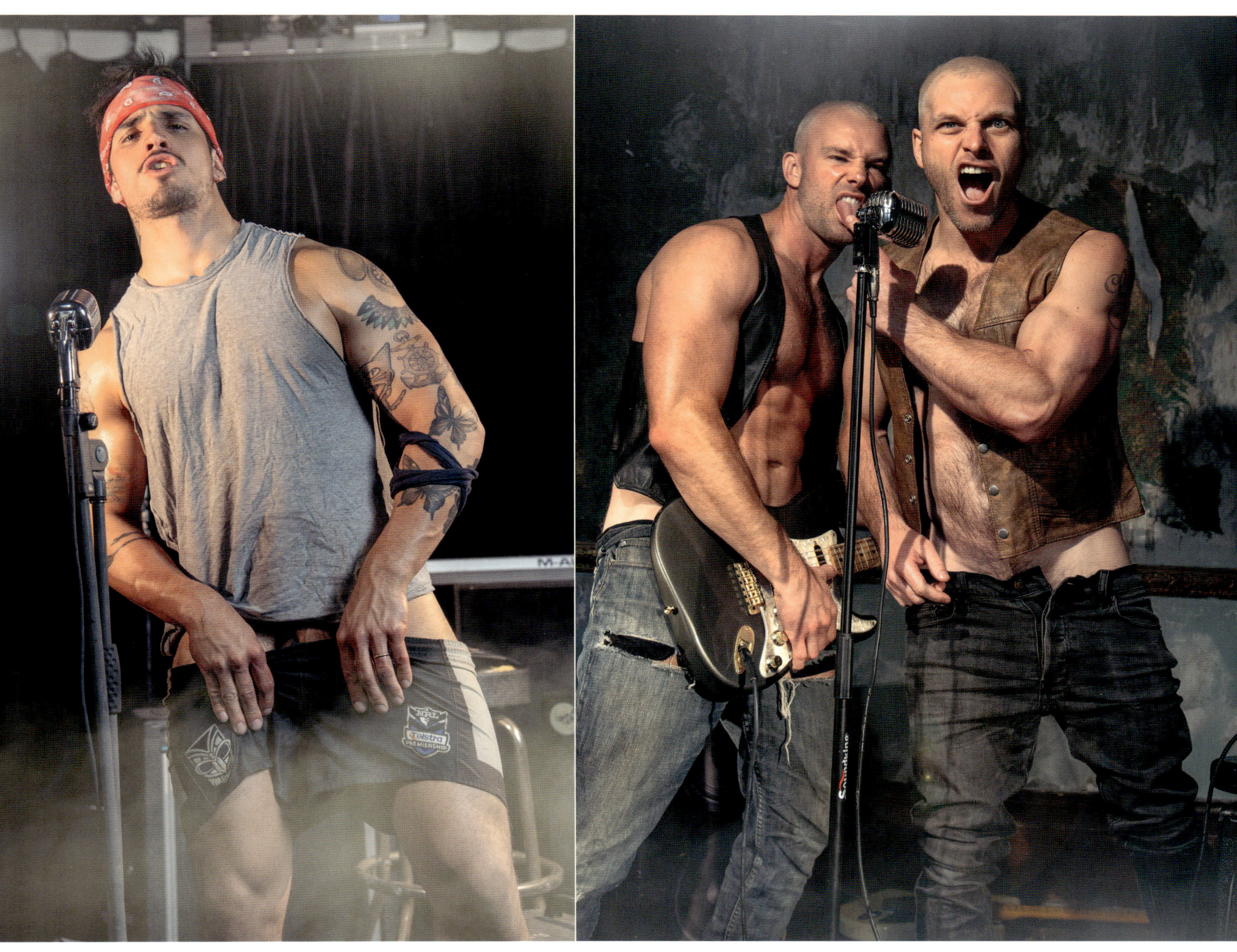
NRL
Telstra
PREMIERSHIP

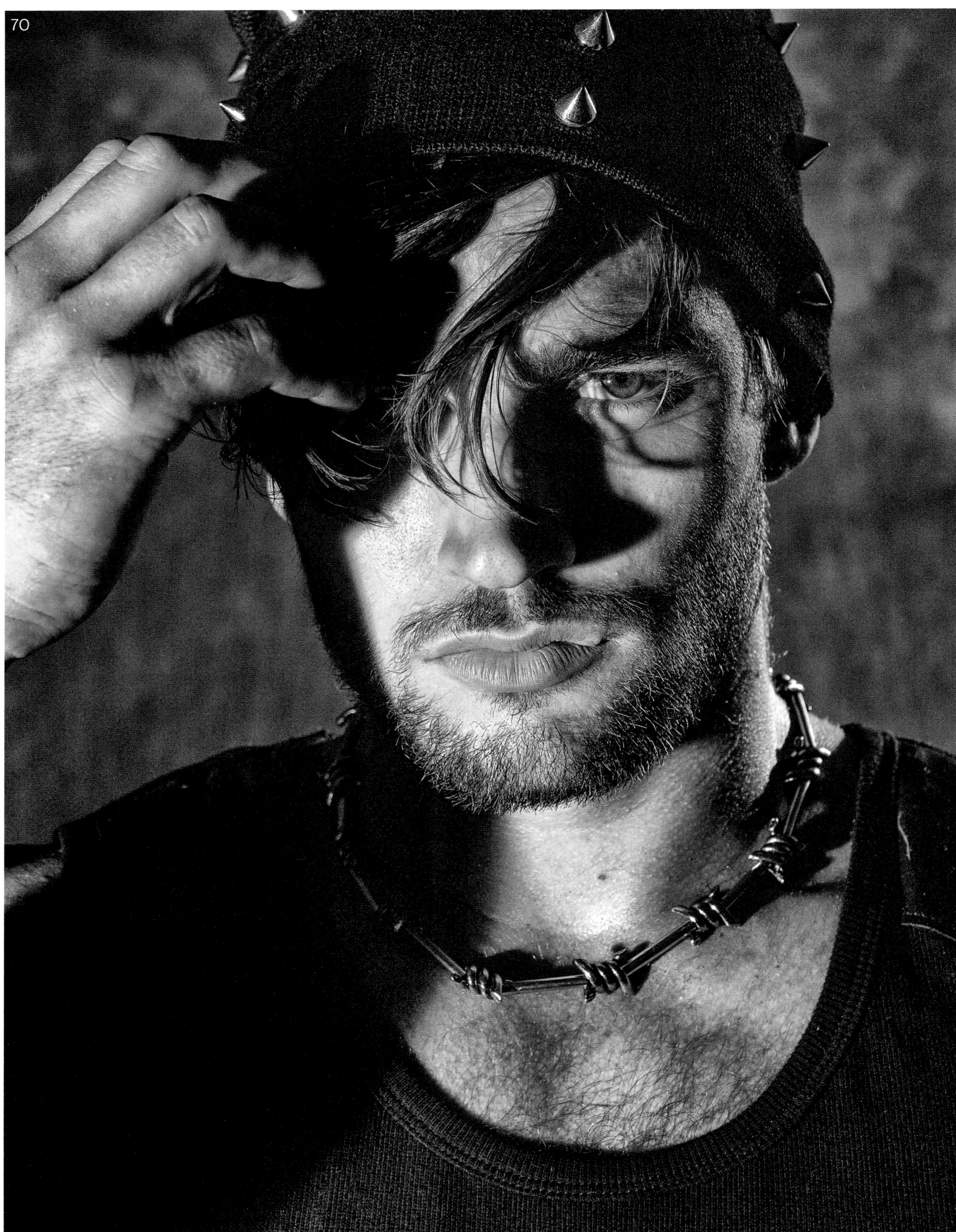

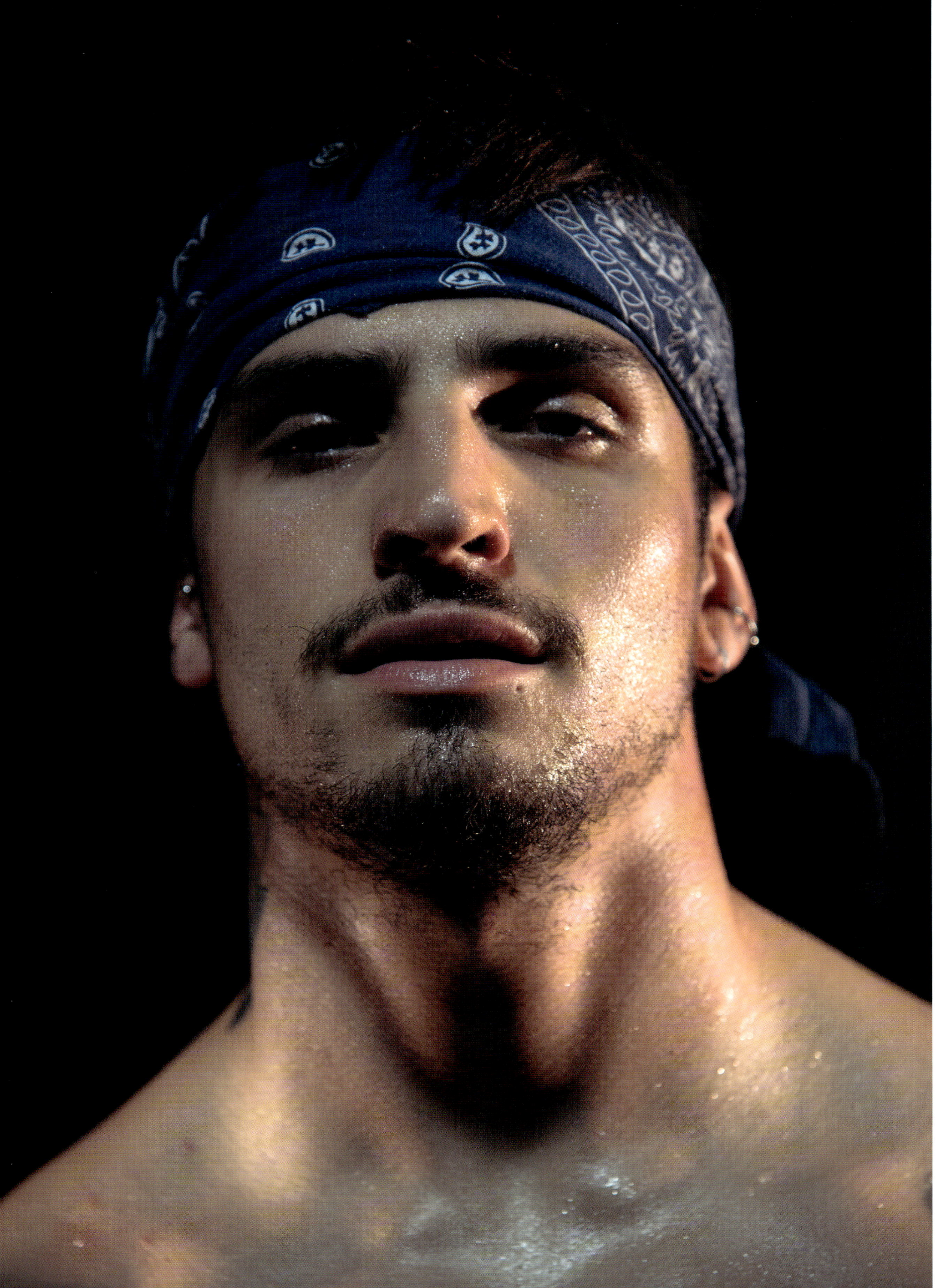

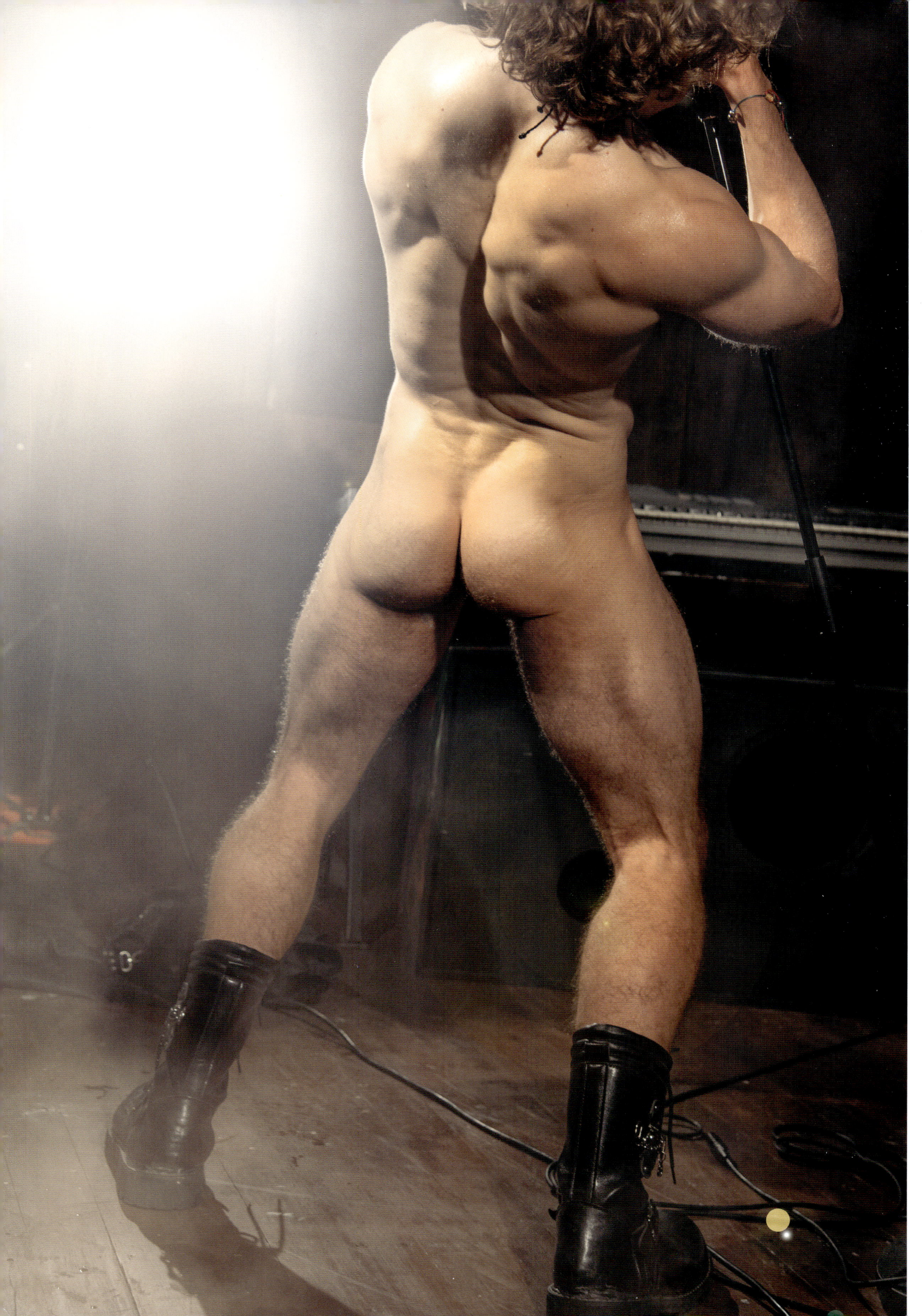

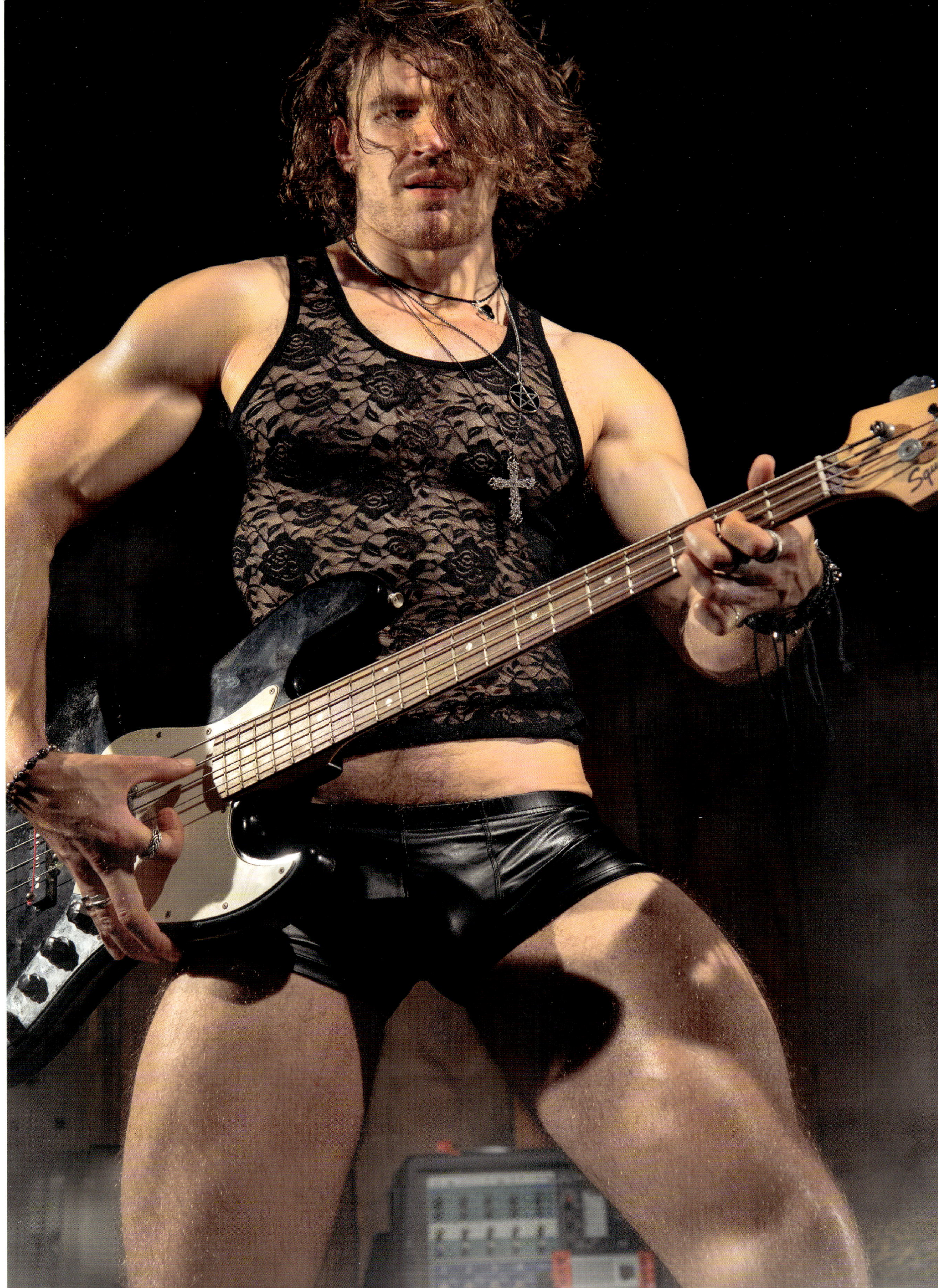

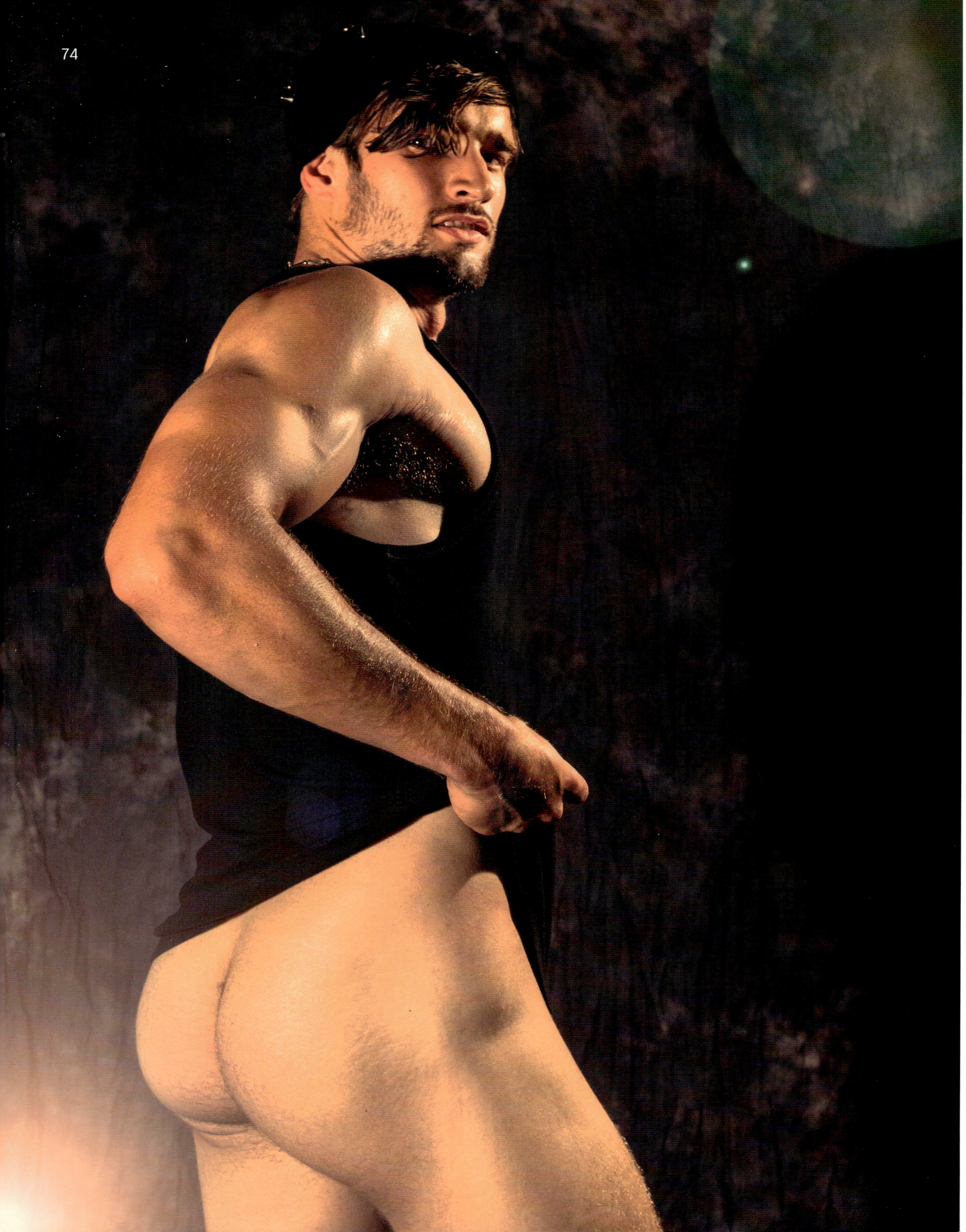

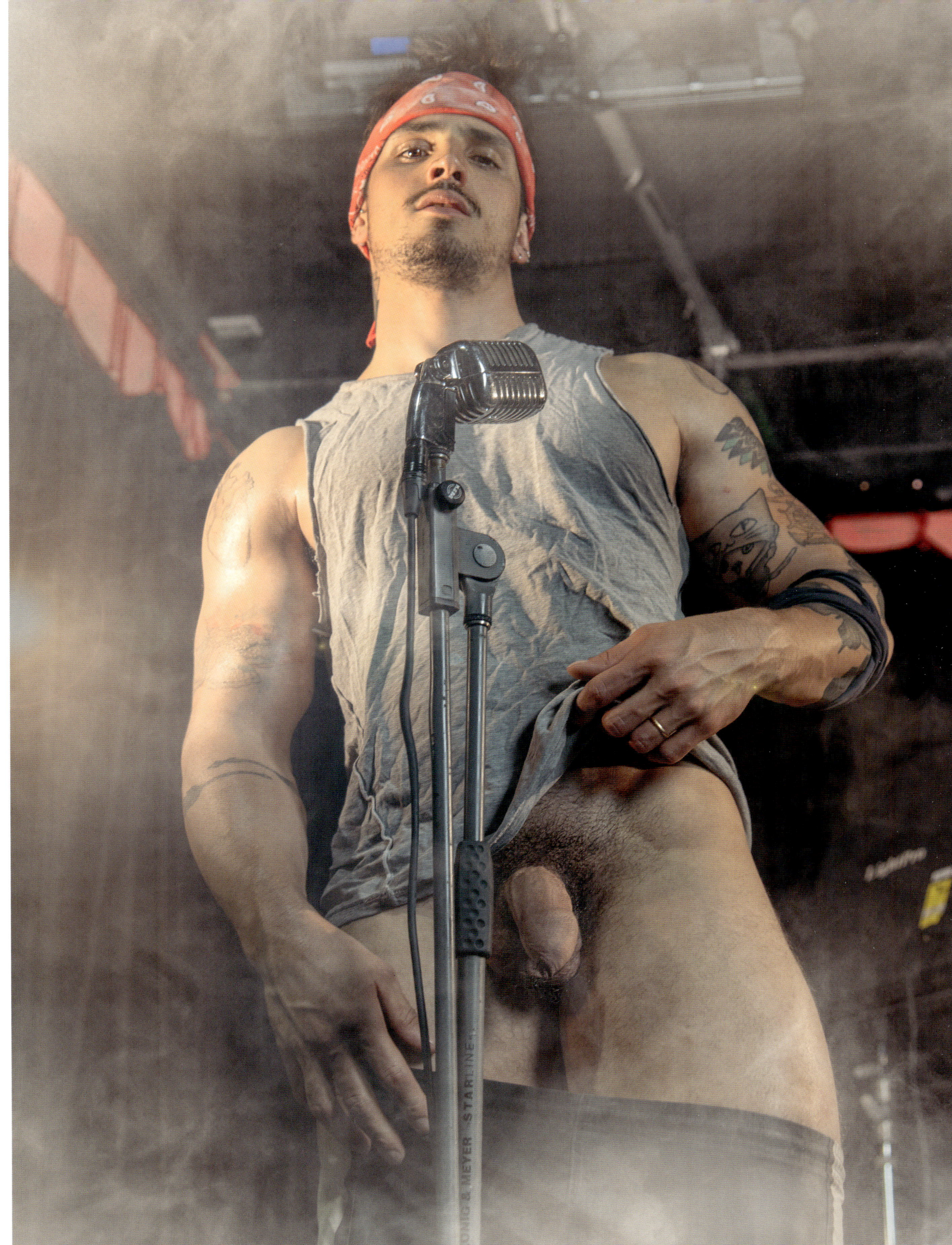
STARLINE

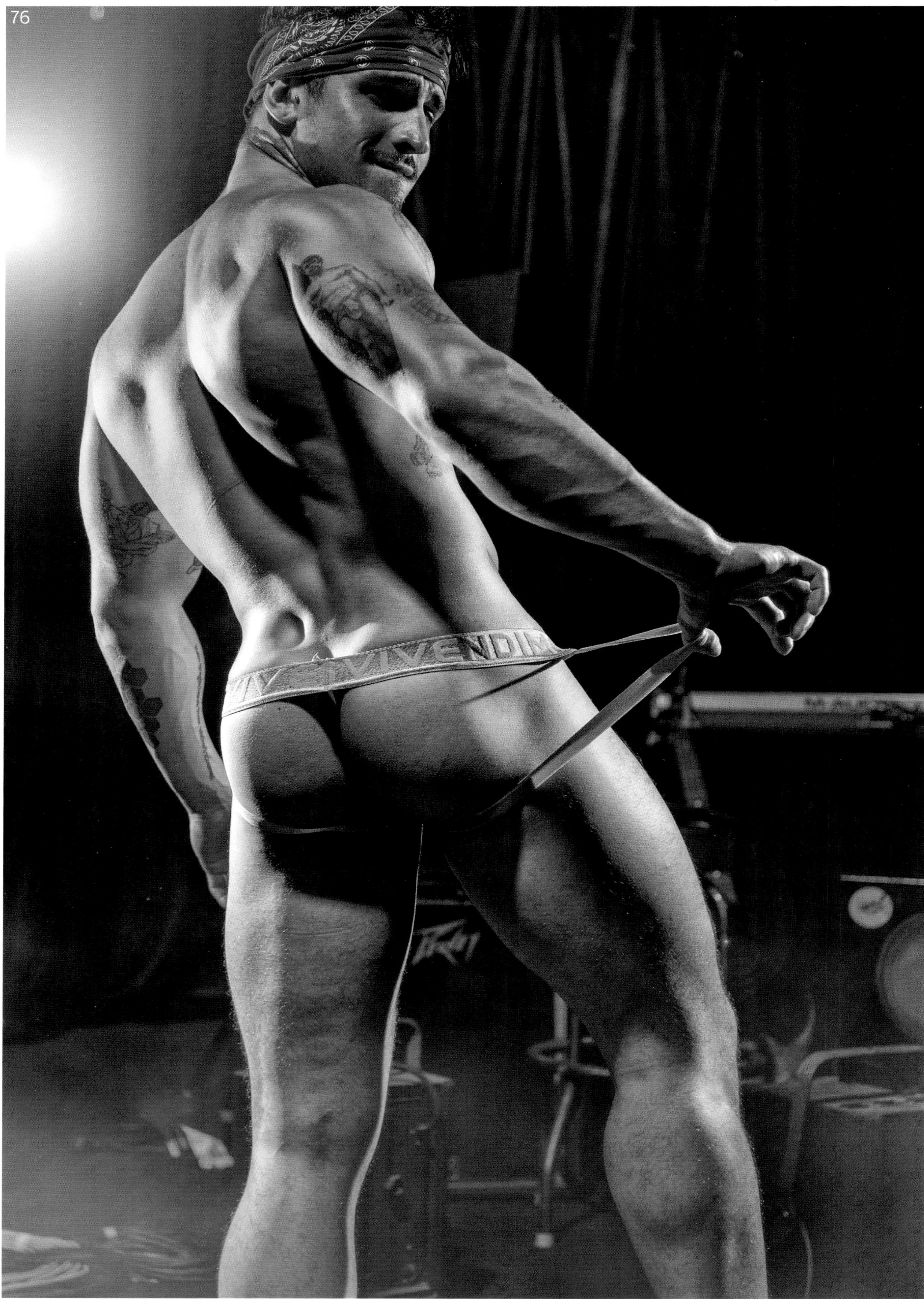
VIVENDI

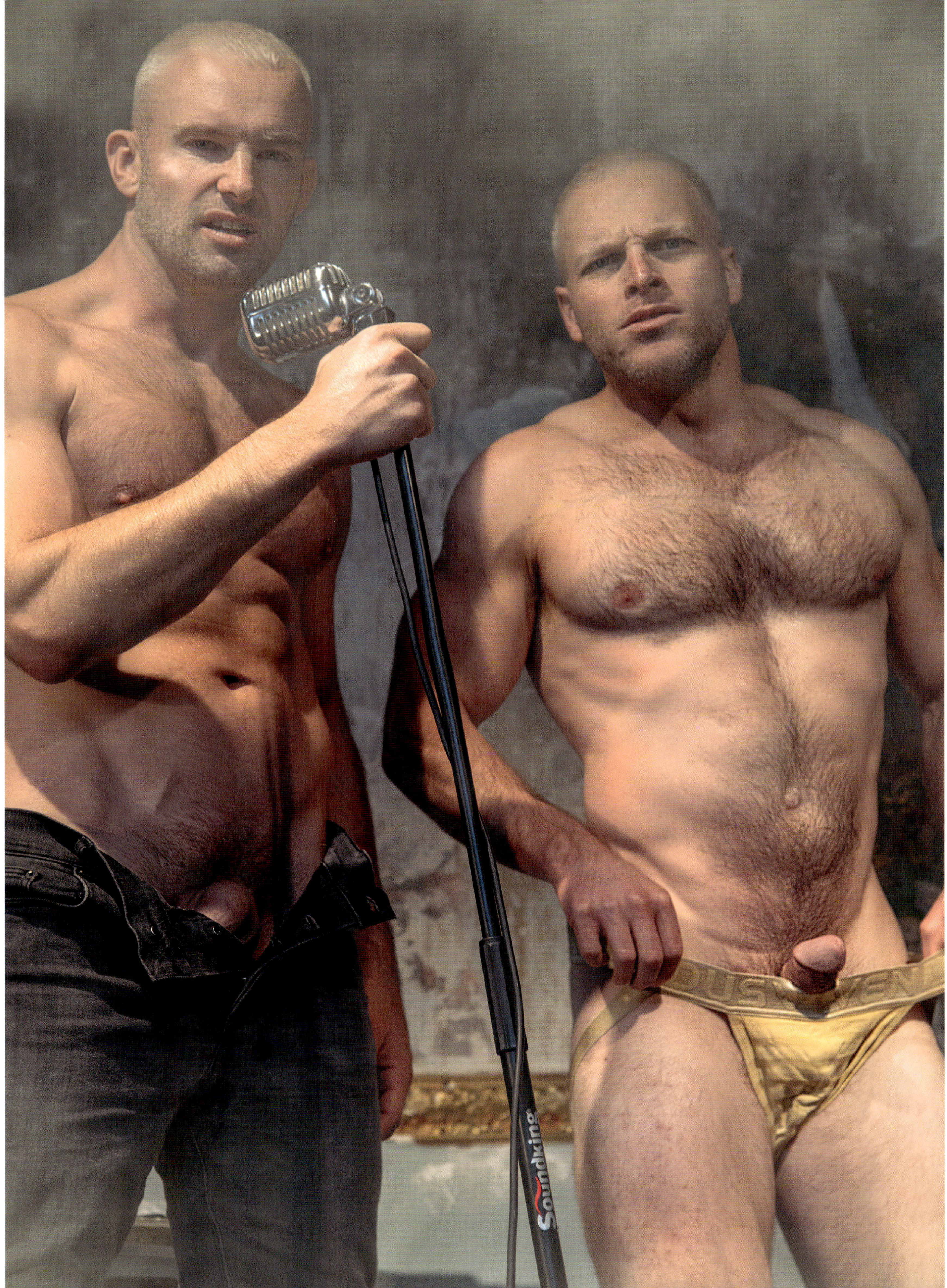
Soundking

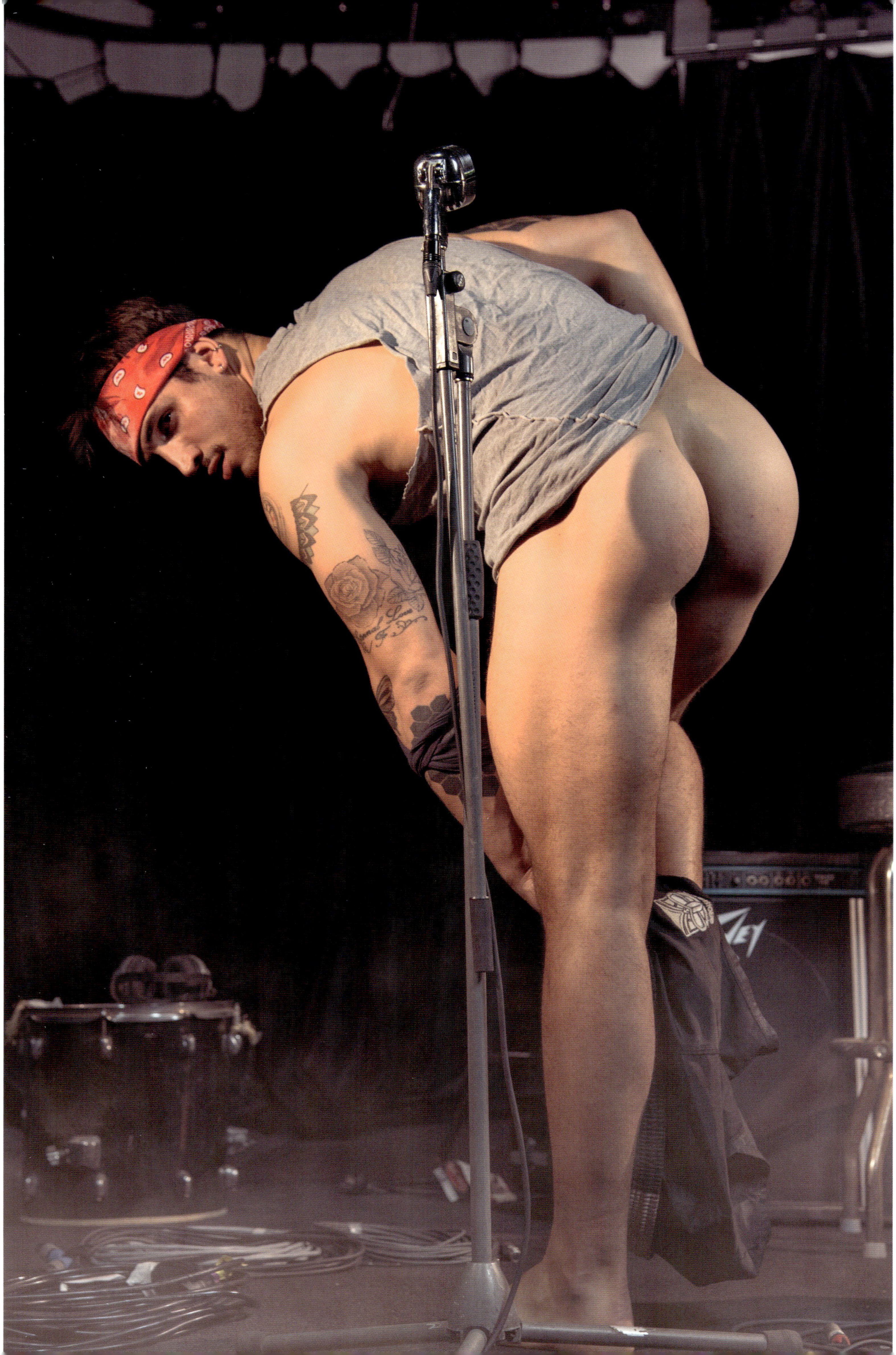

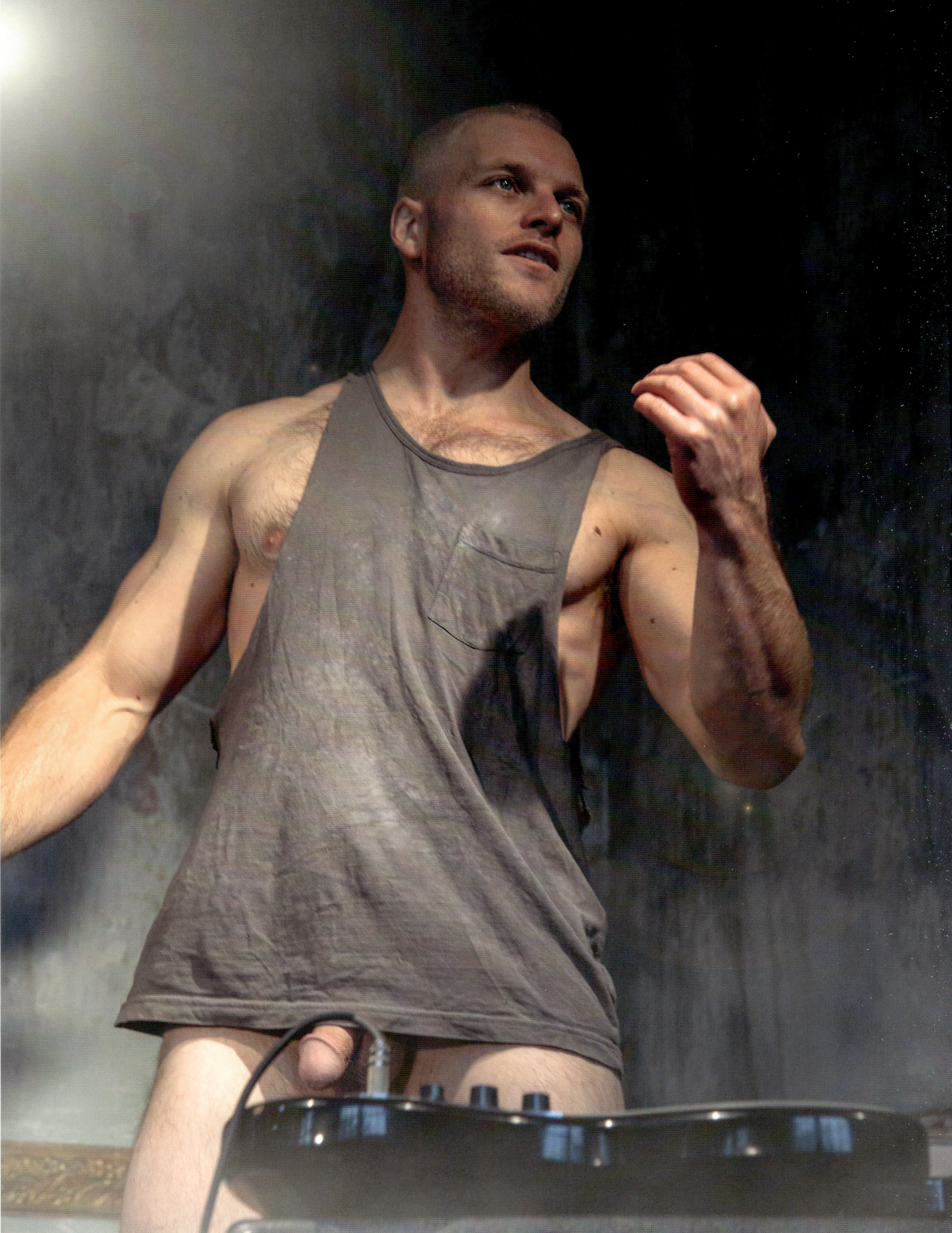

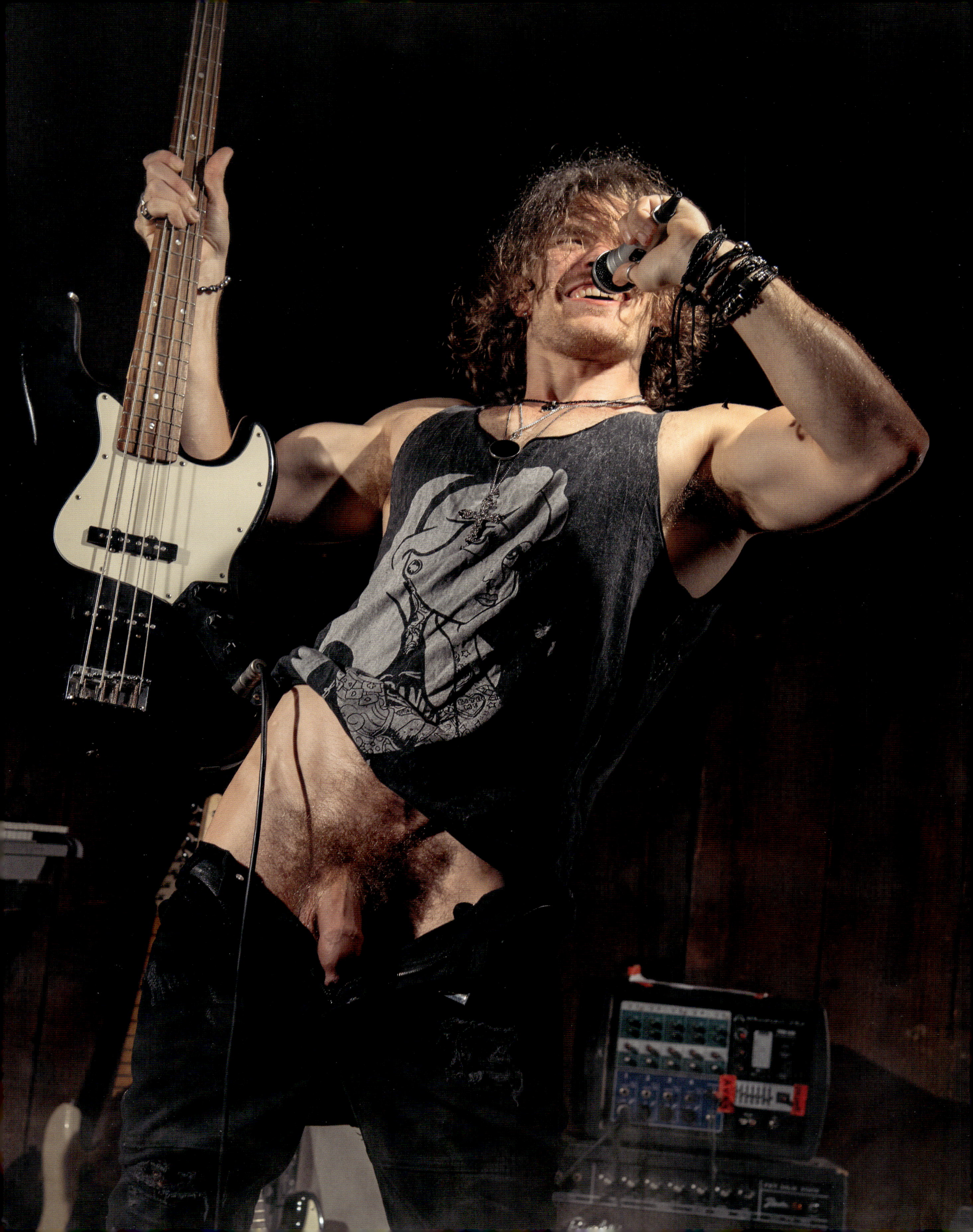

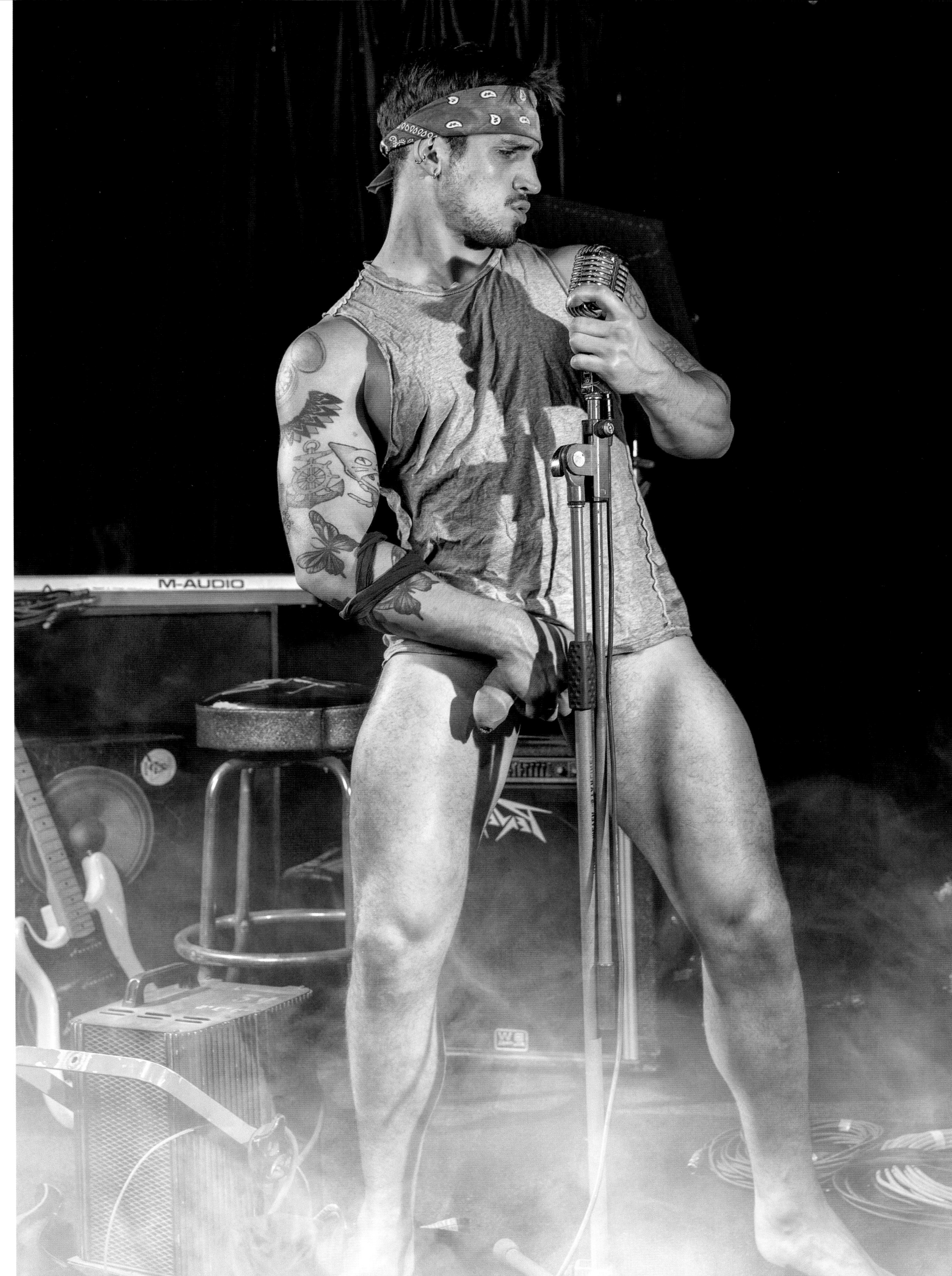
M-AUDIO

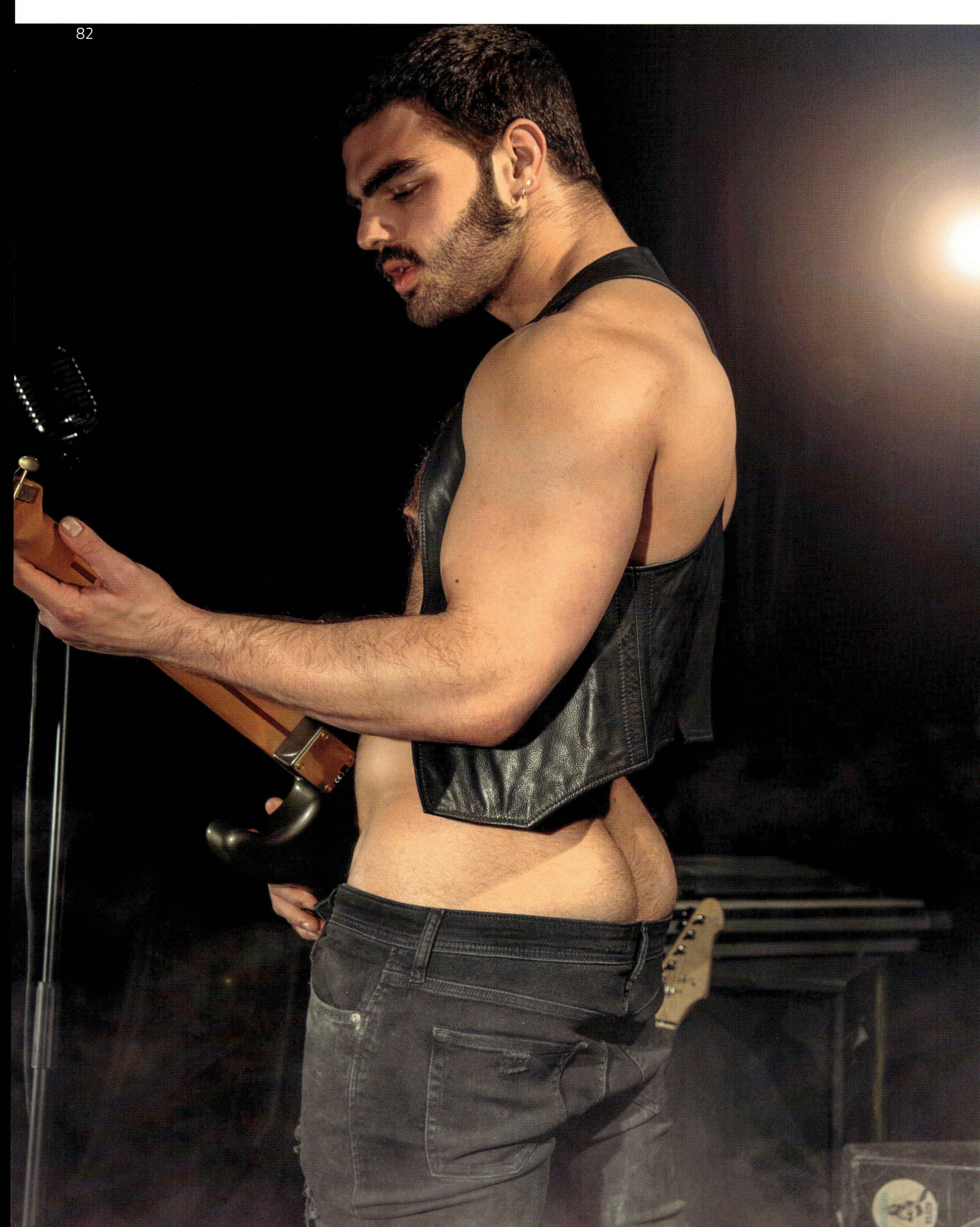

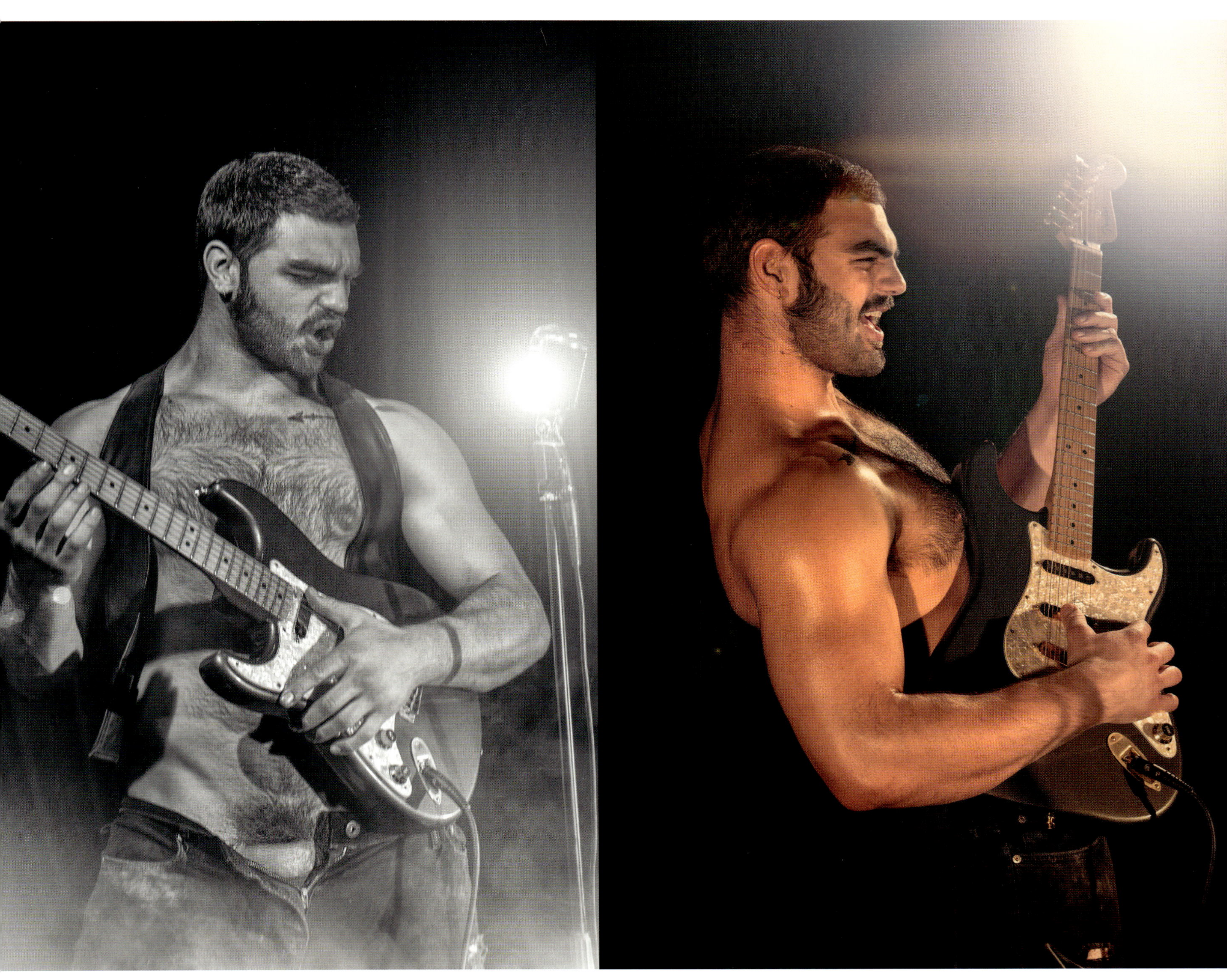

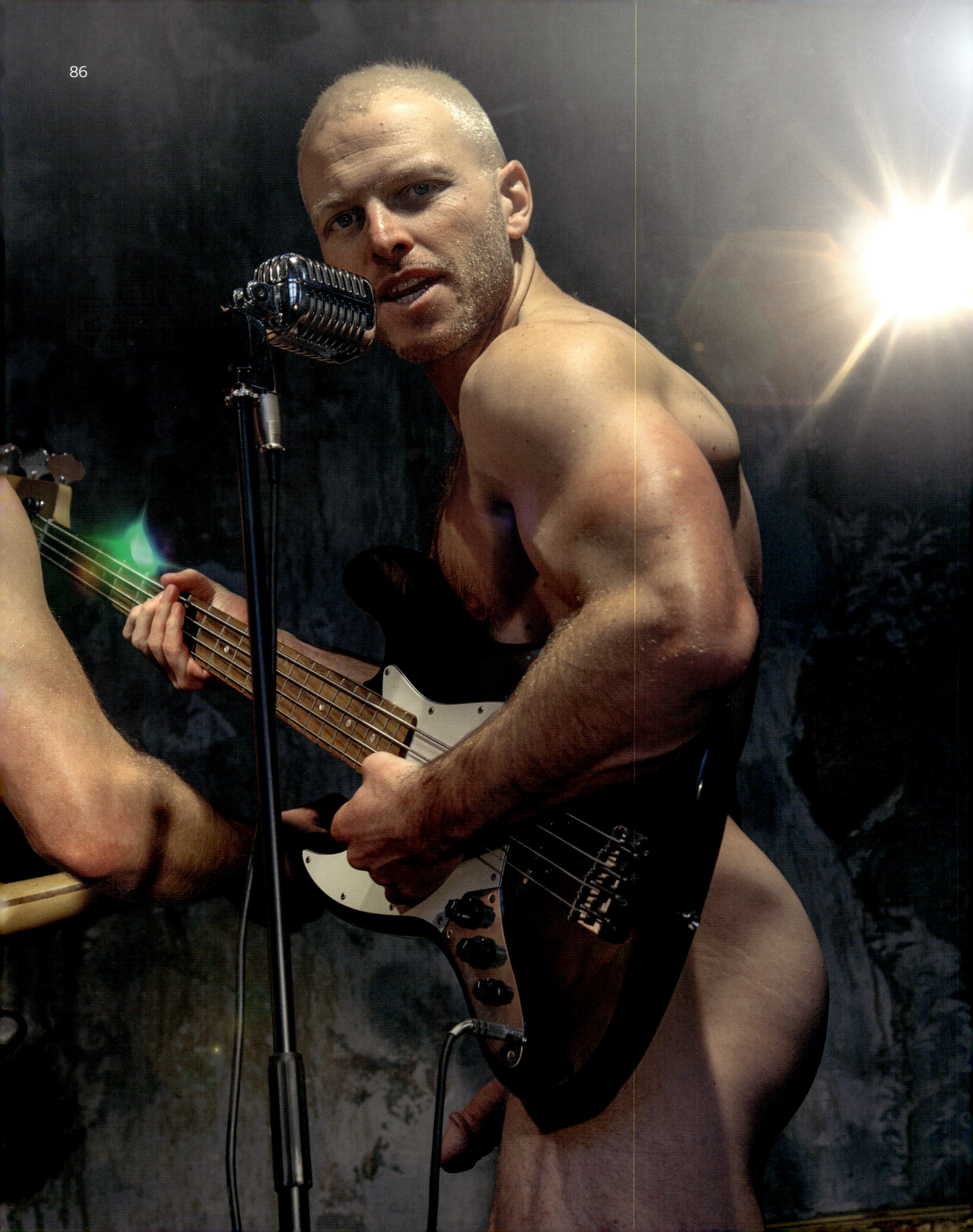

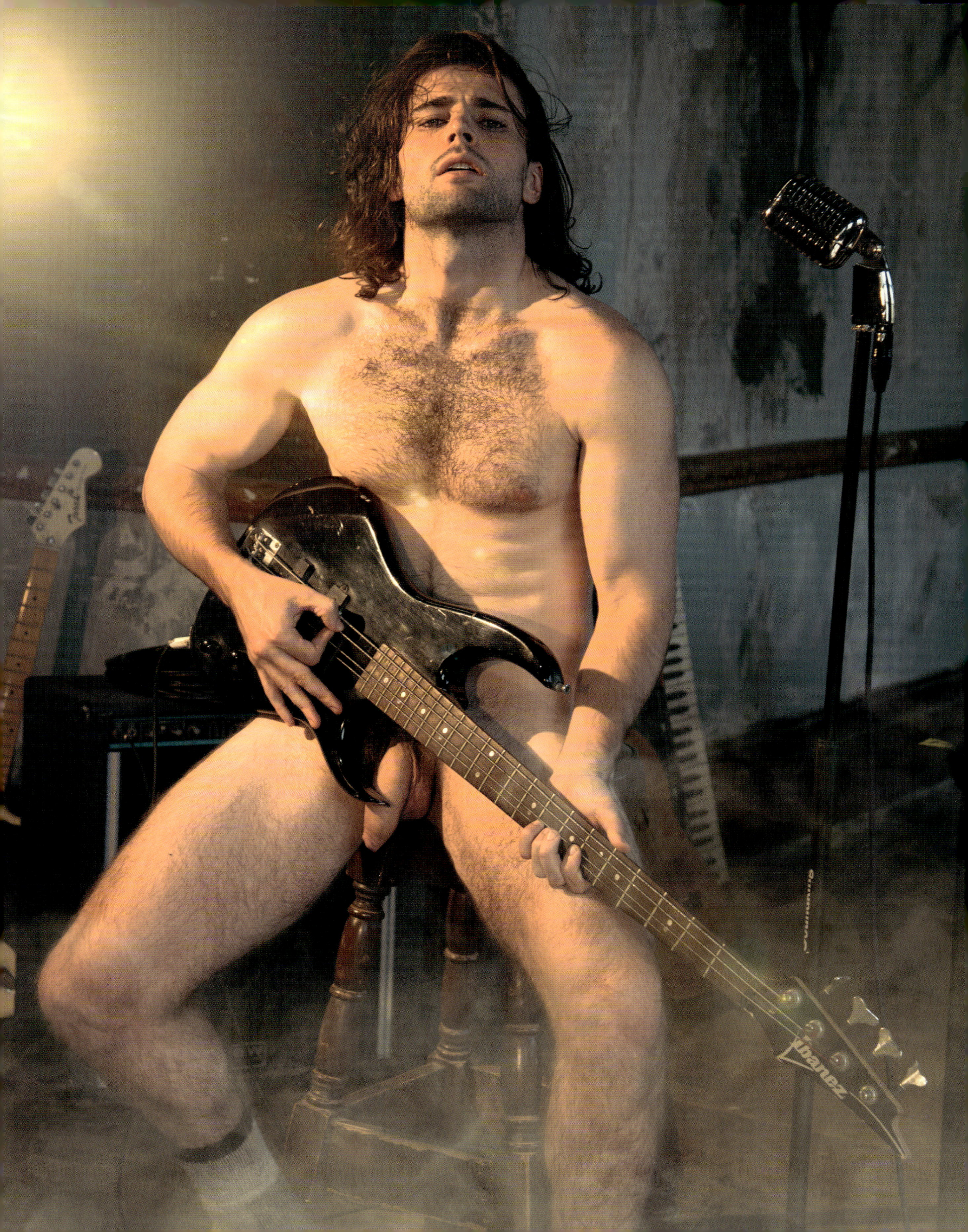
Ibanez

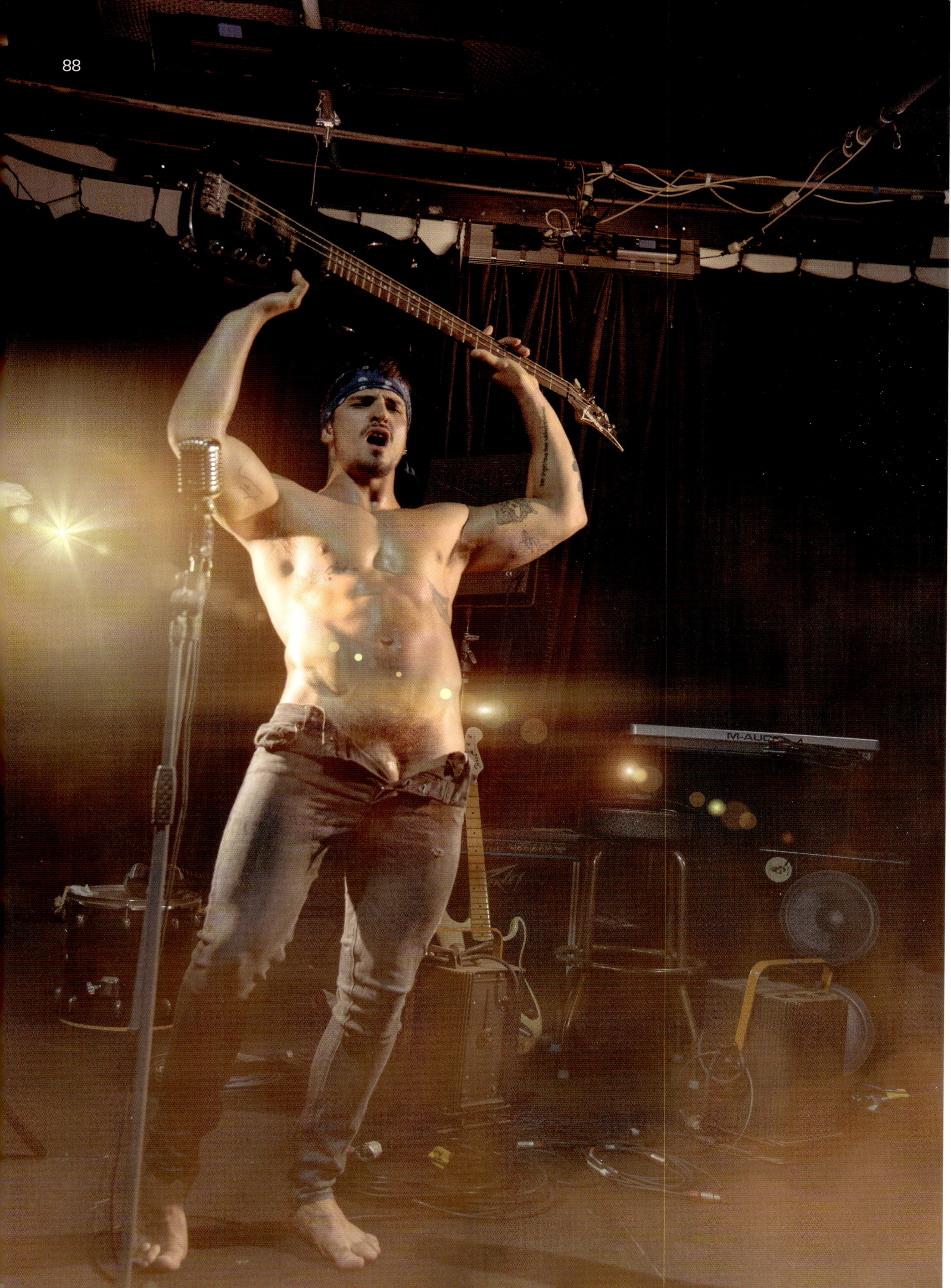

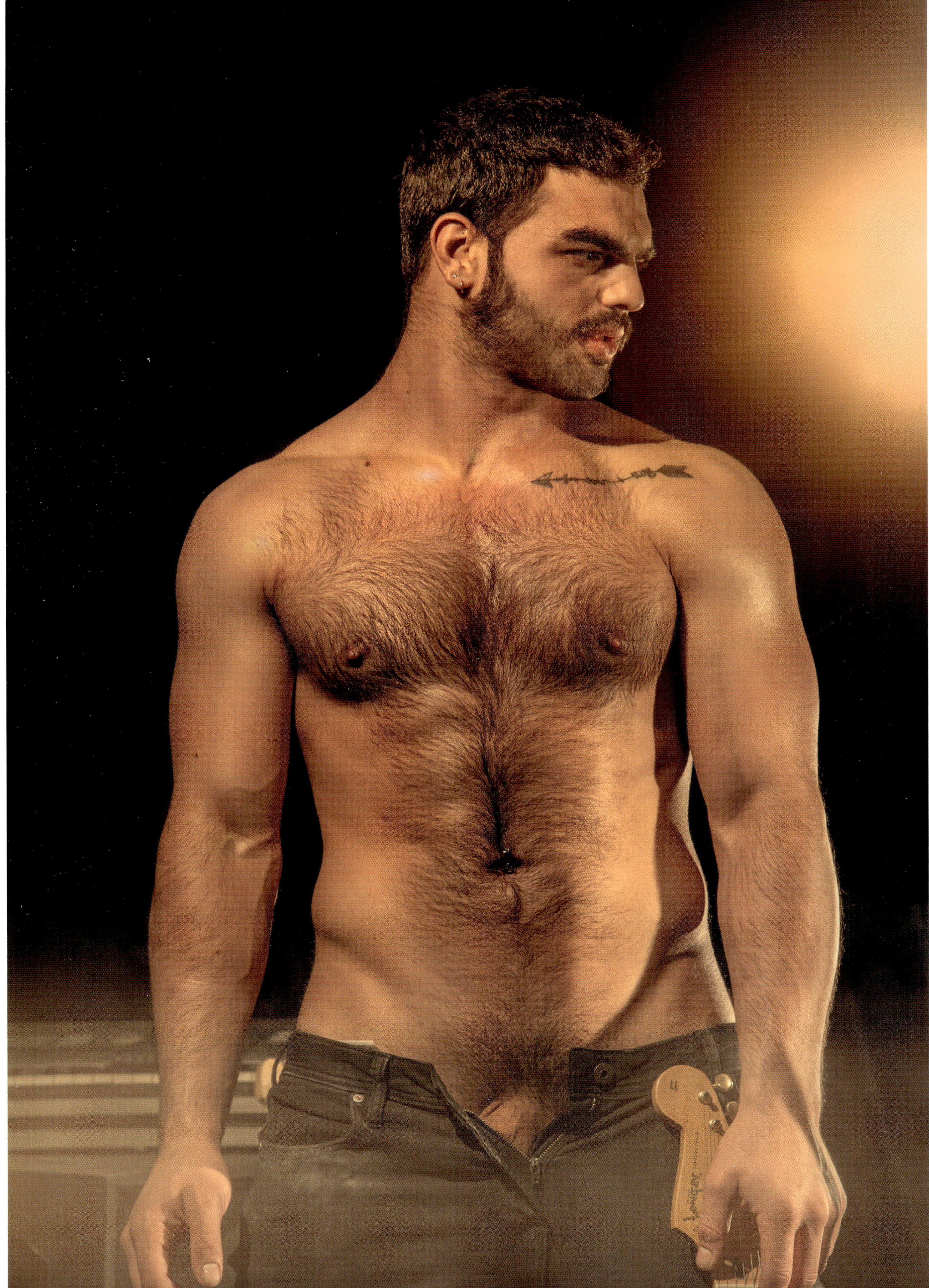

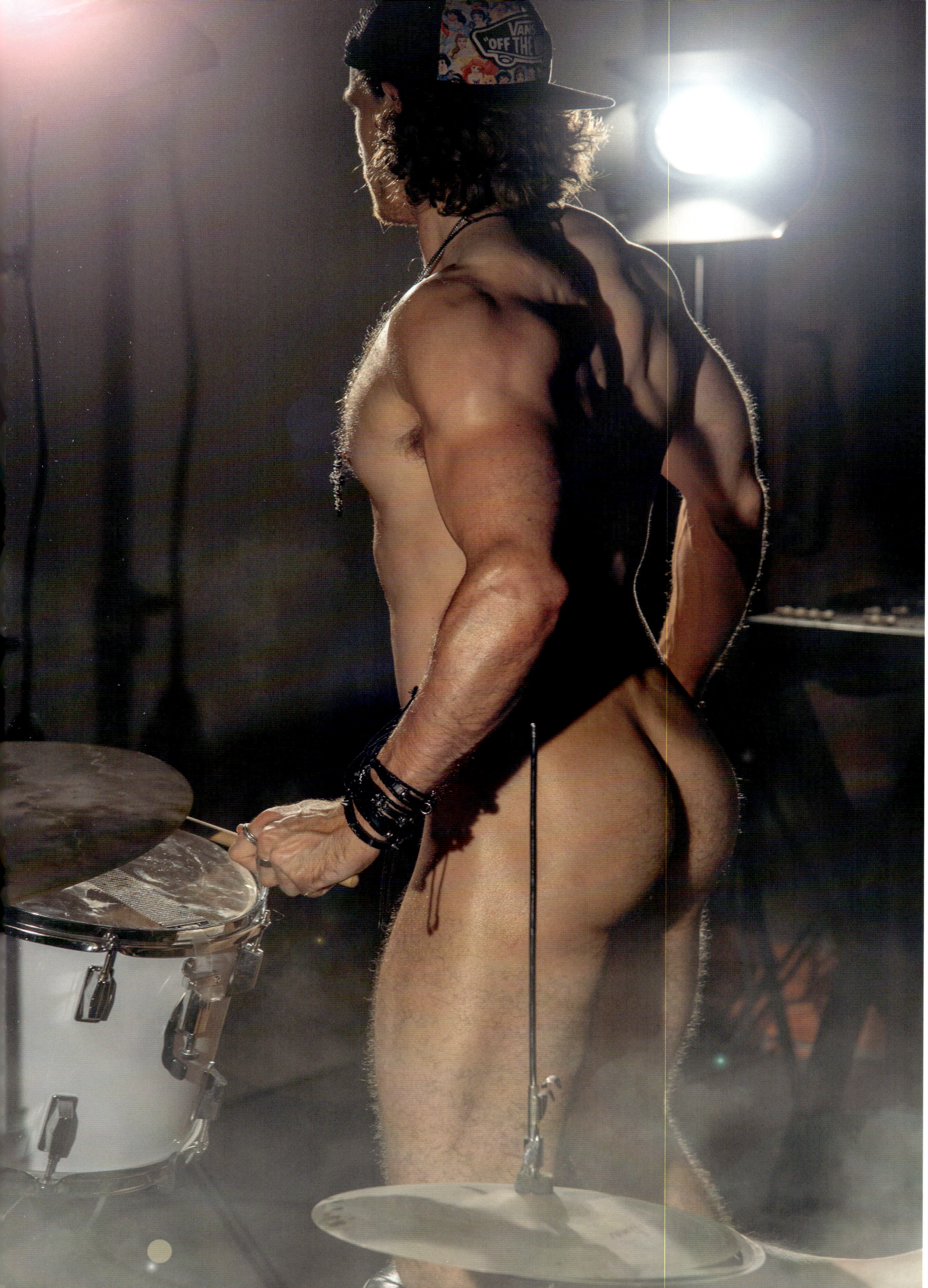
VANS
OFF THE

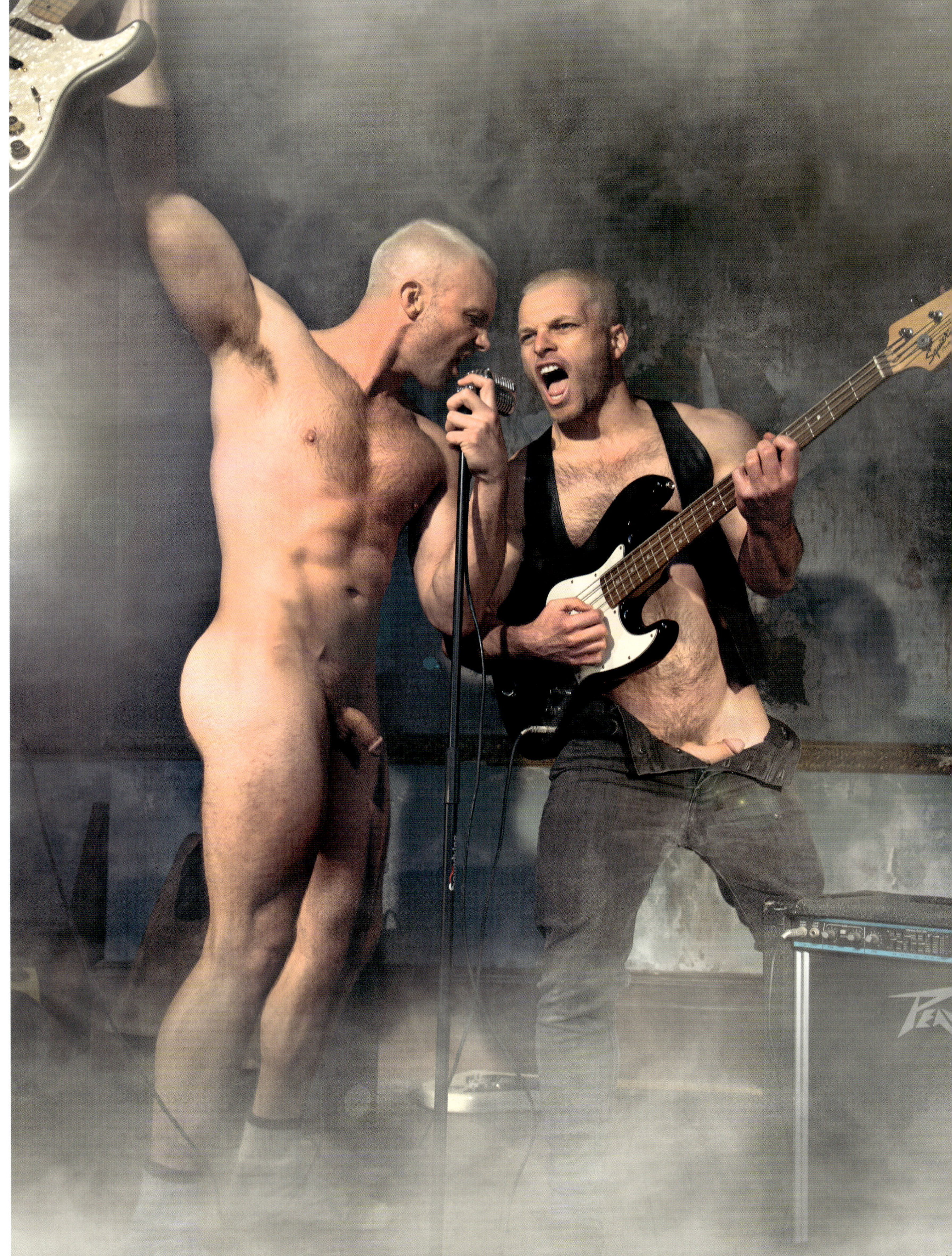

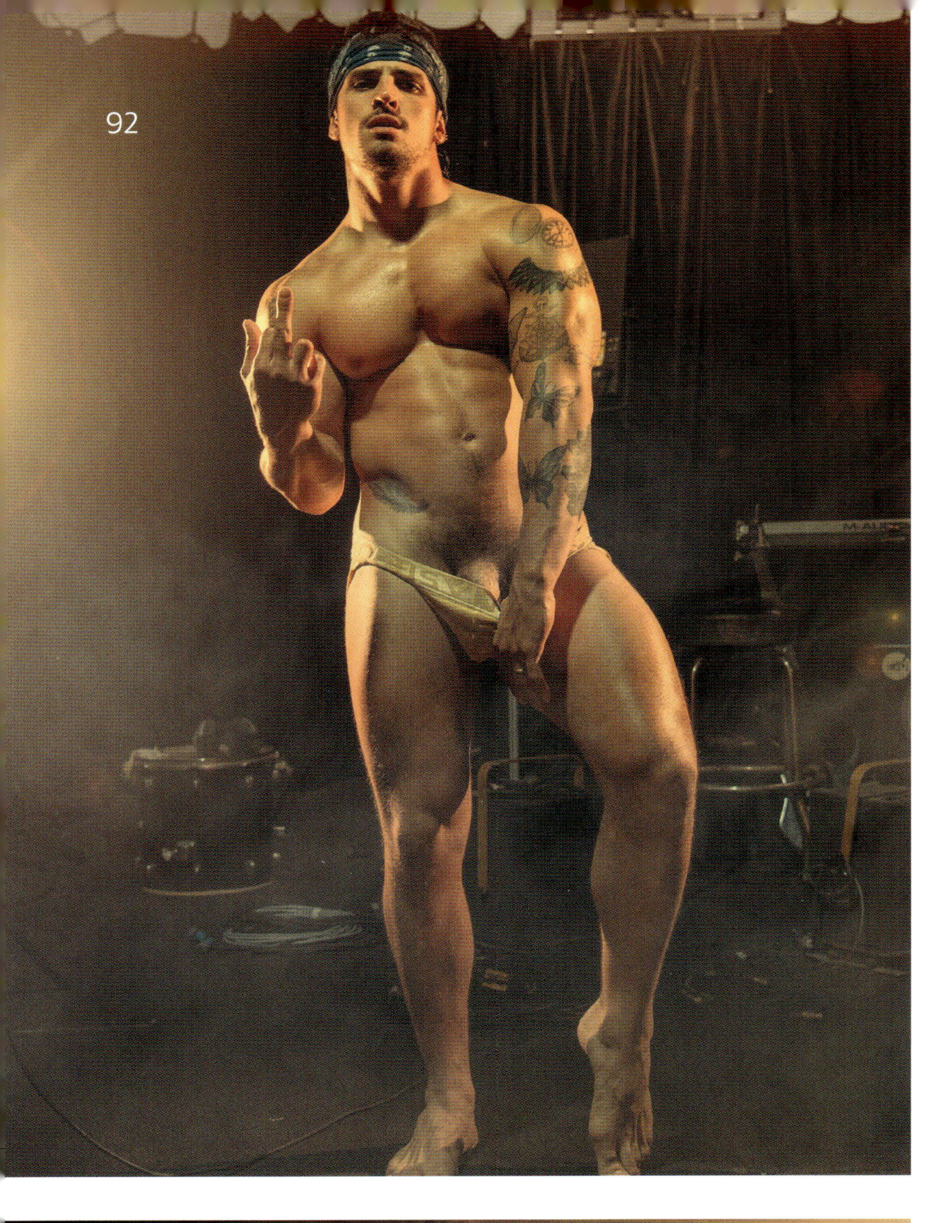

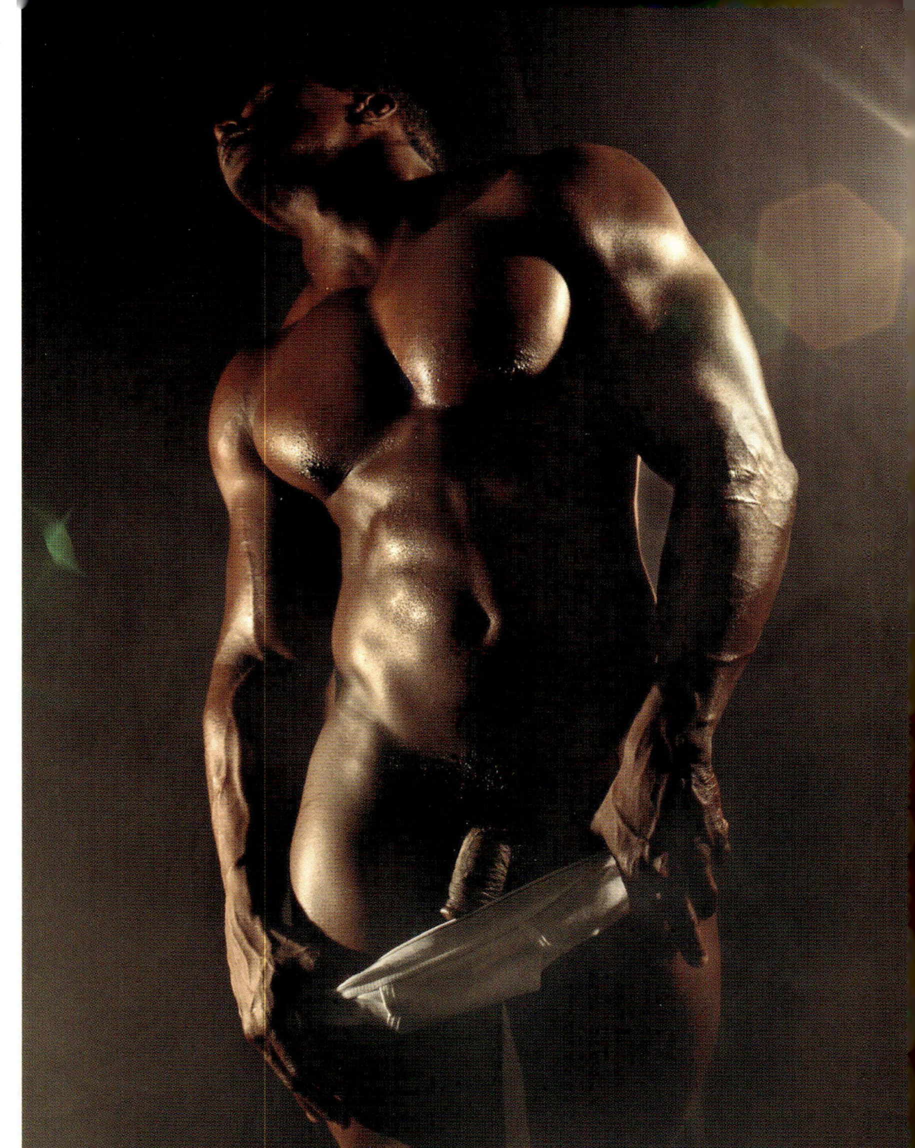

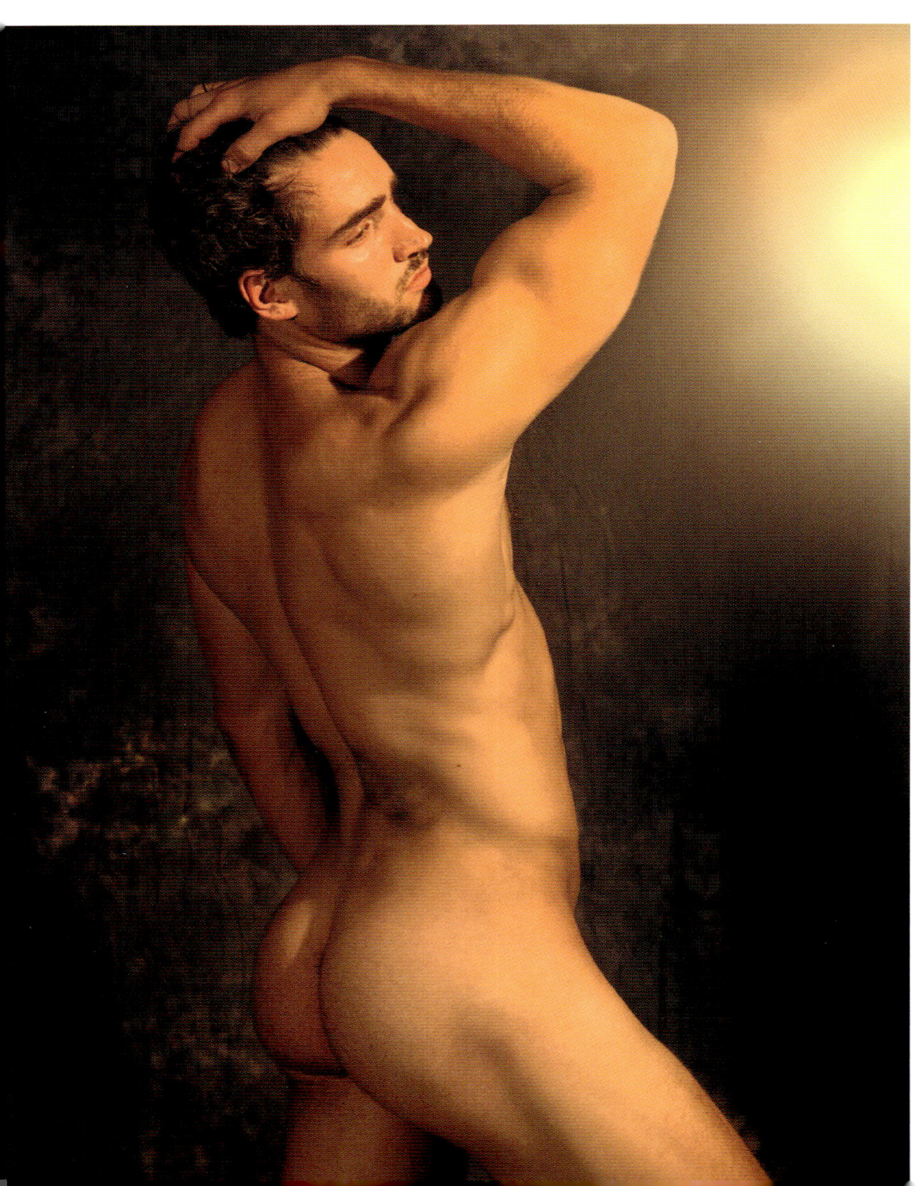

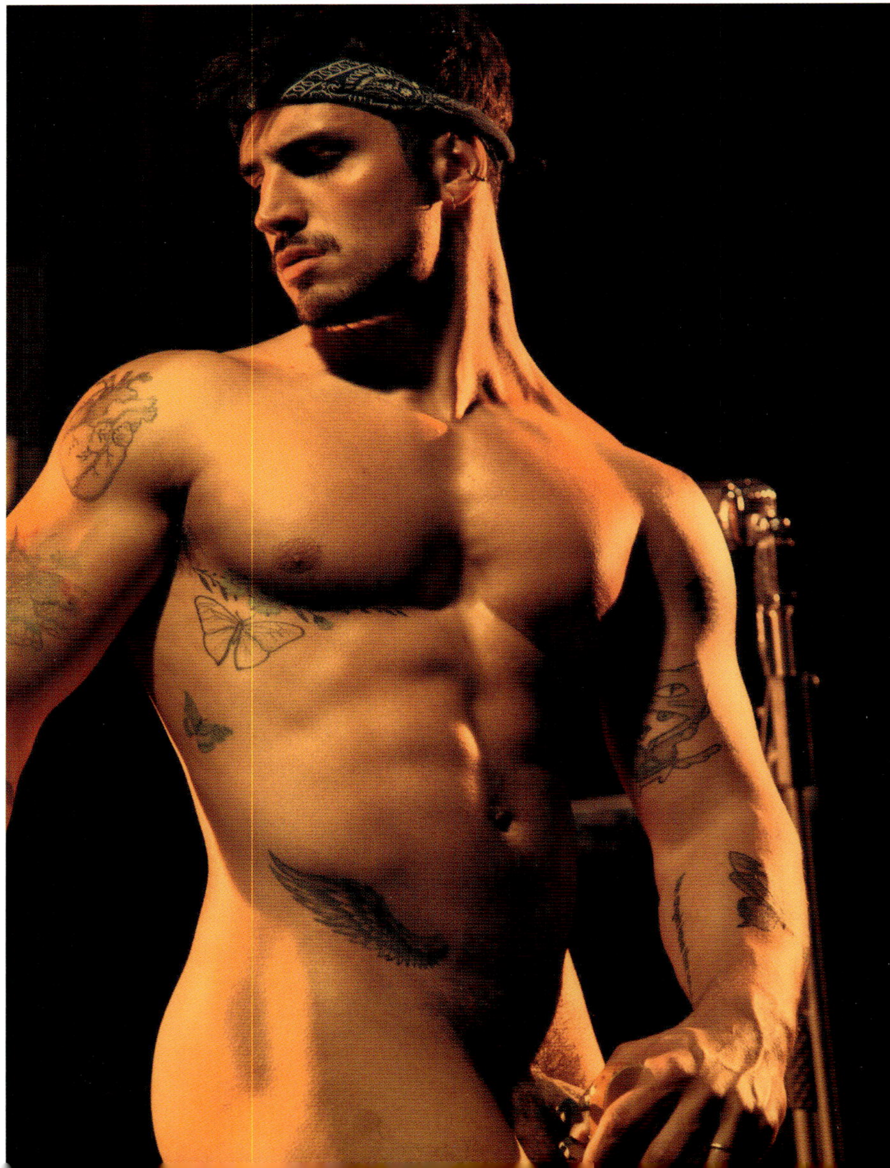

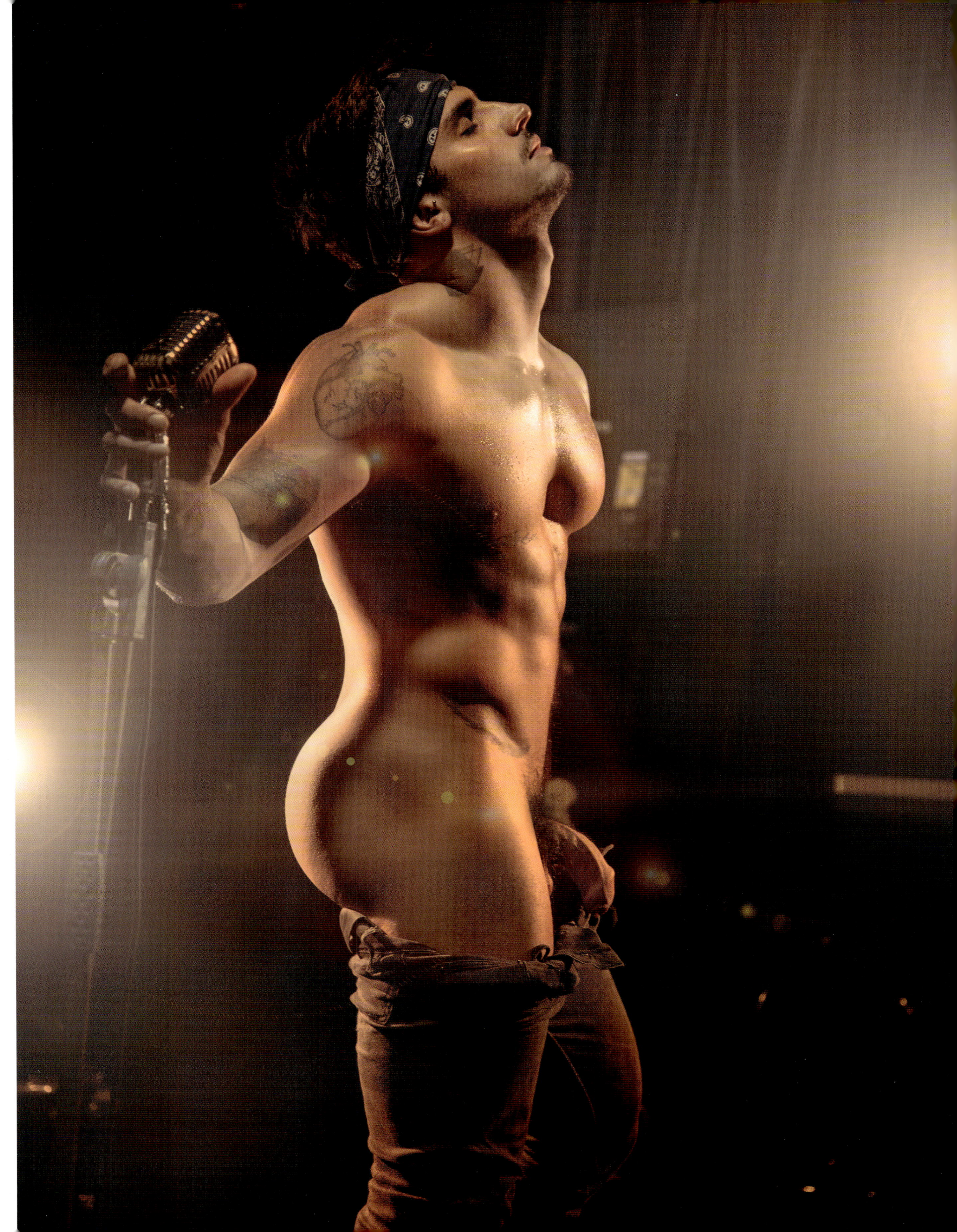

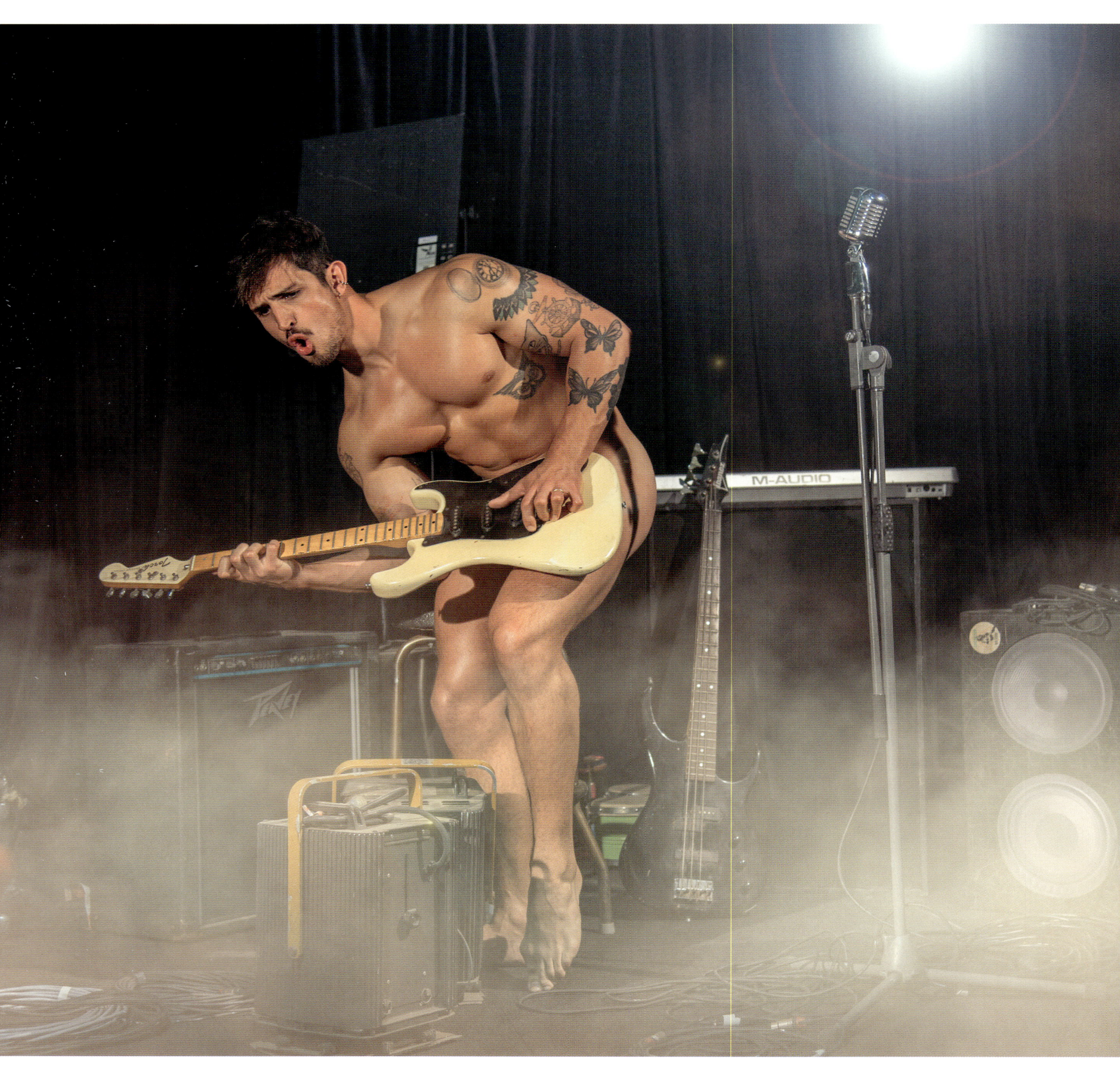
M-AUDIO

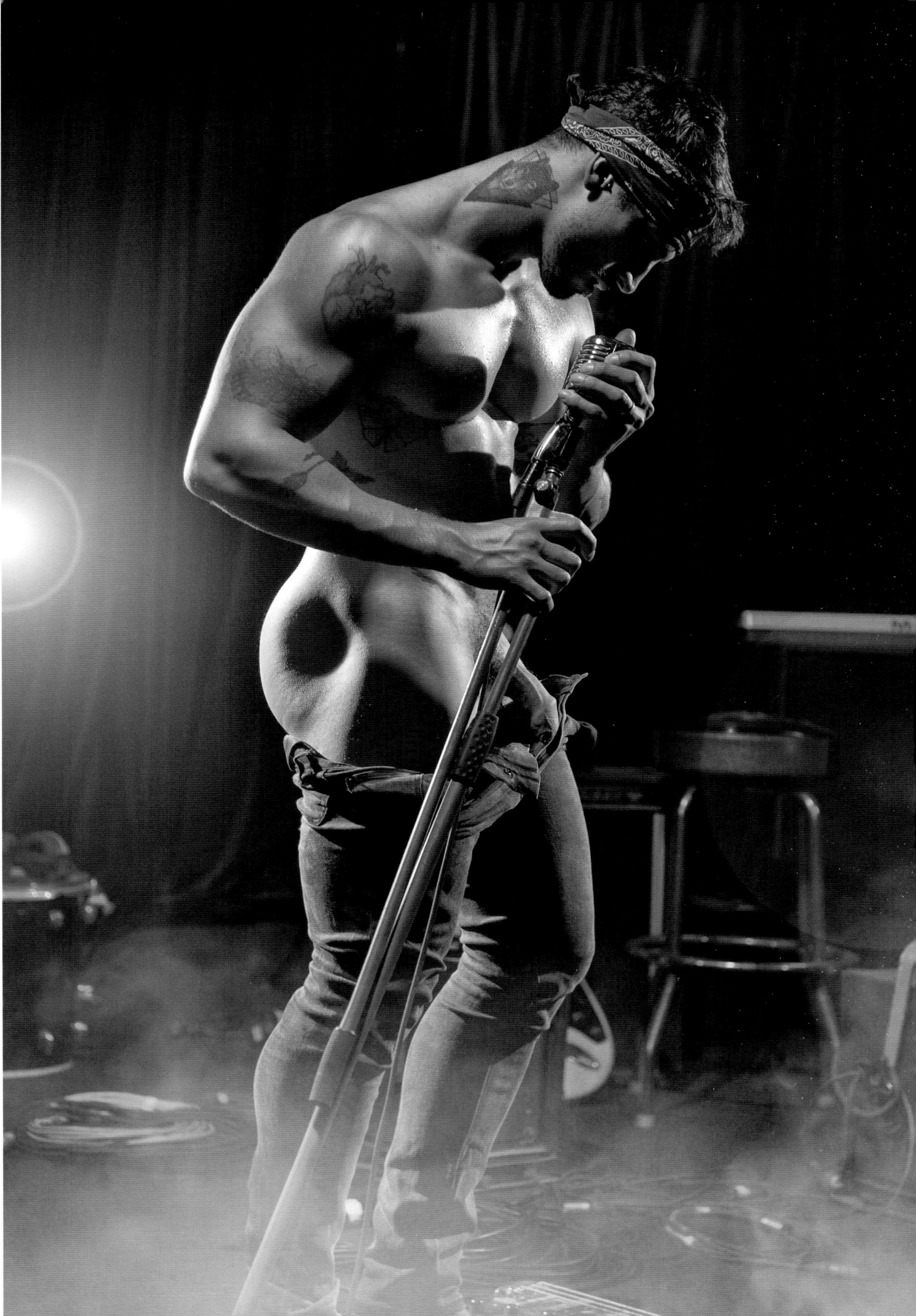

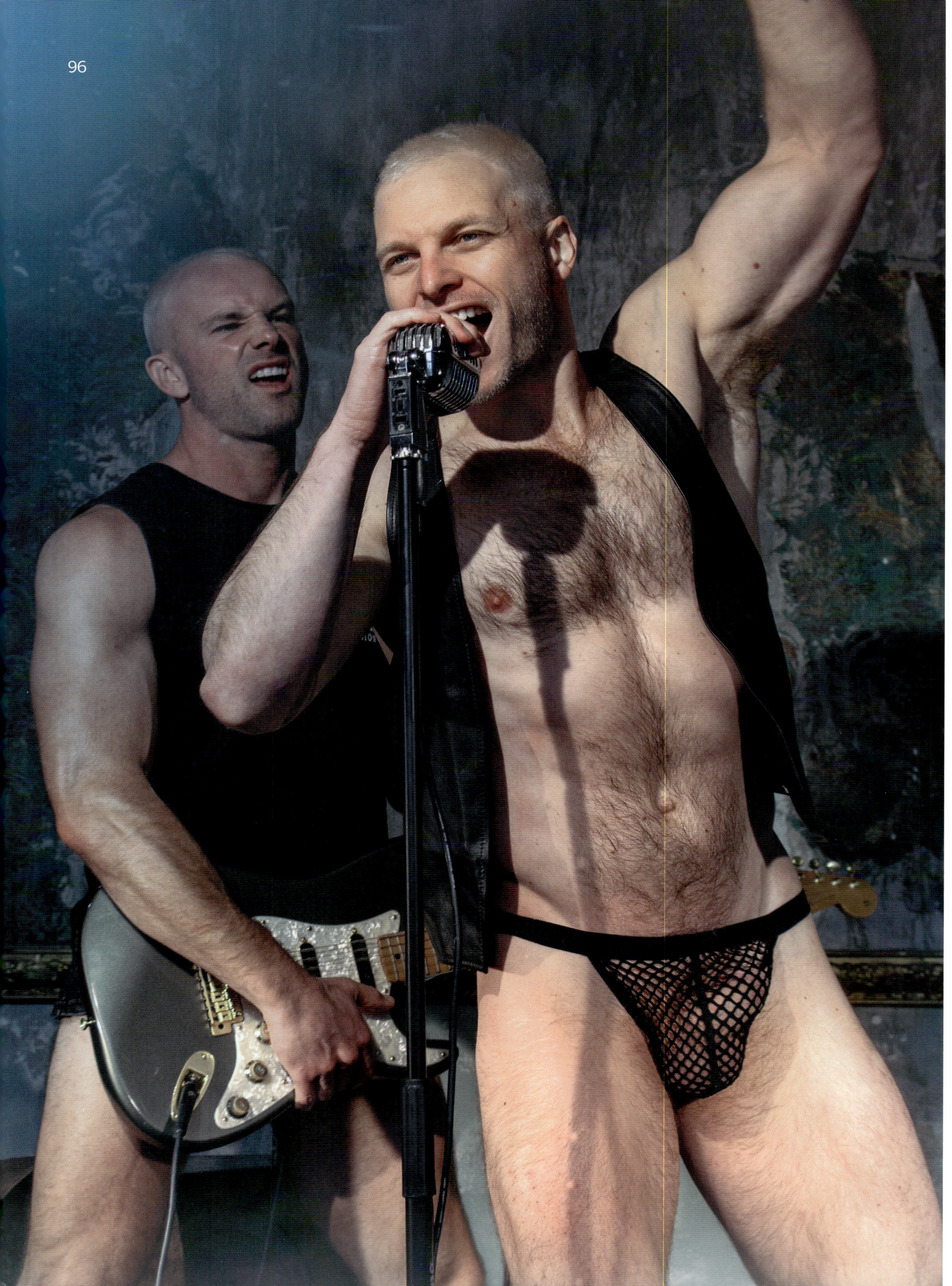

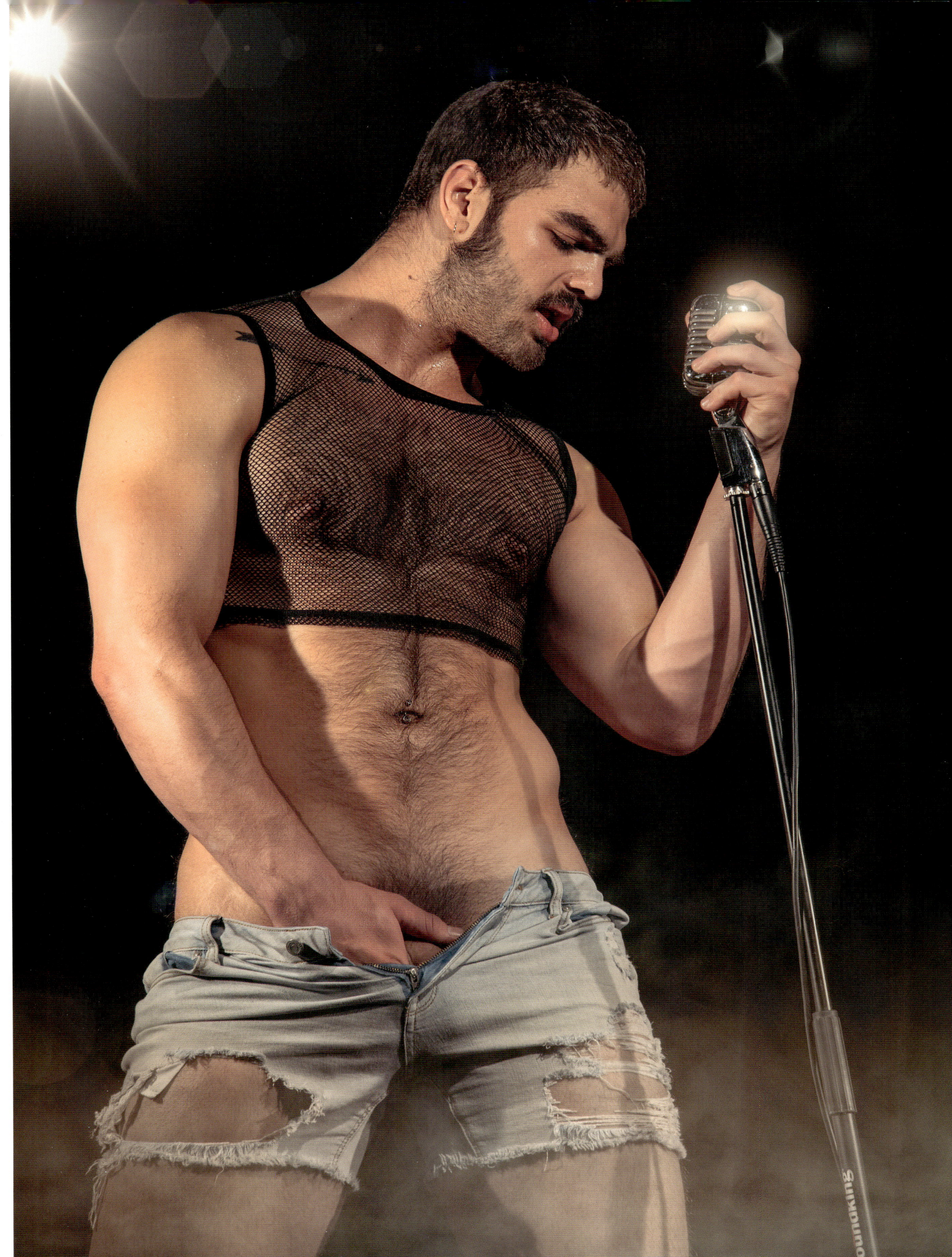

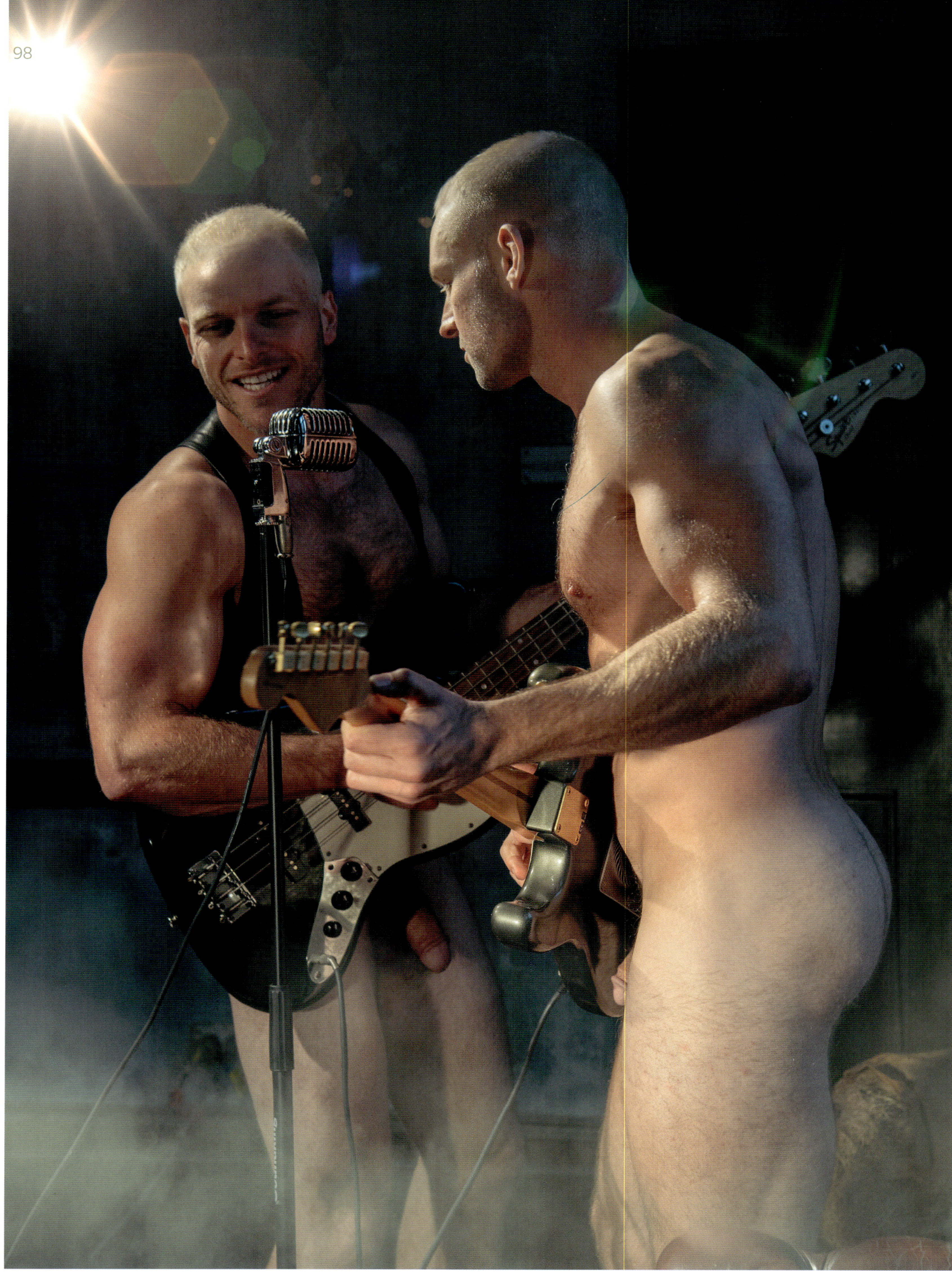

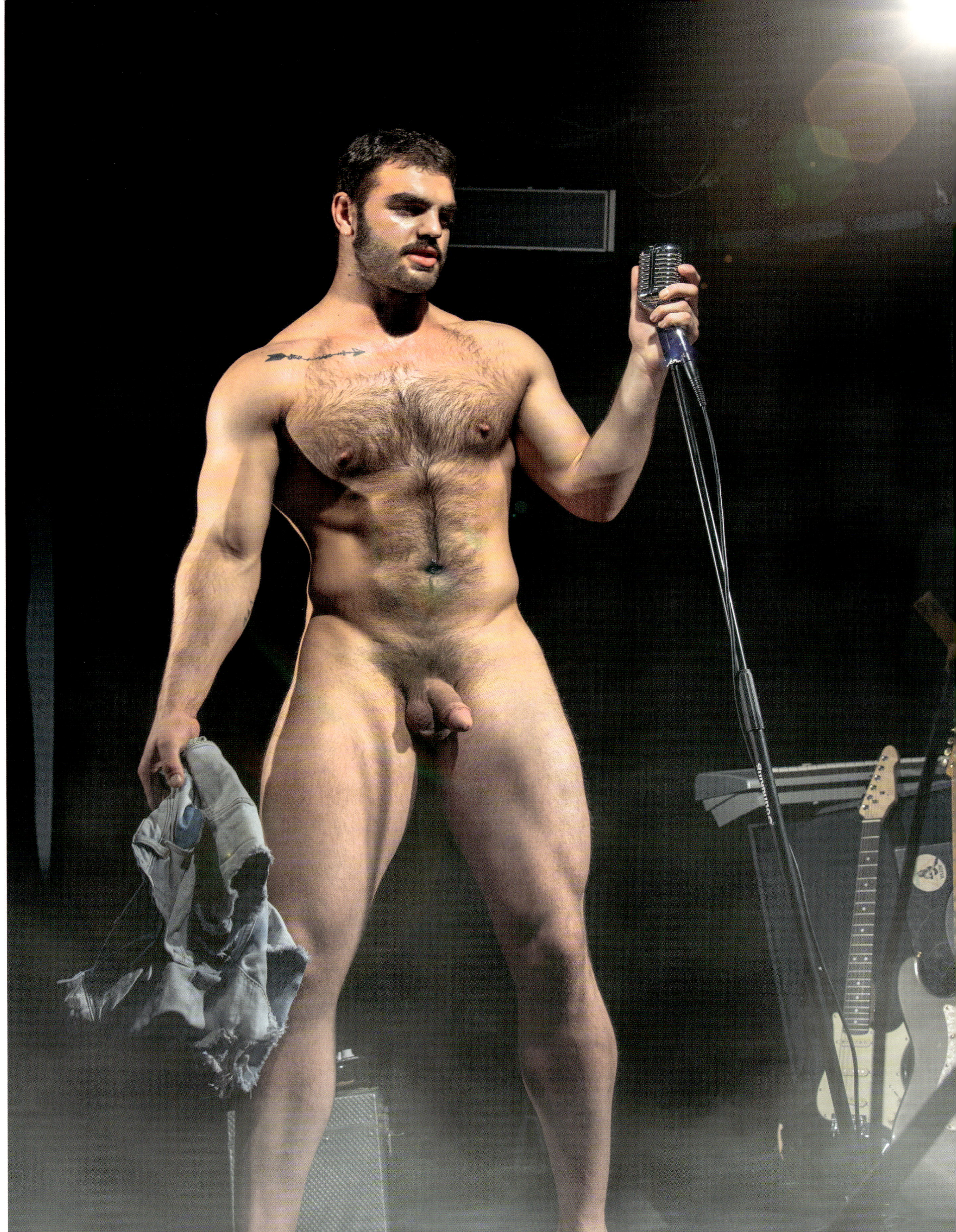

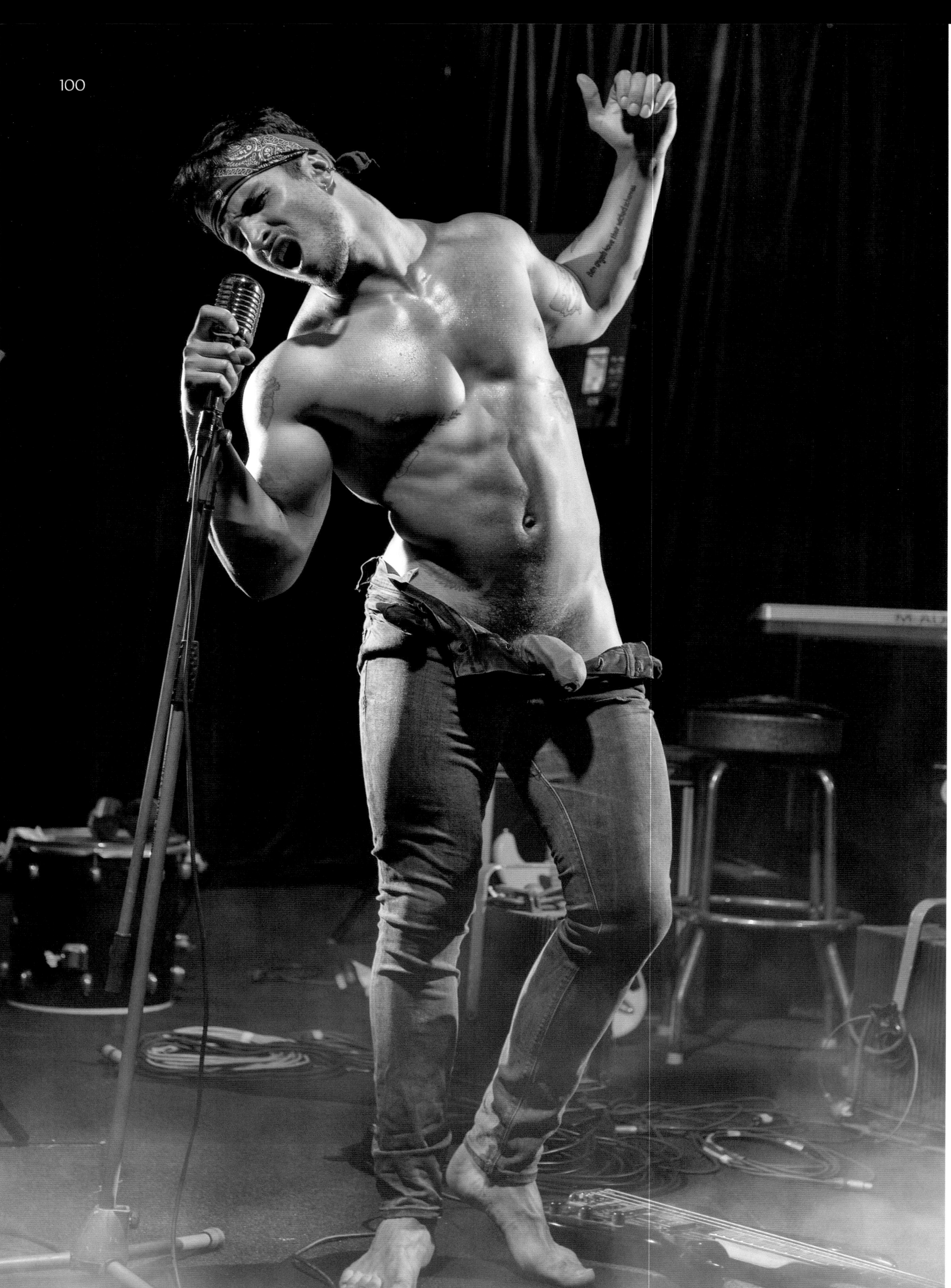

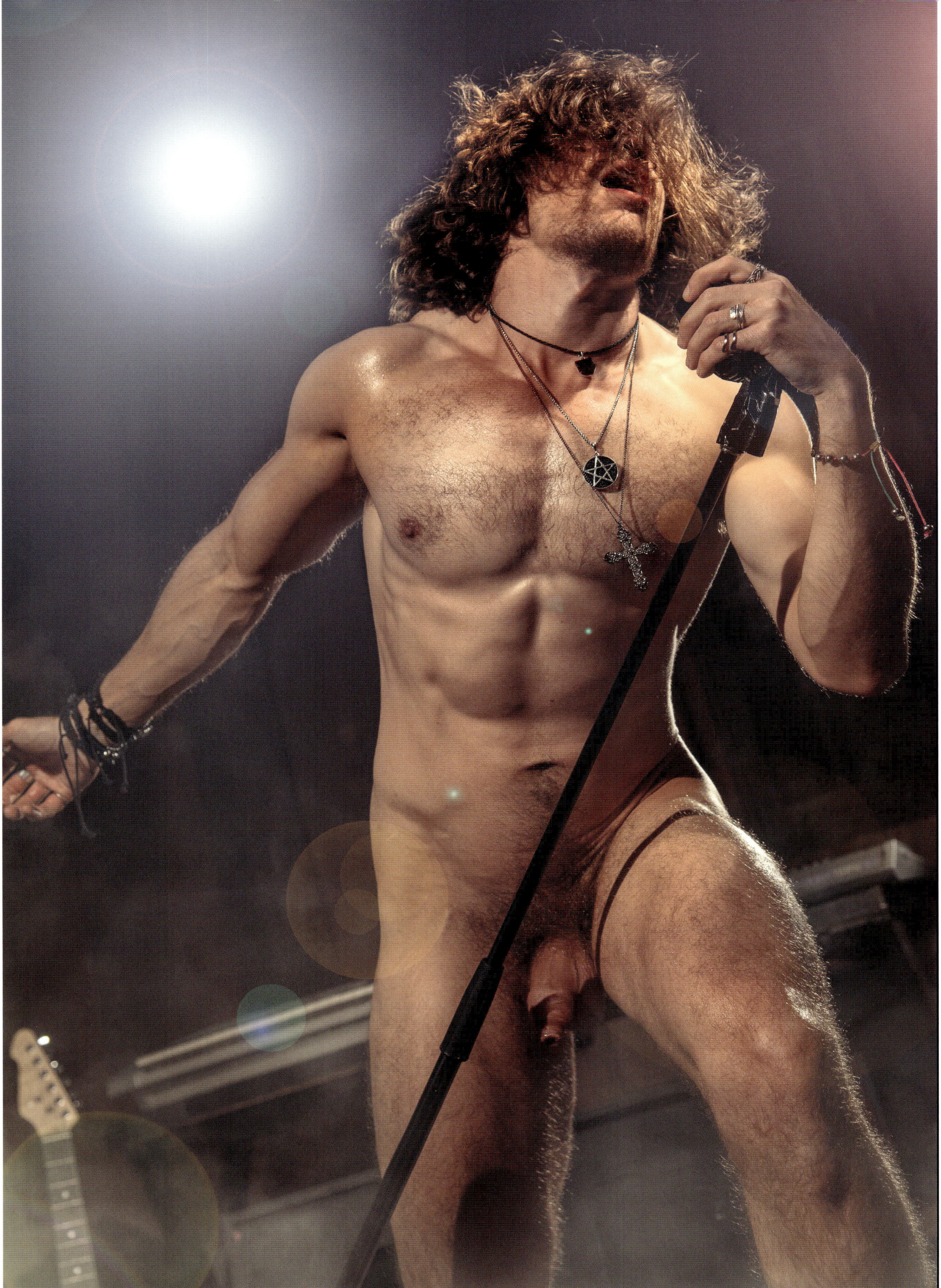

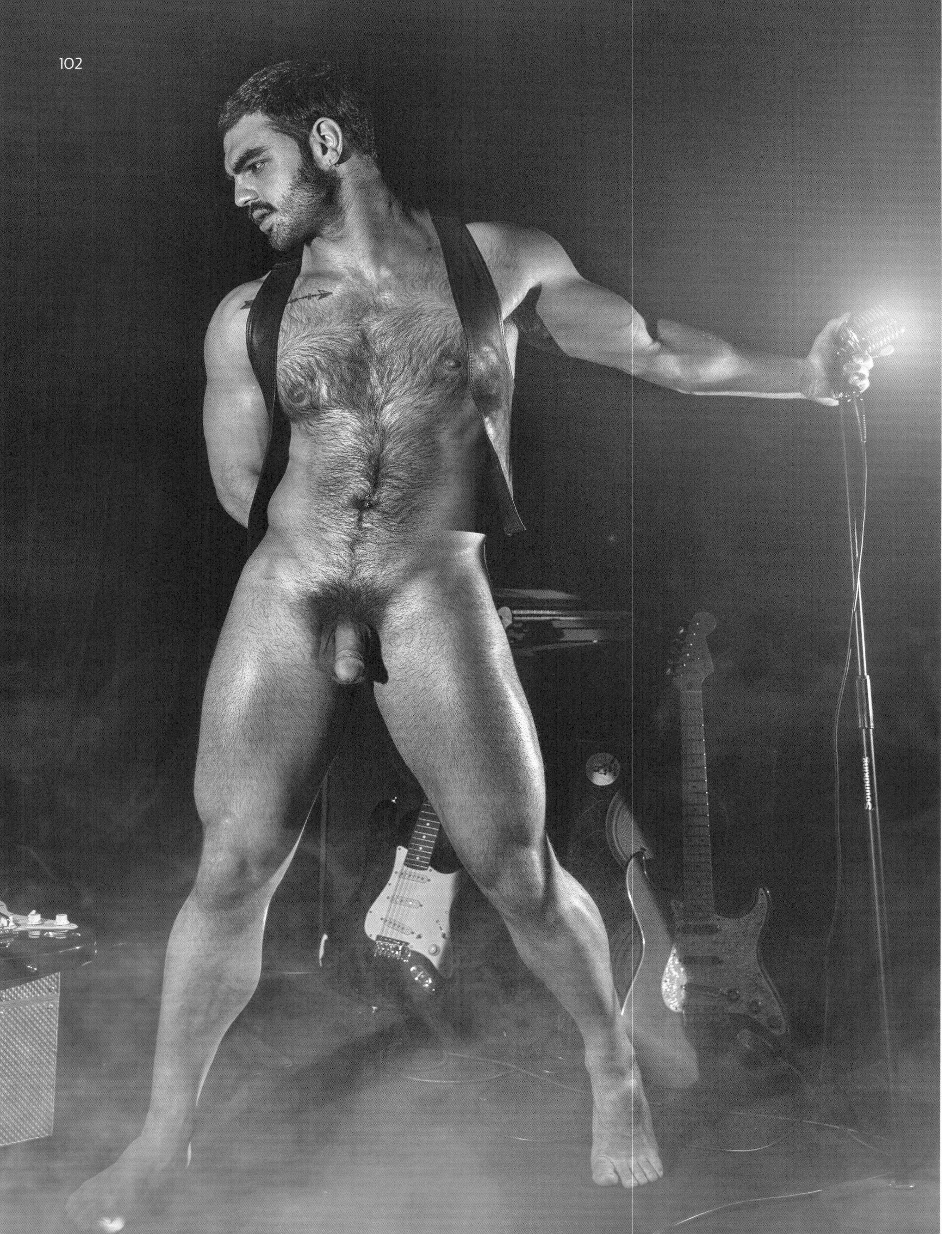
Soundking

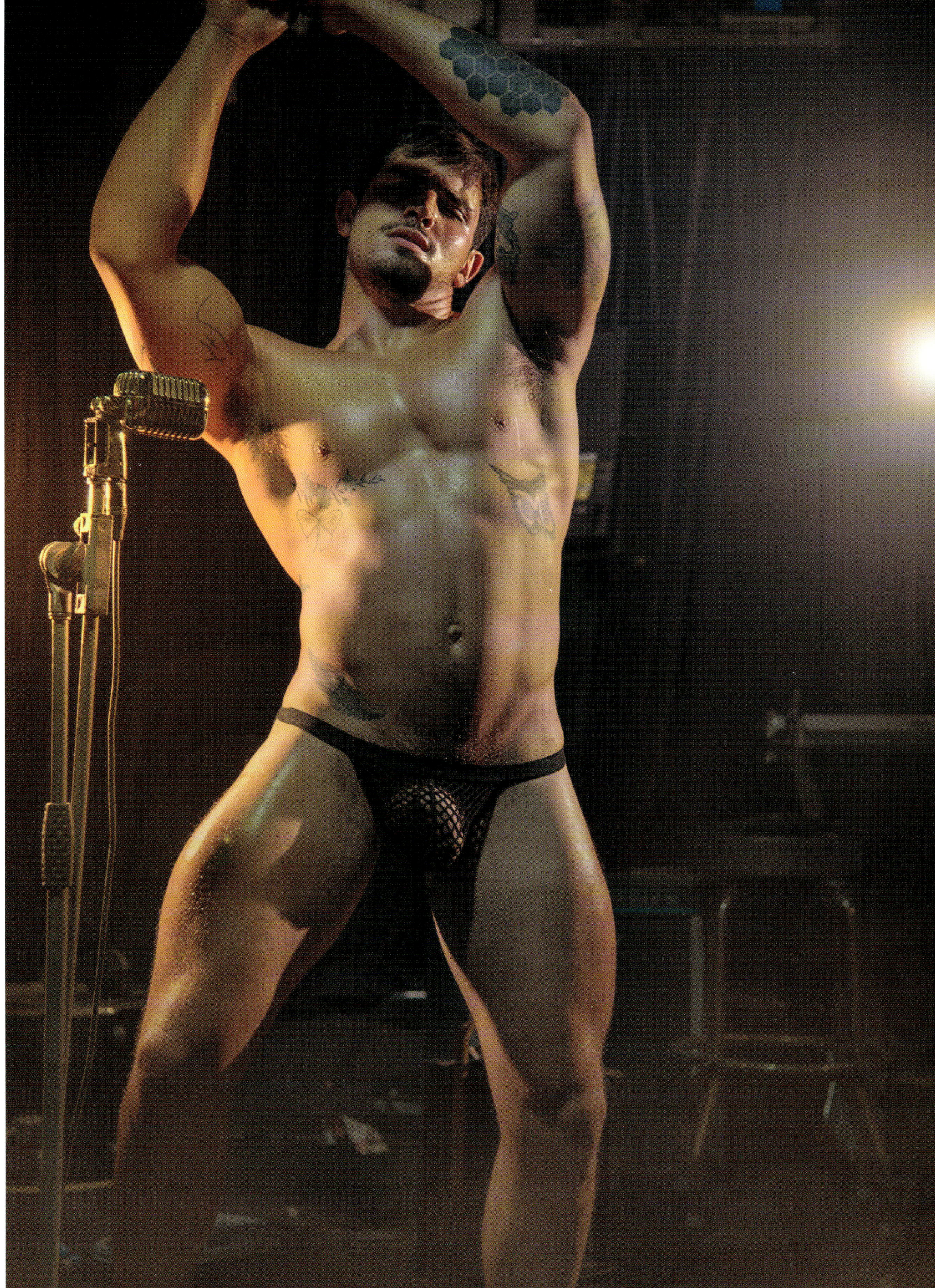

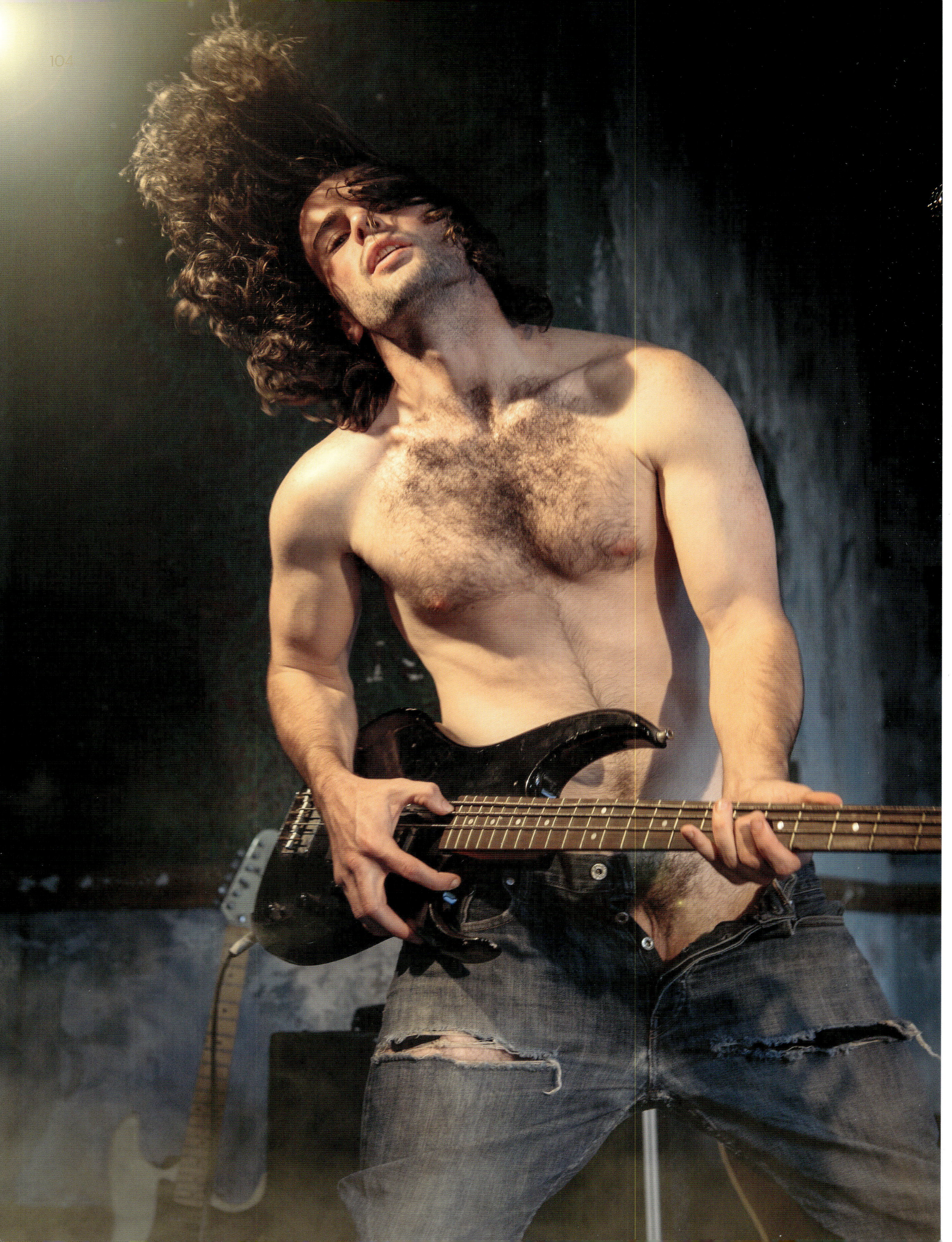

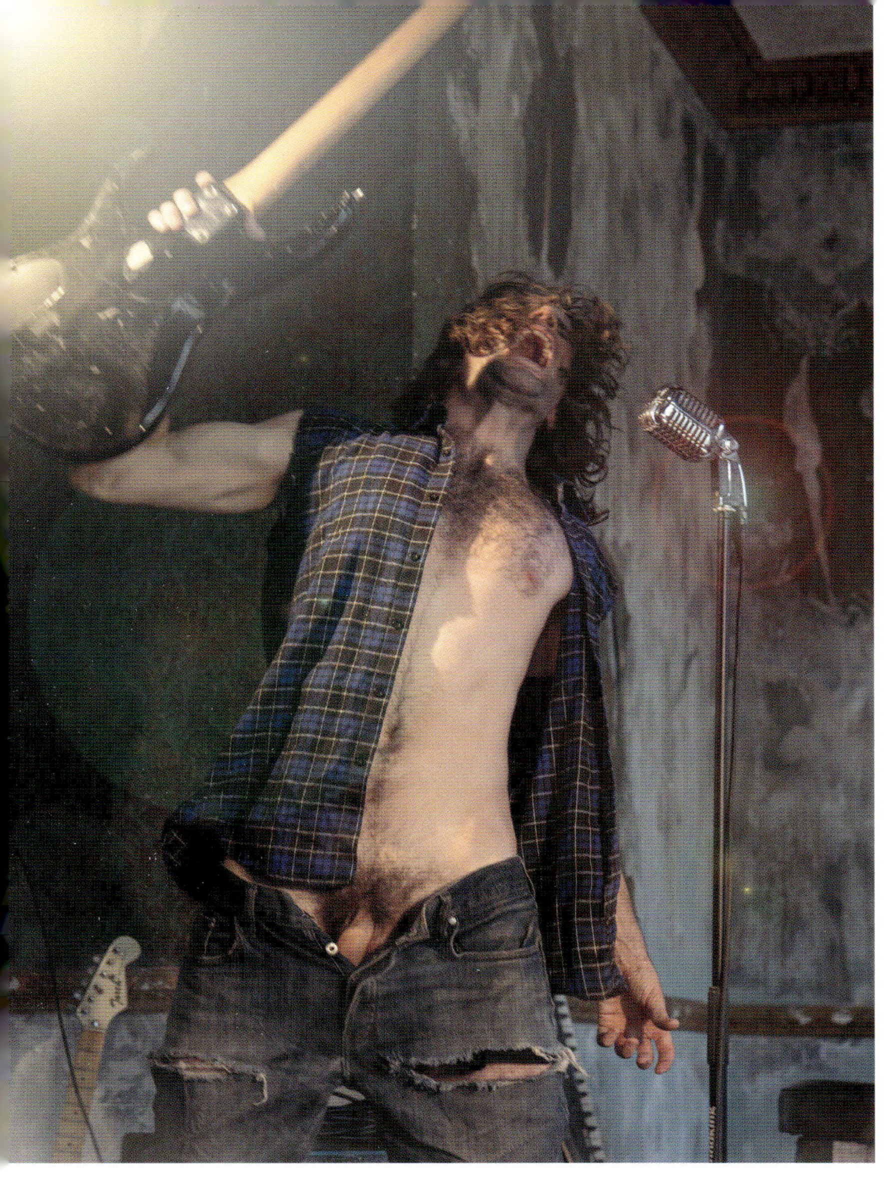

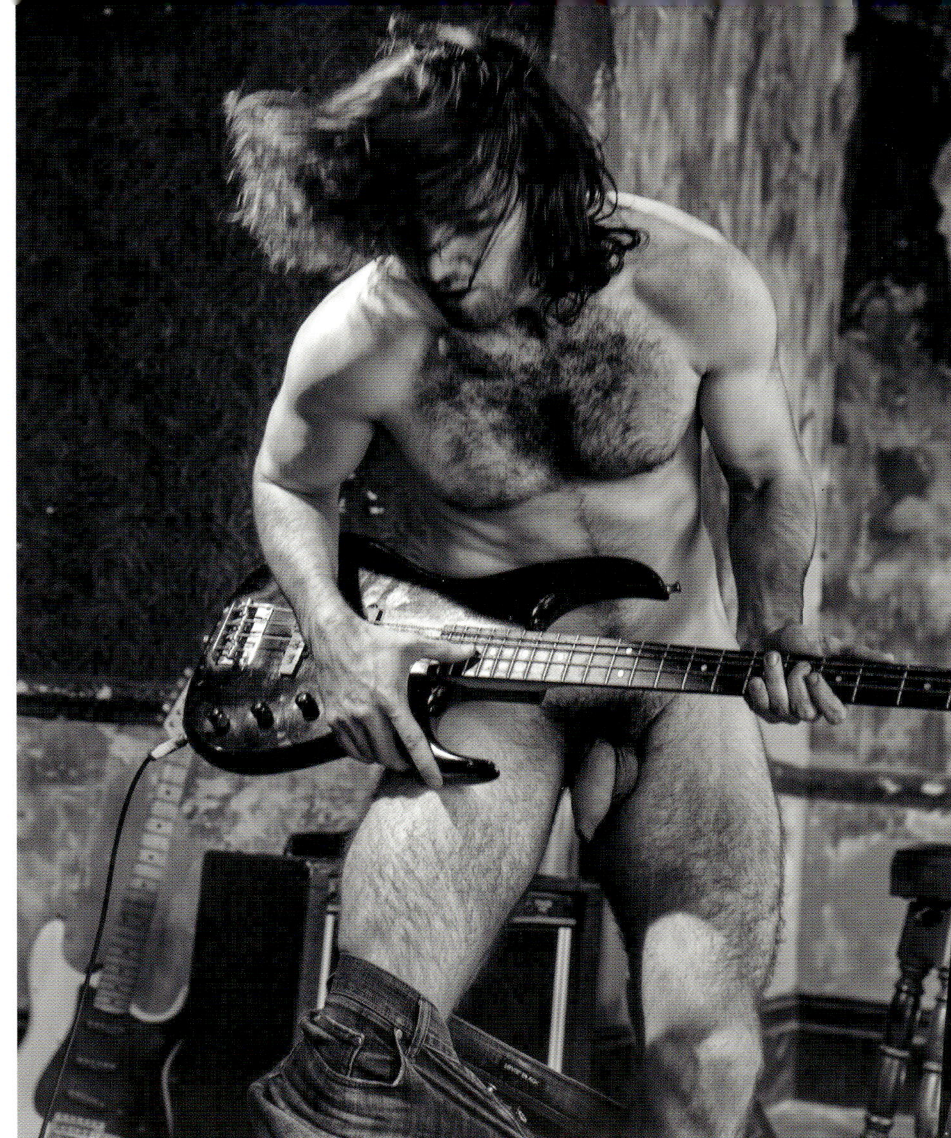

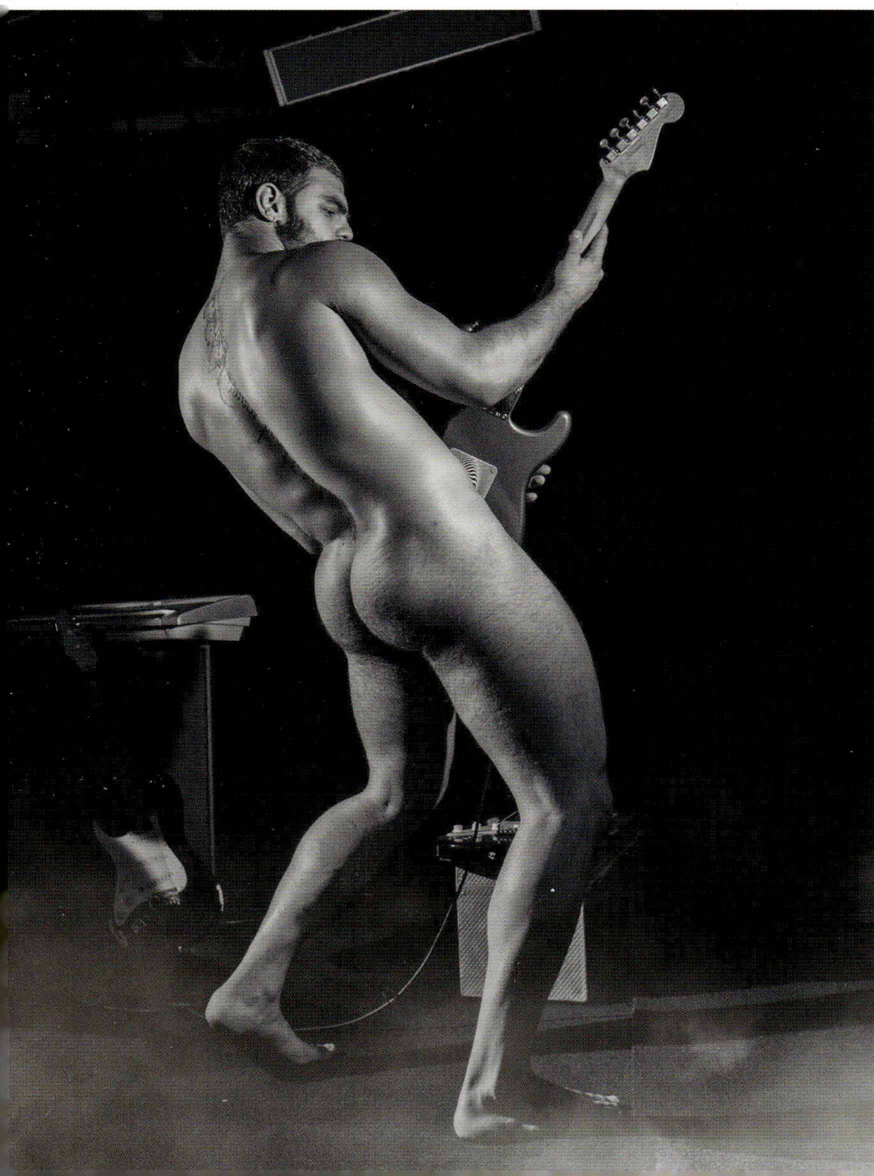

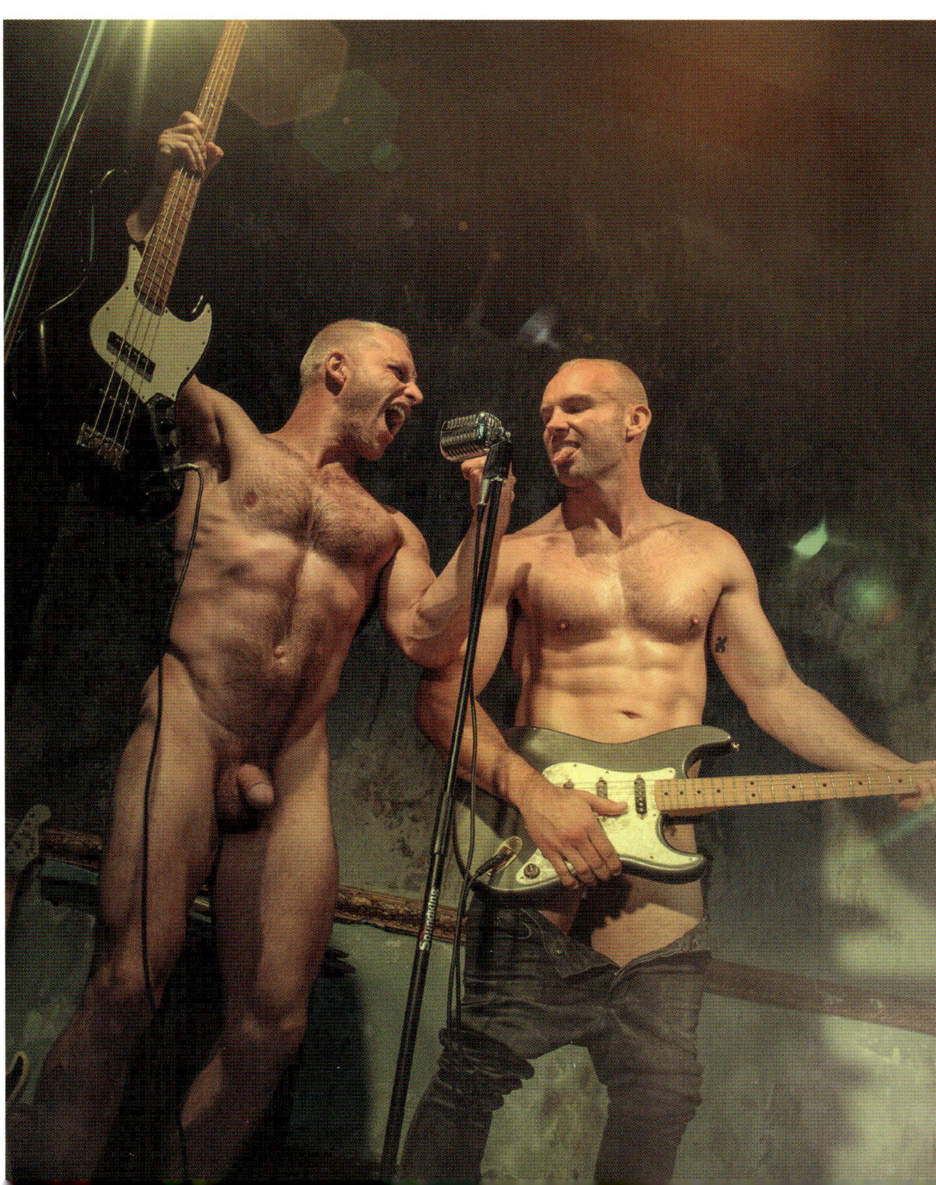

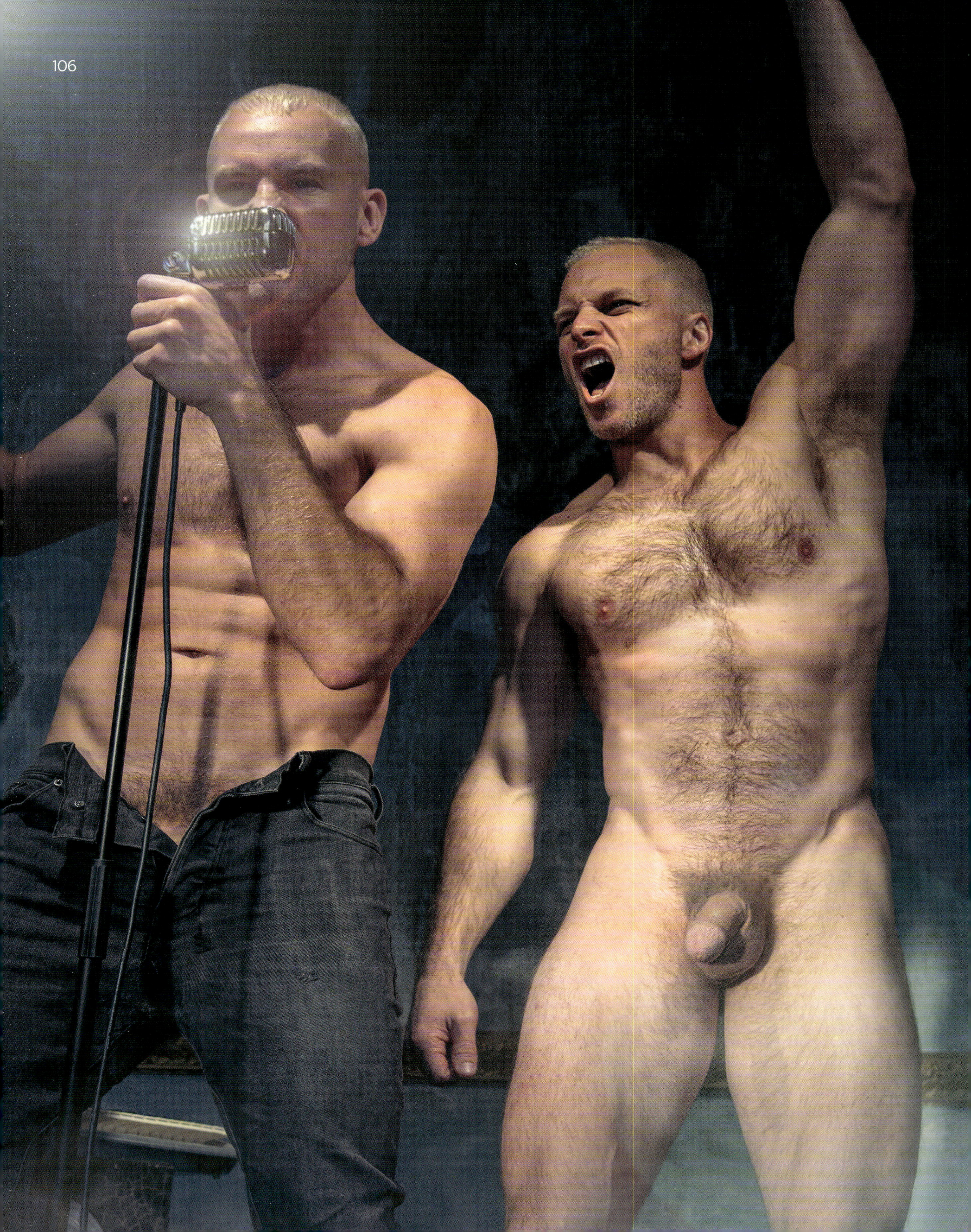

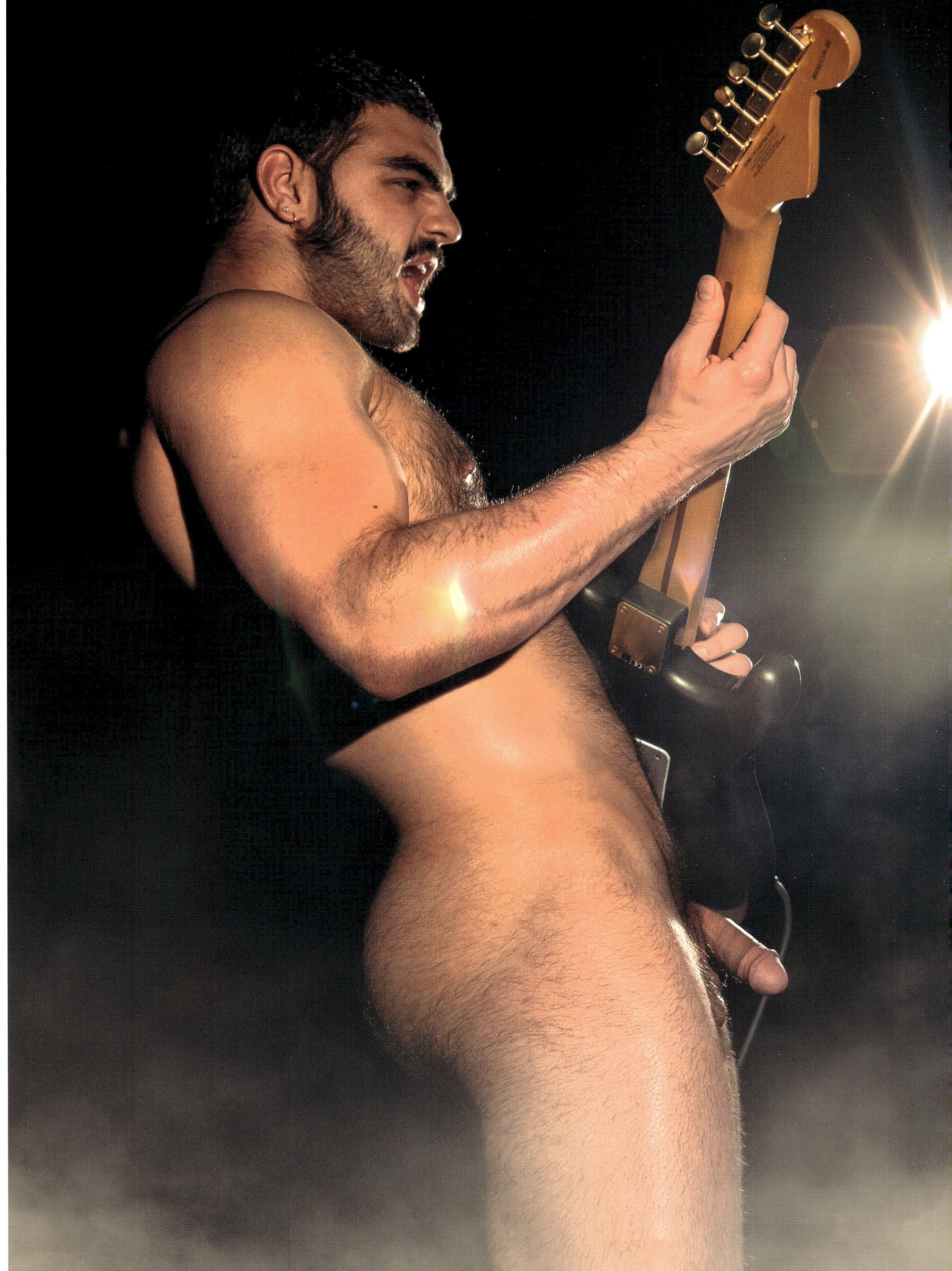

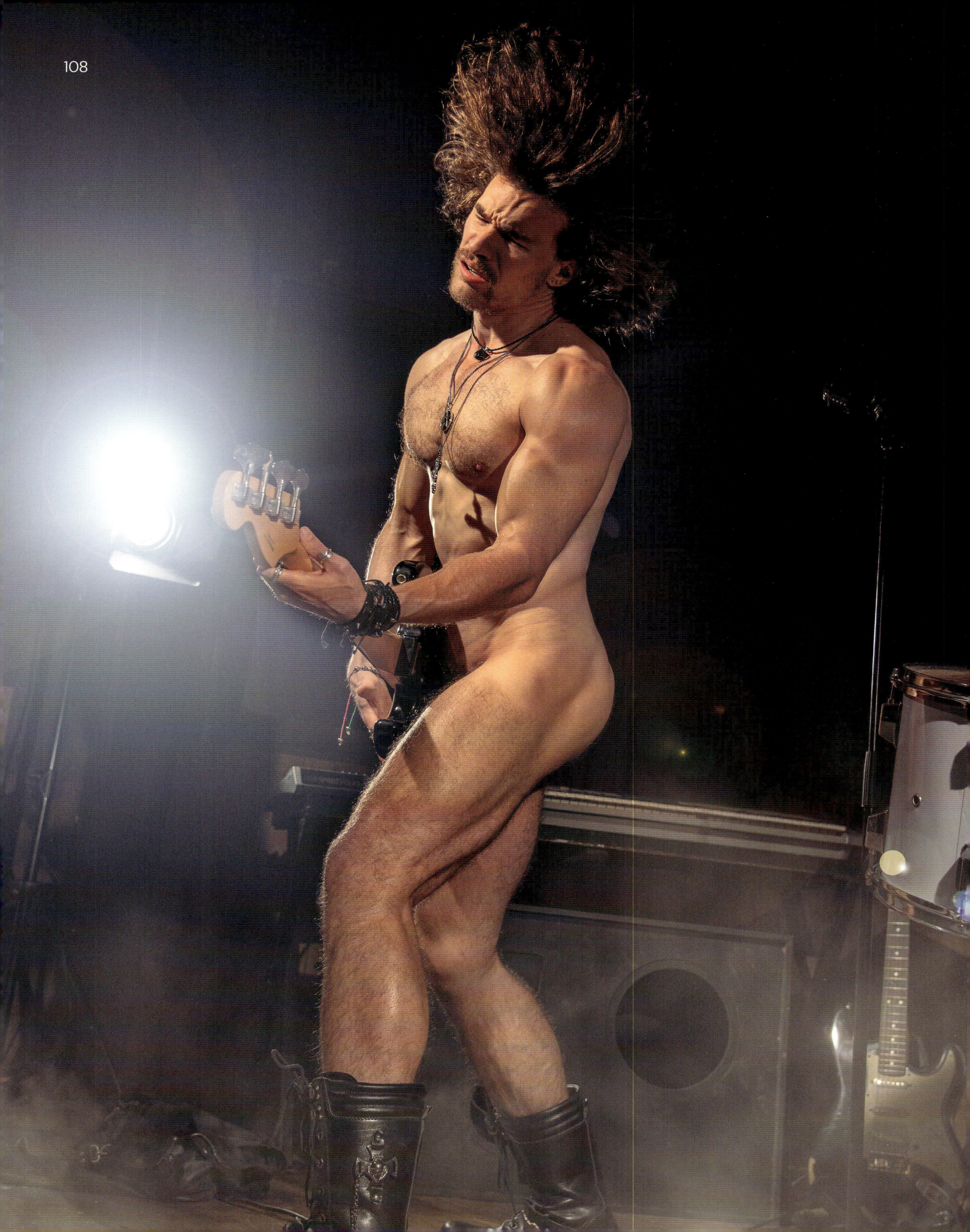

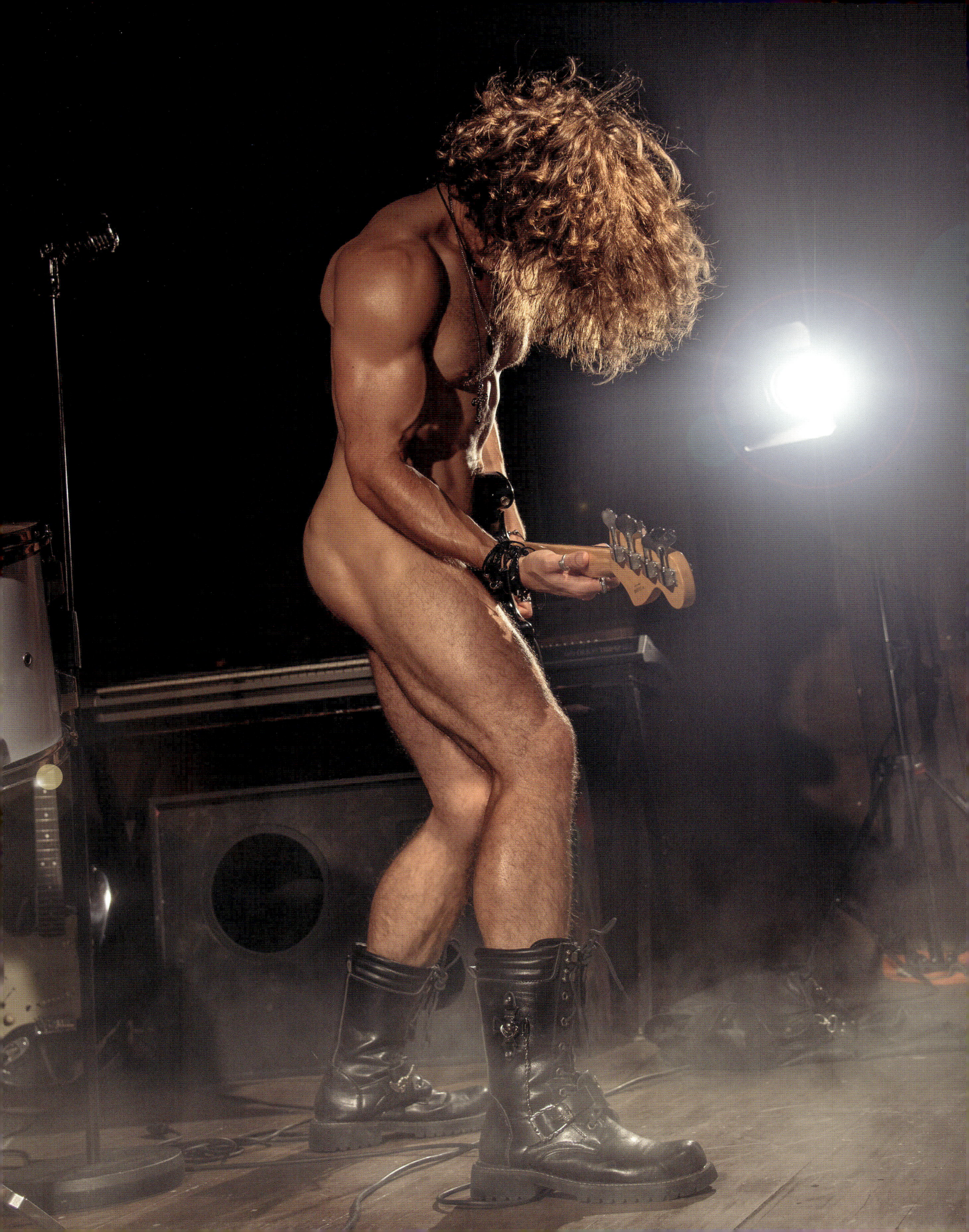

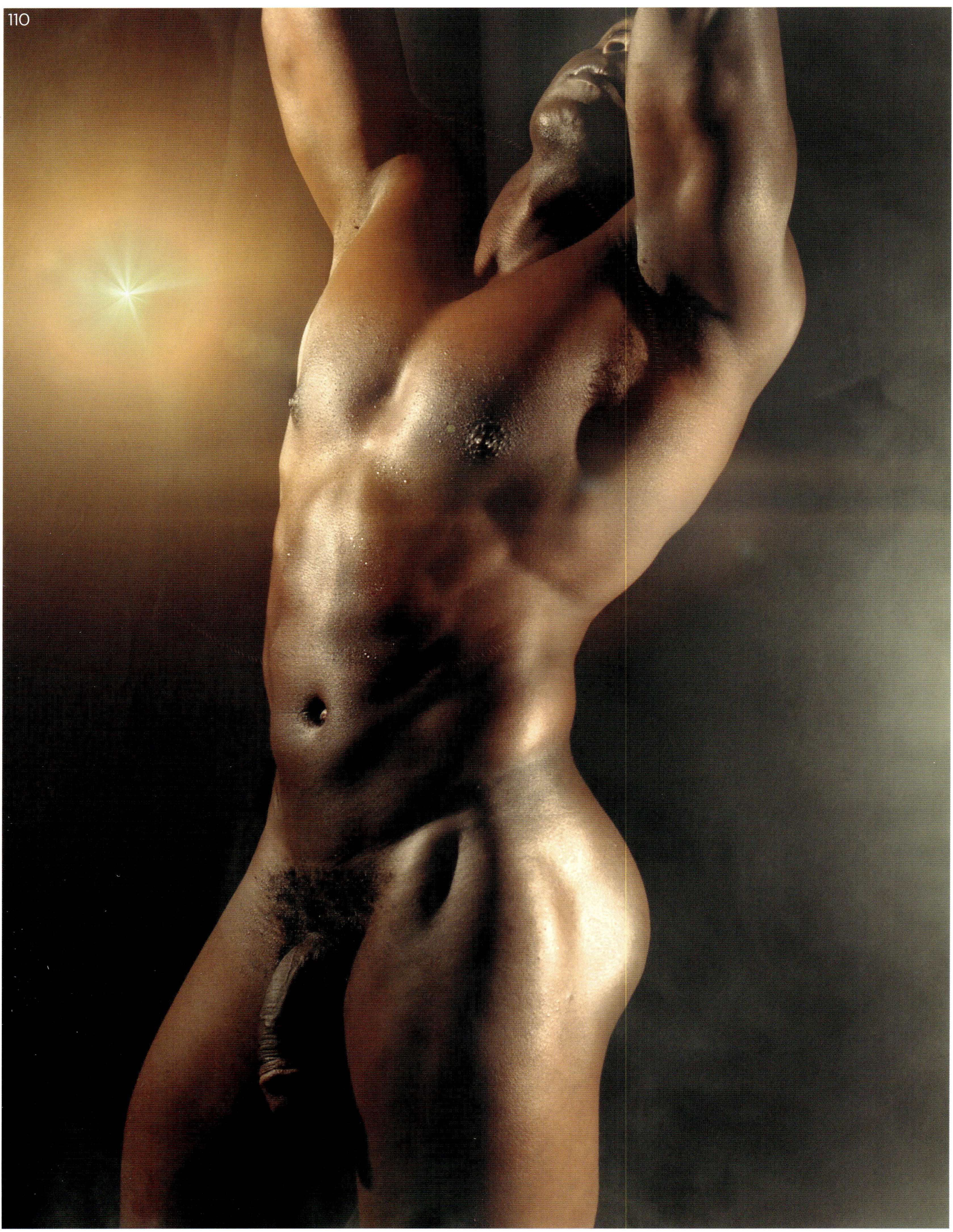

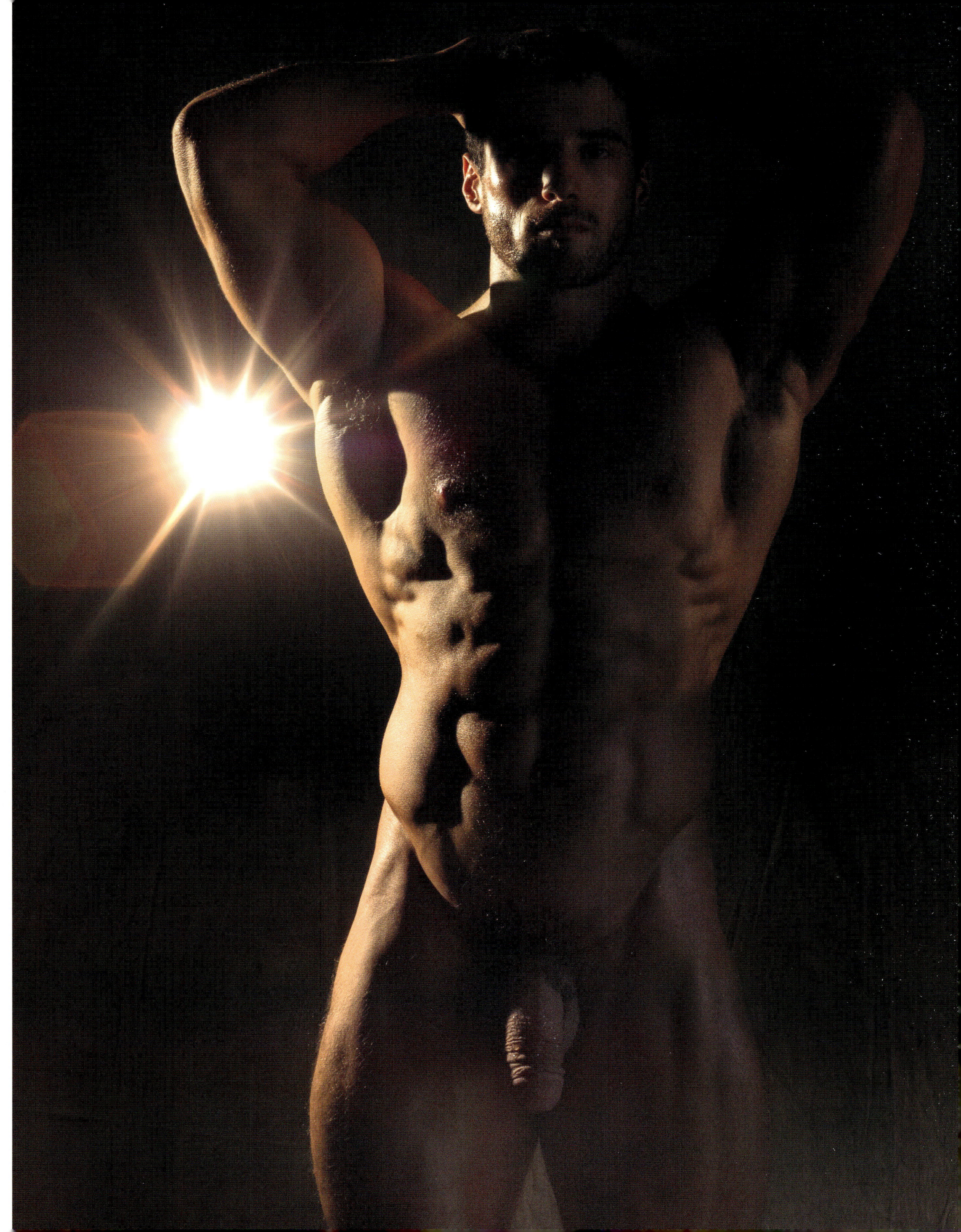

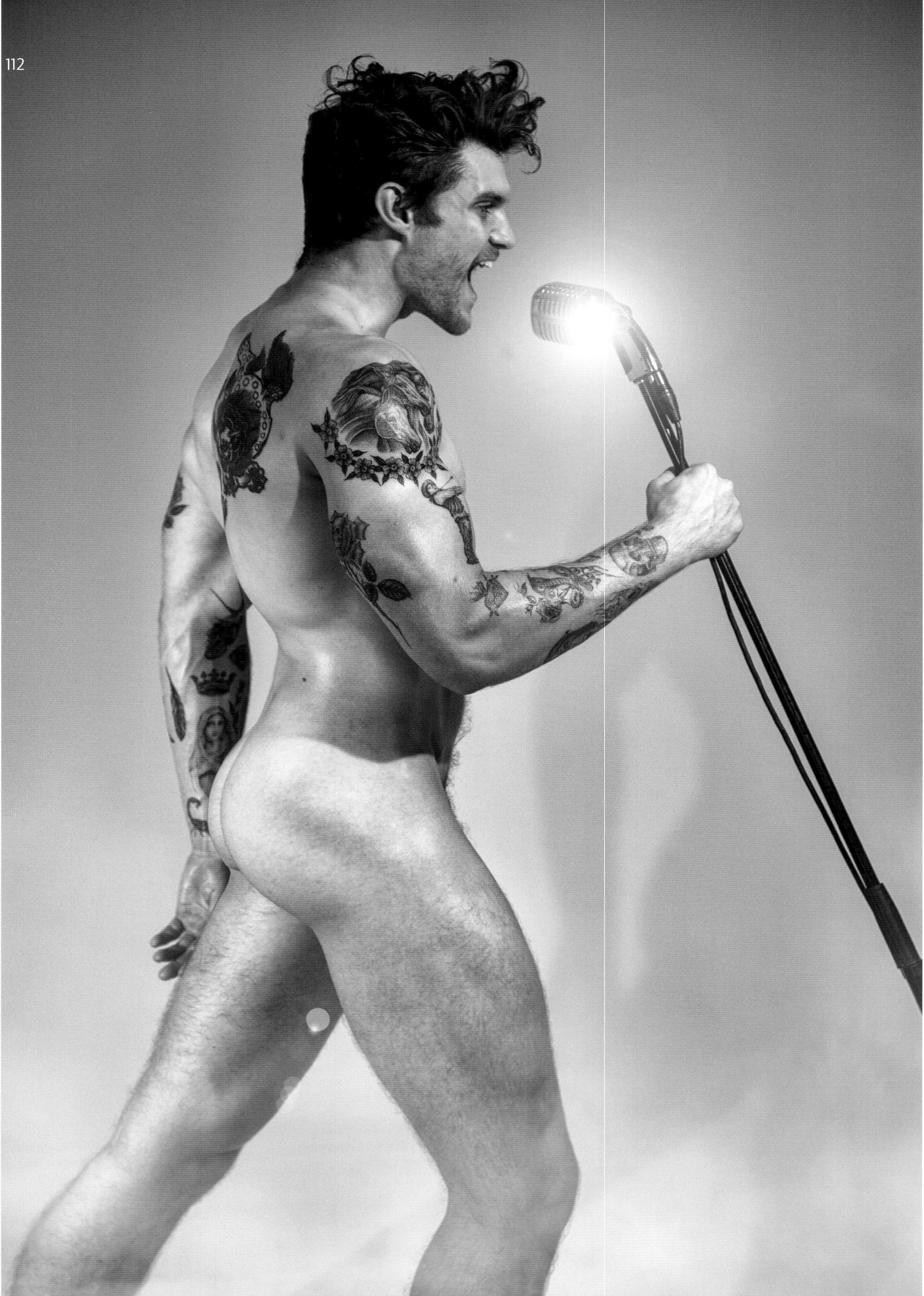

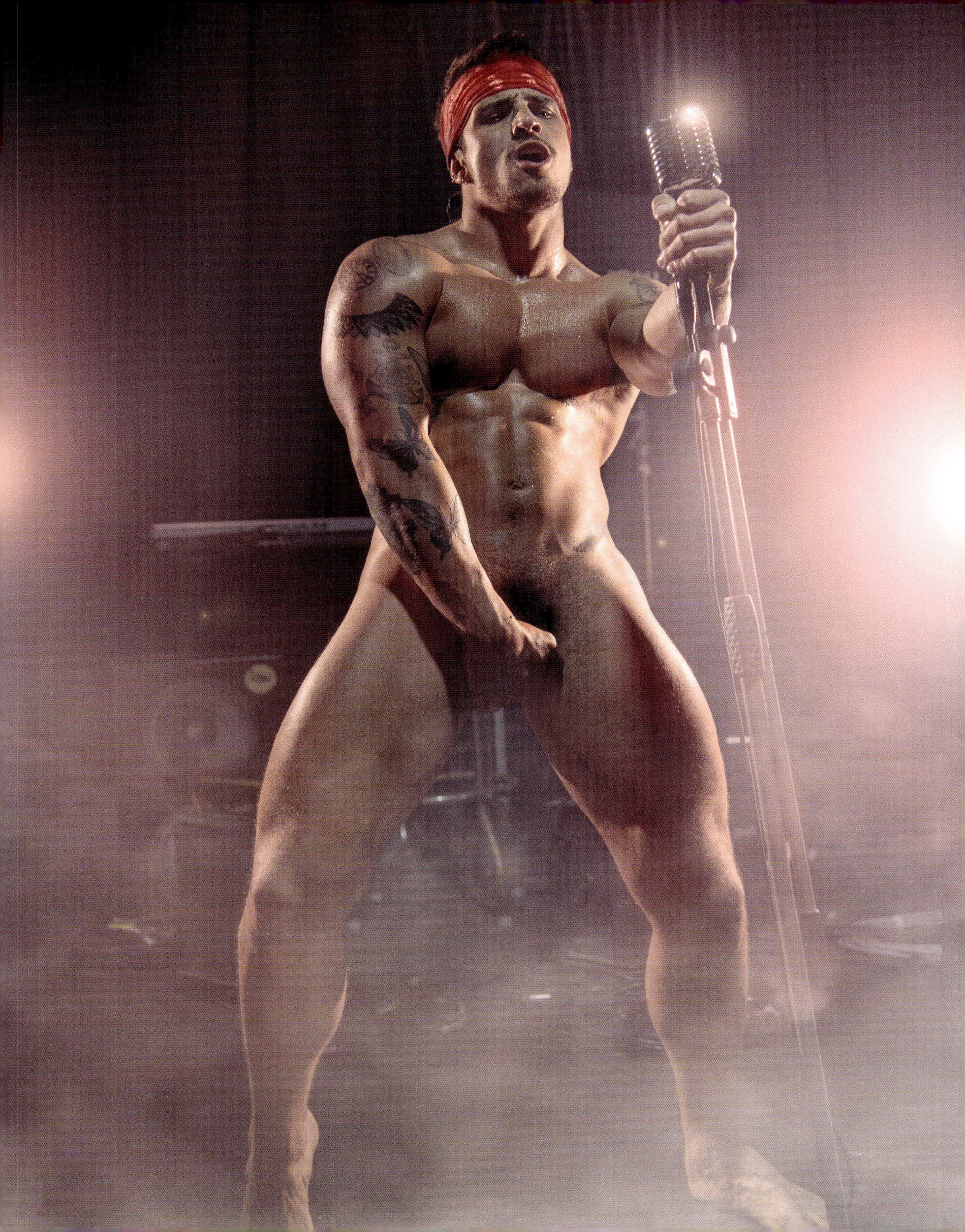

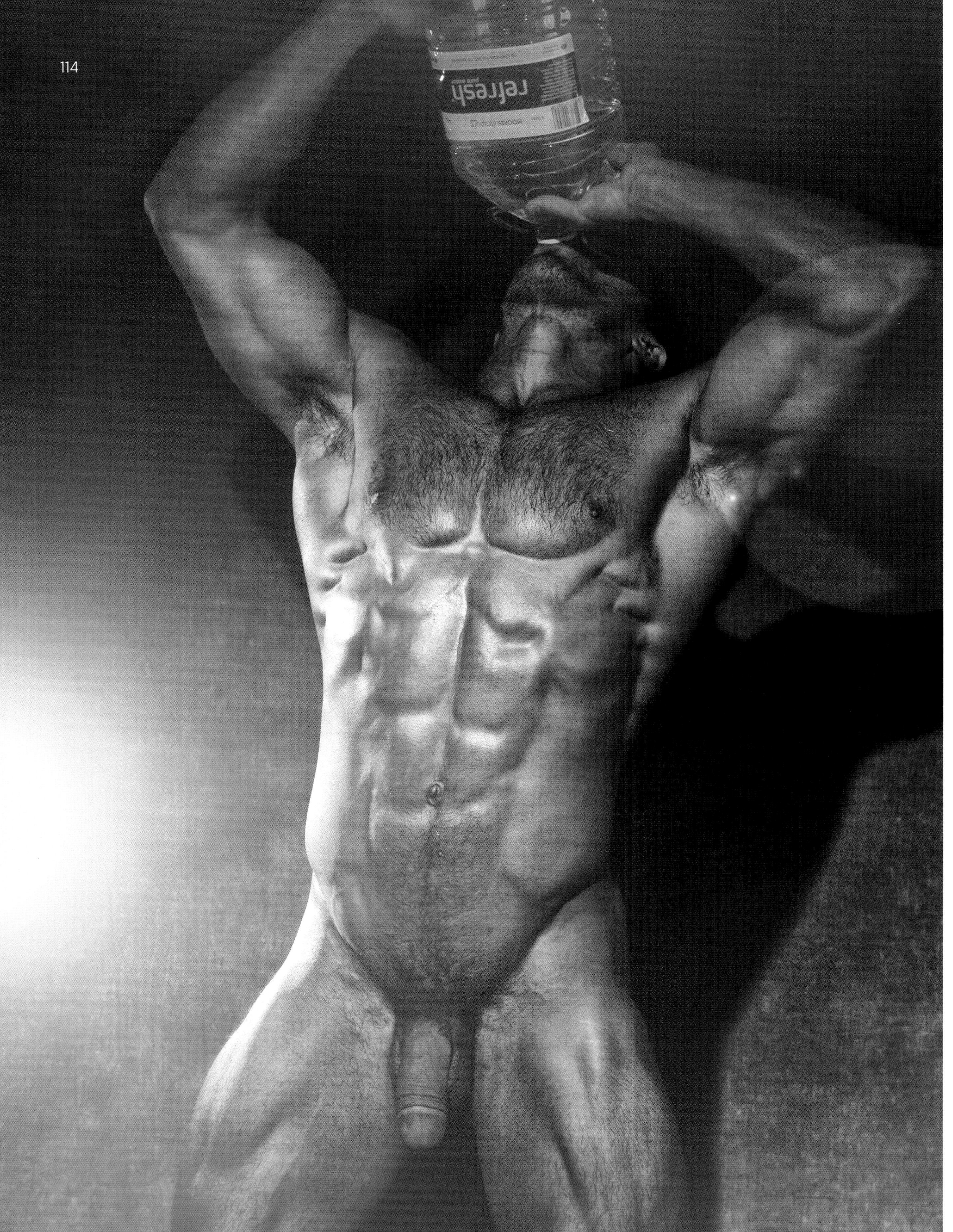
refresh

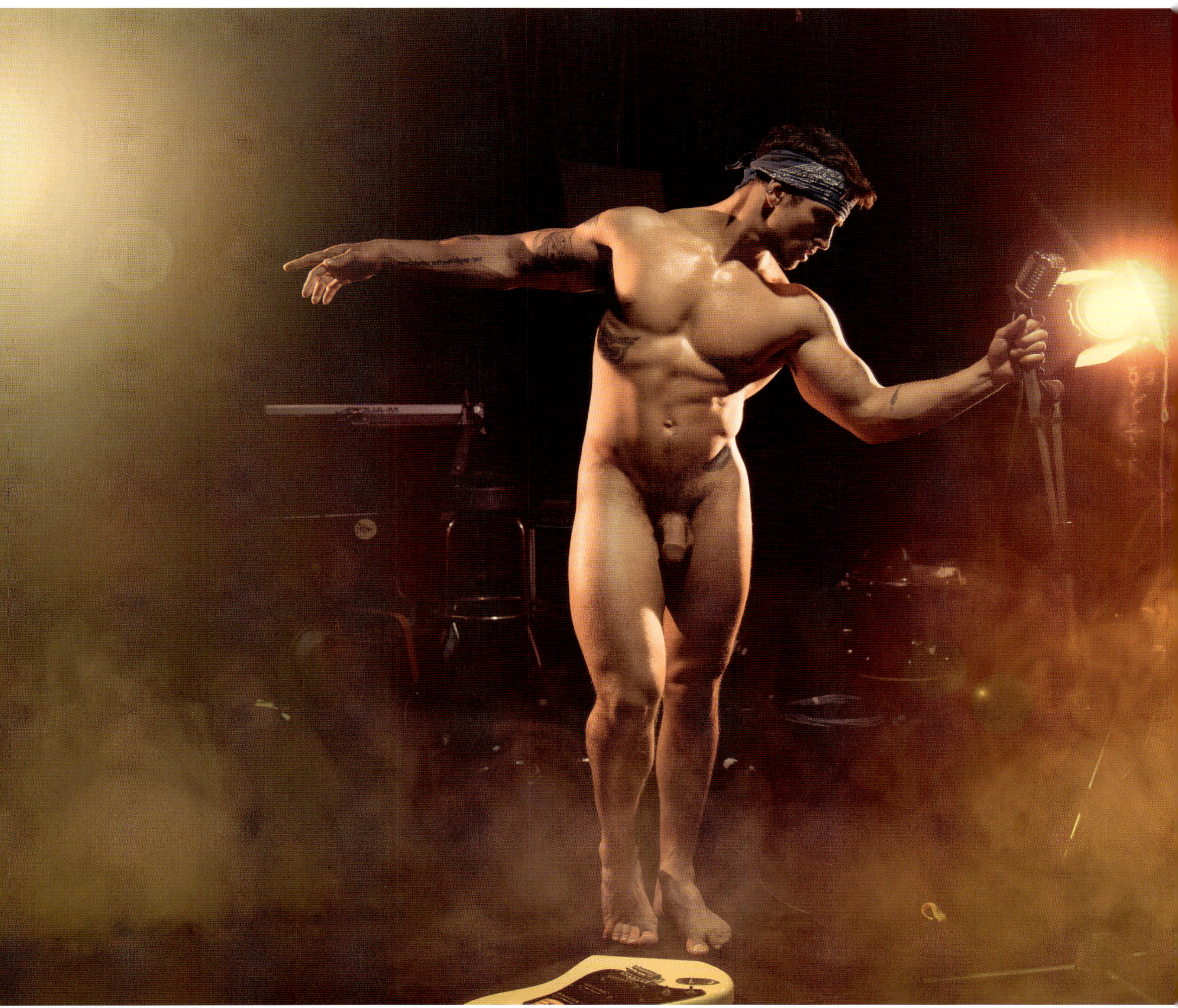

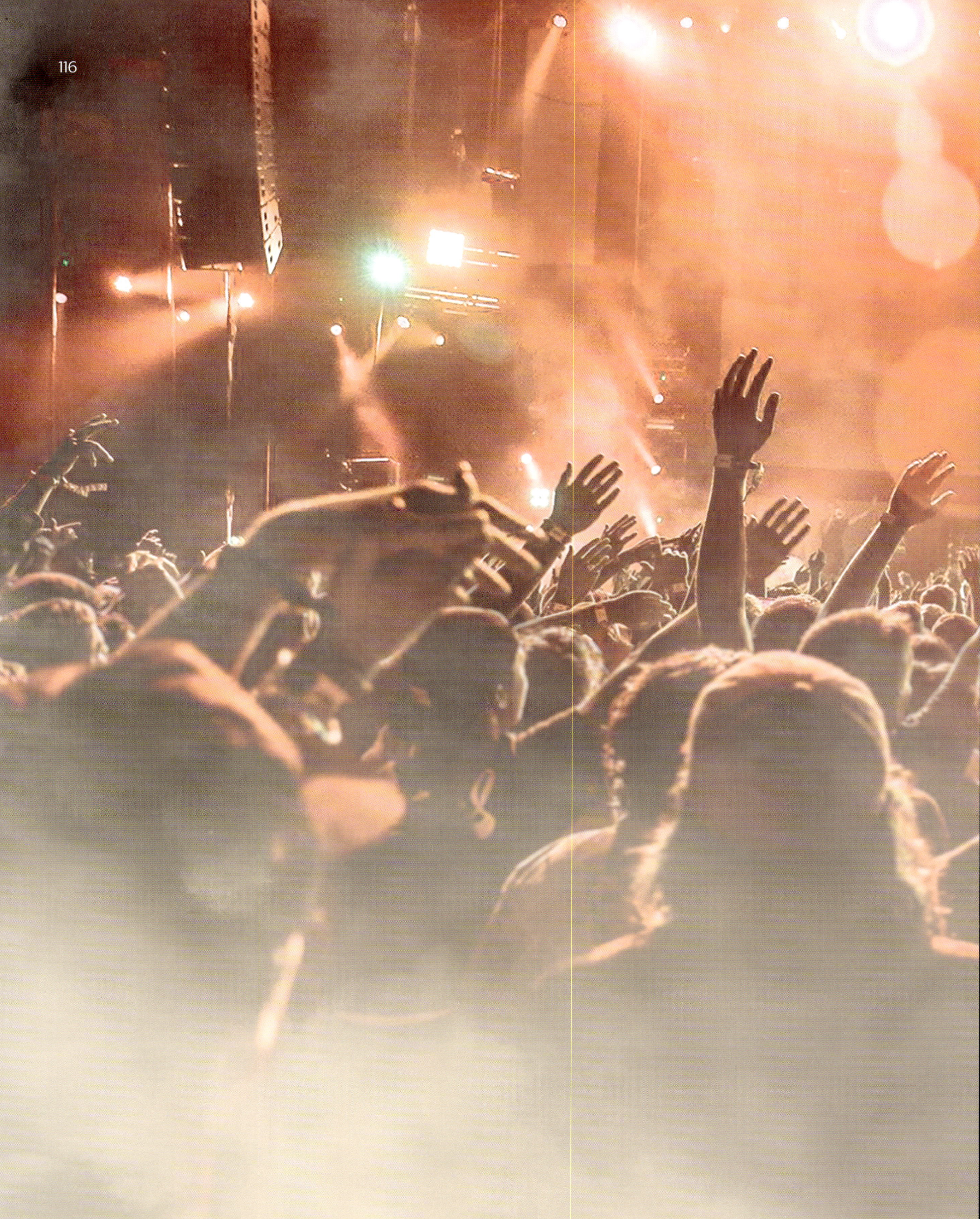

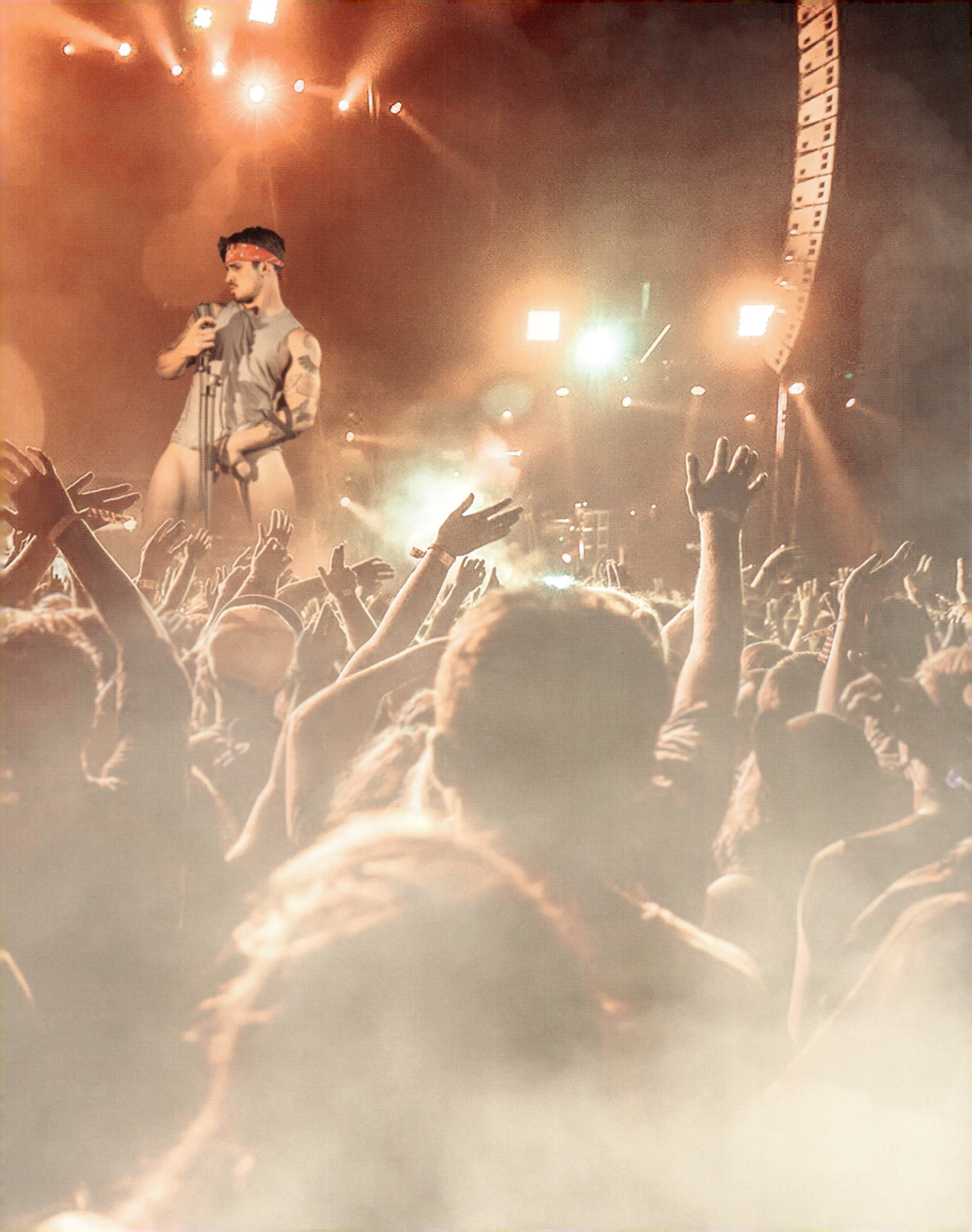

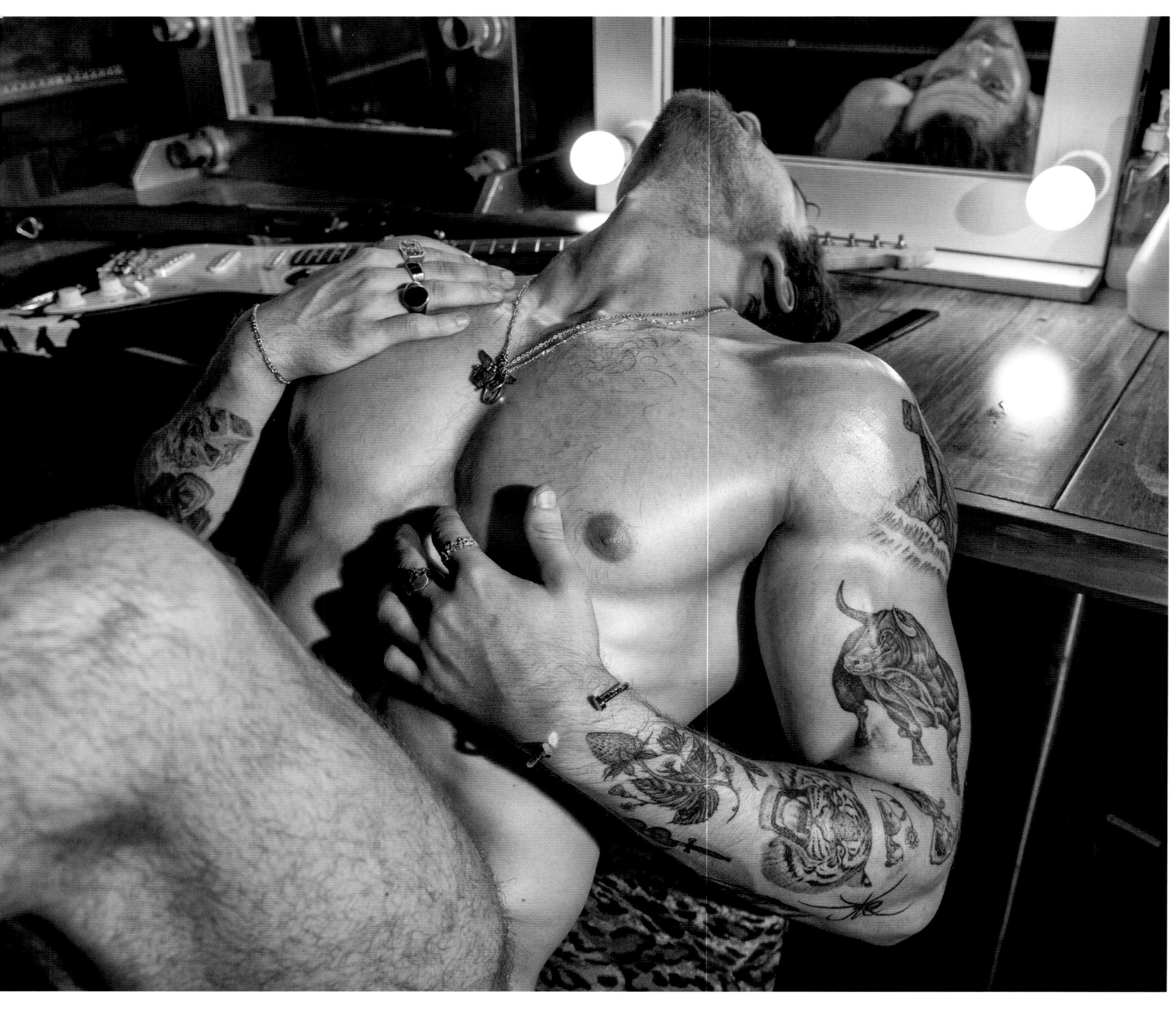

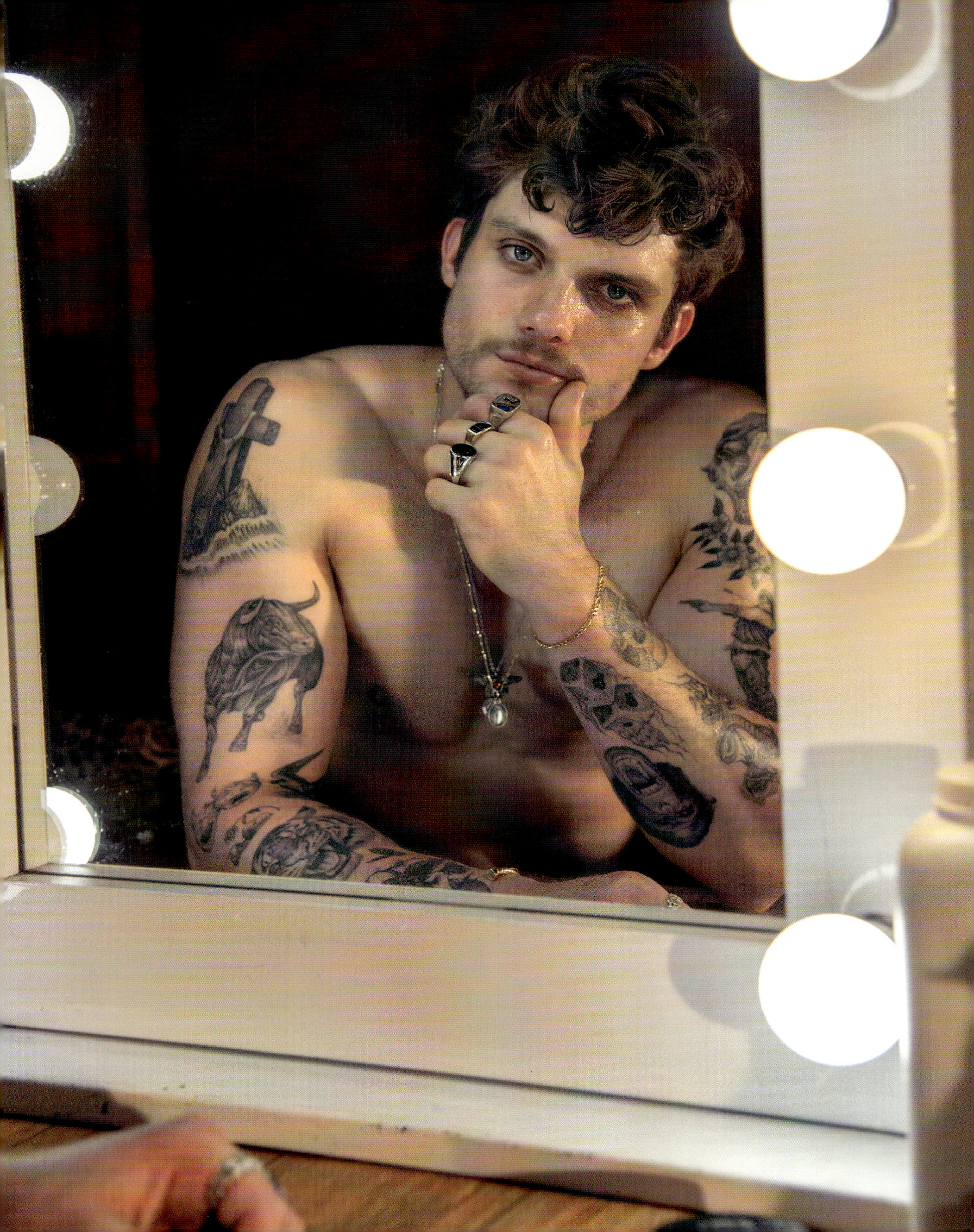

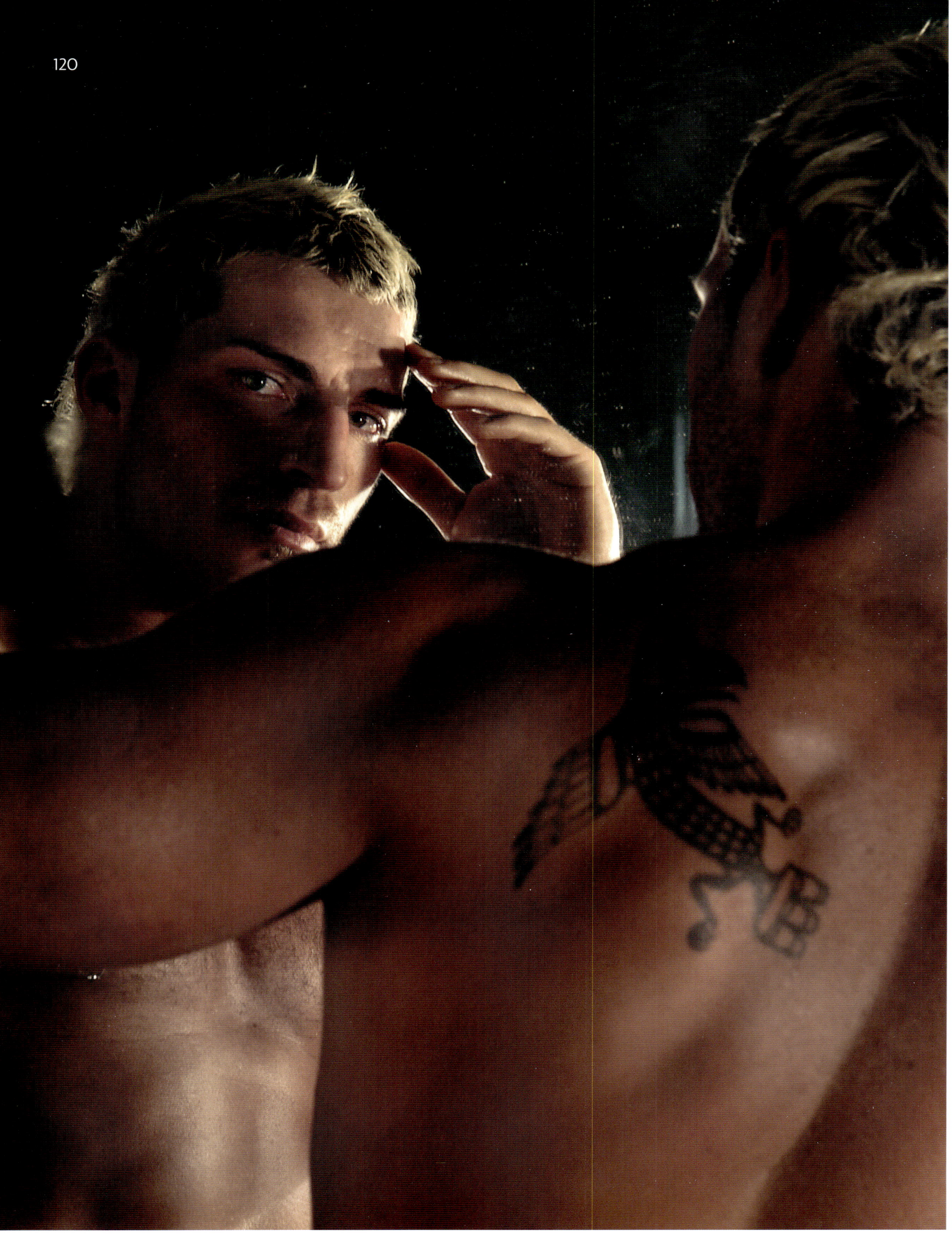

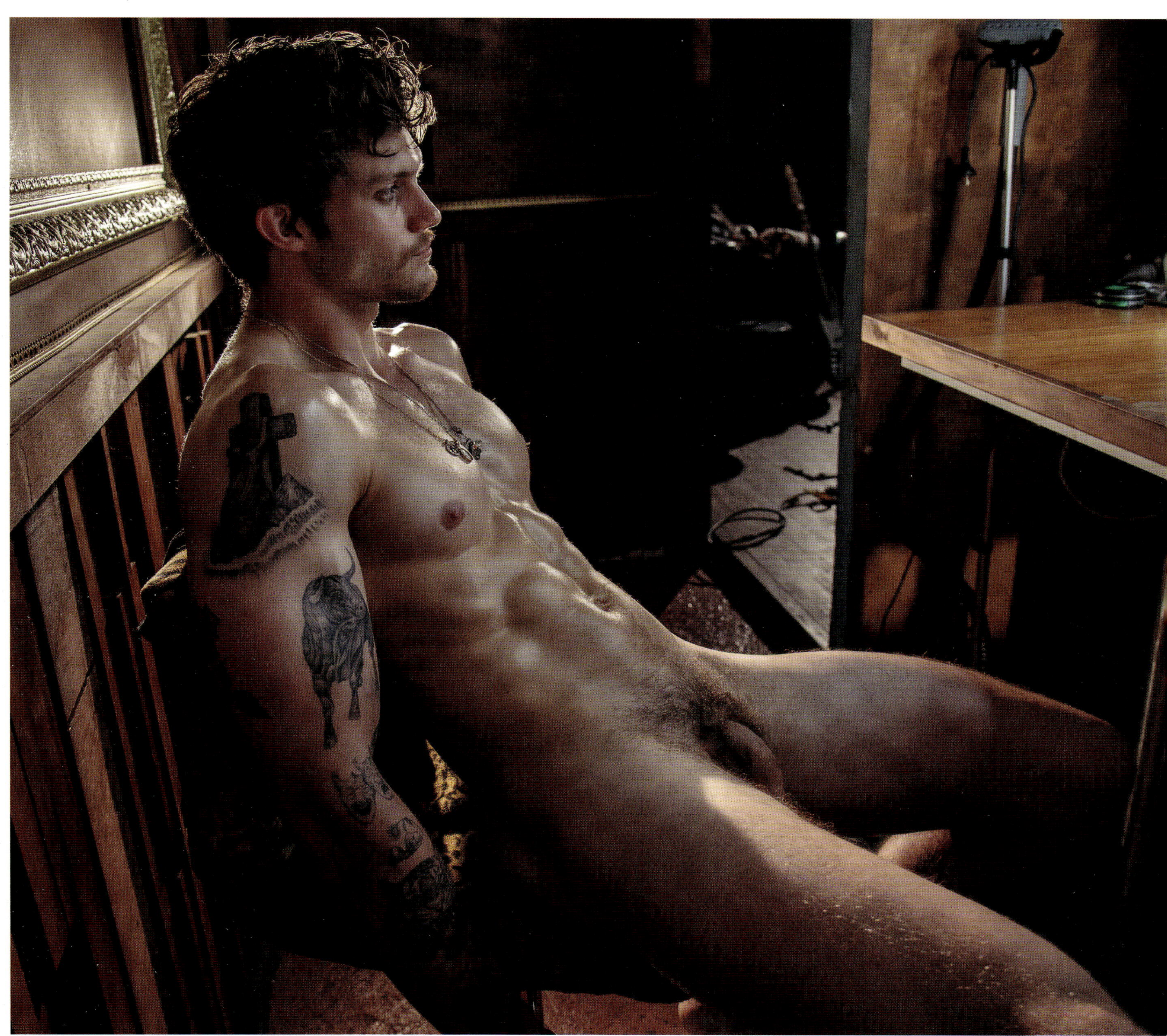

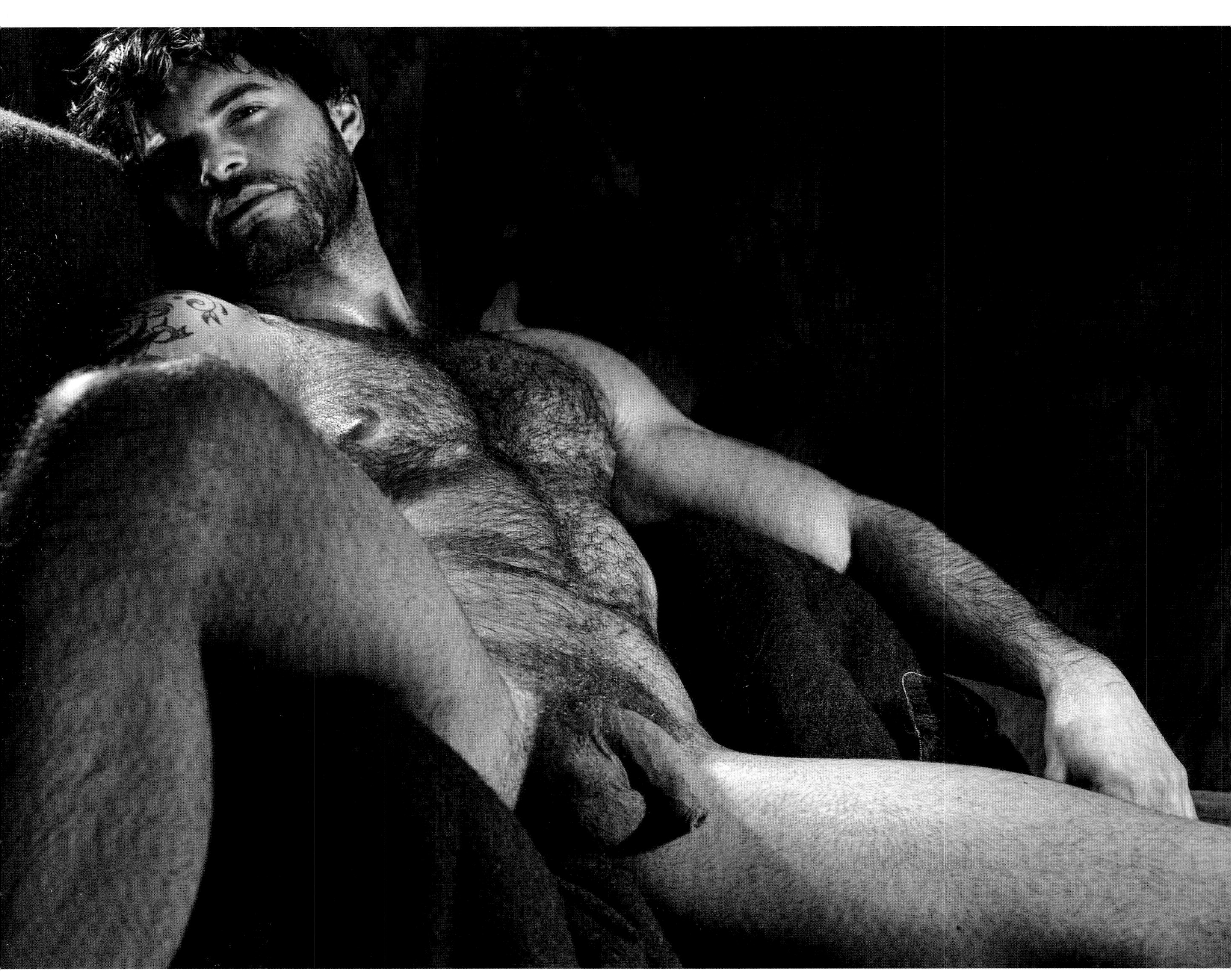

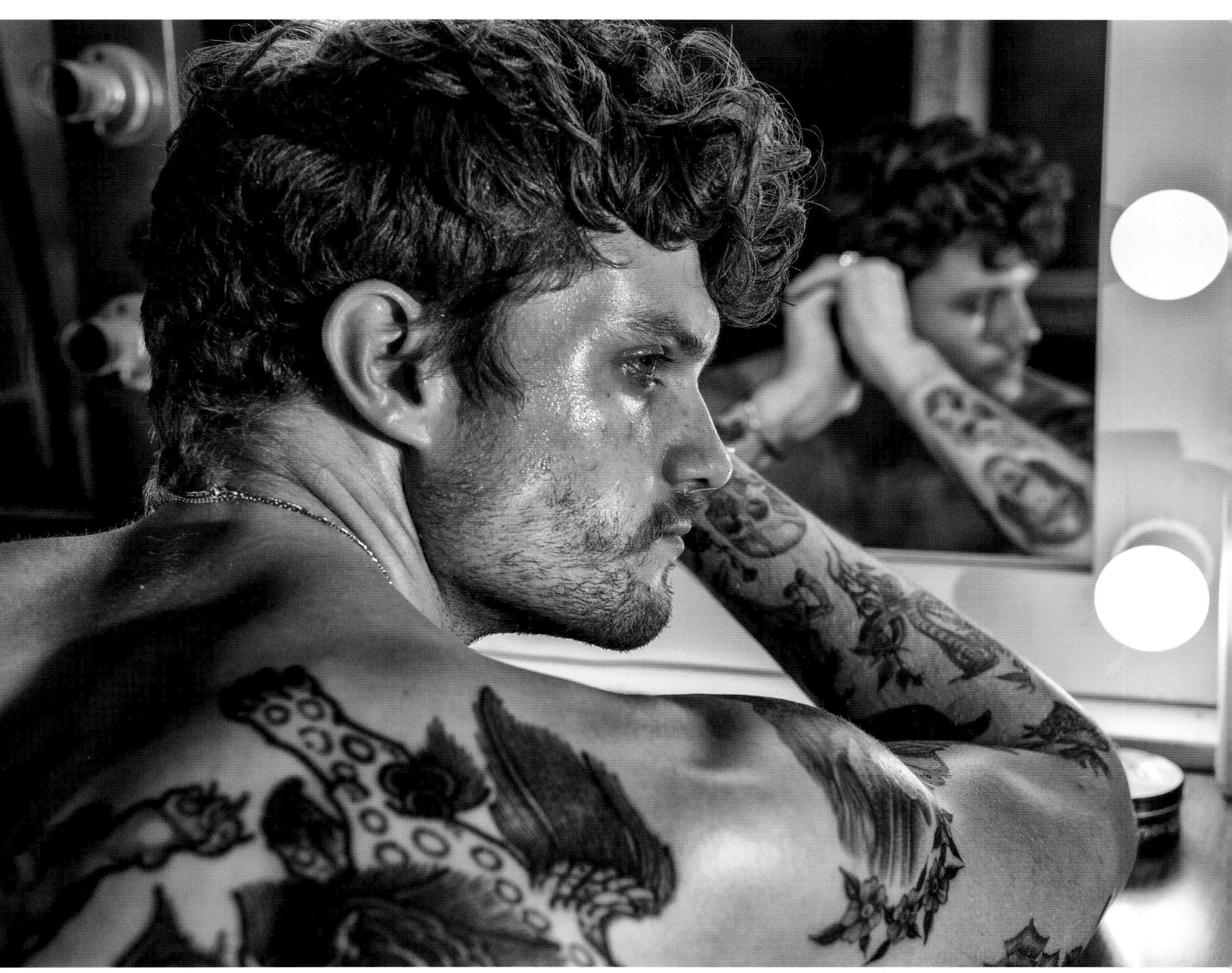

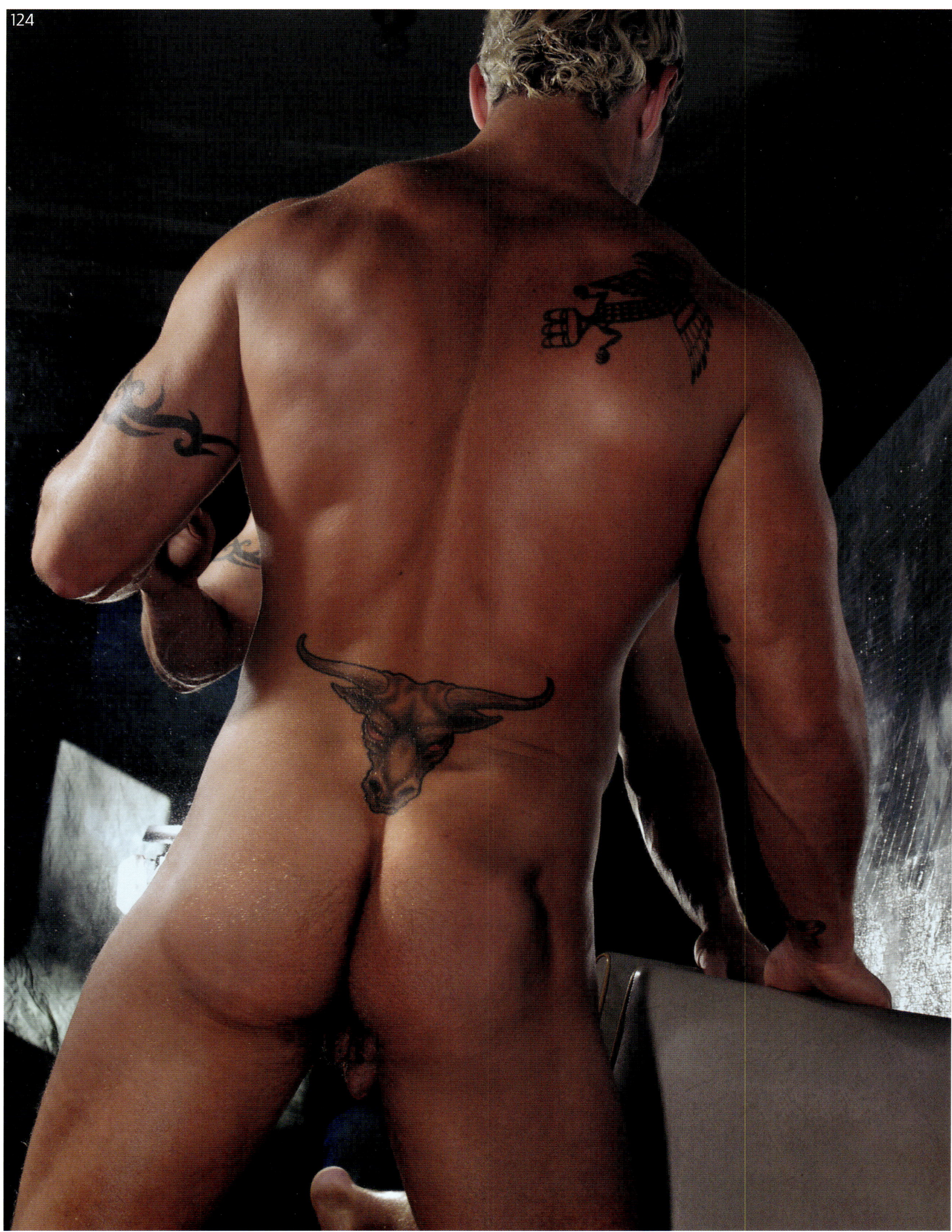

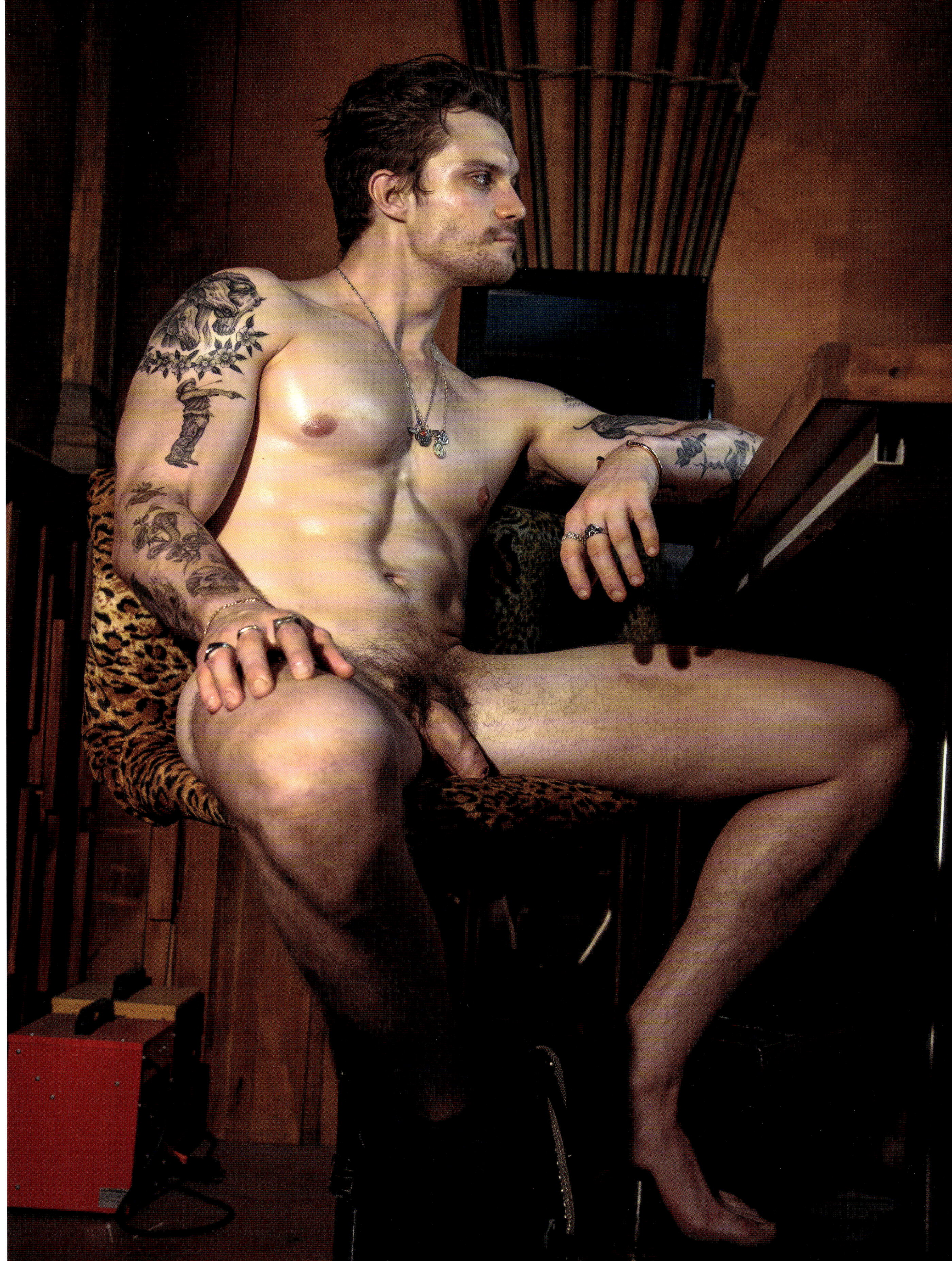

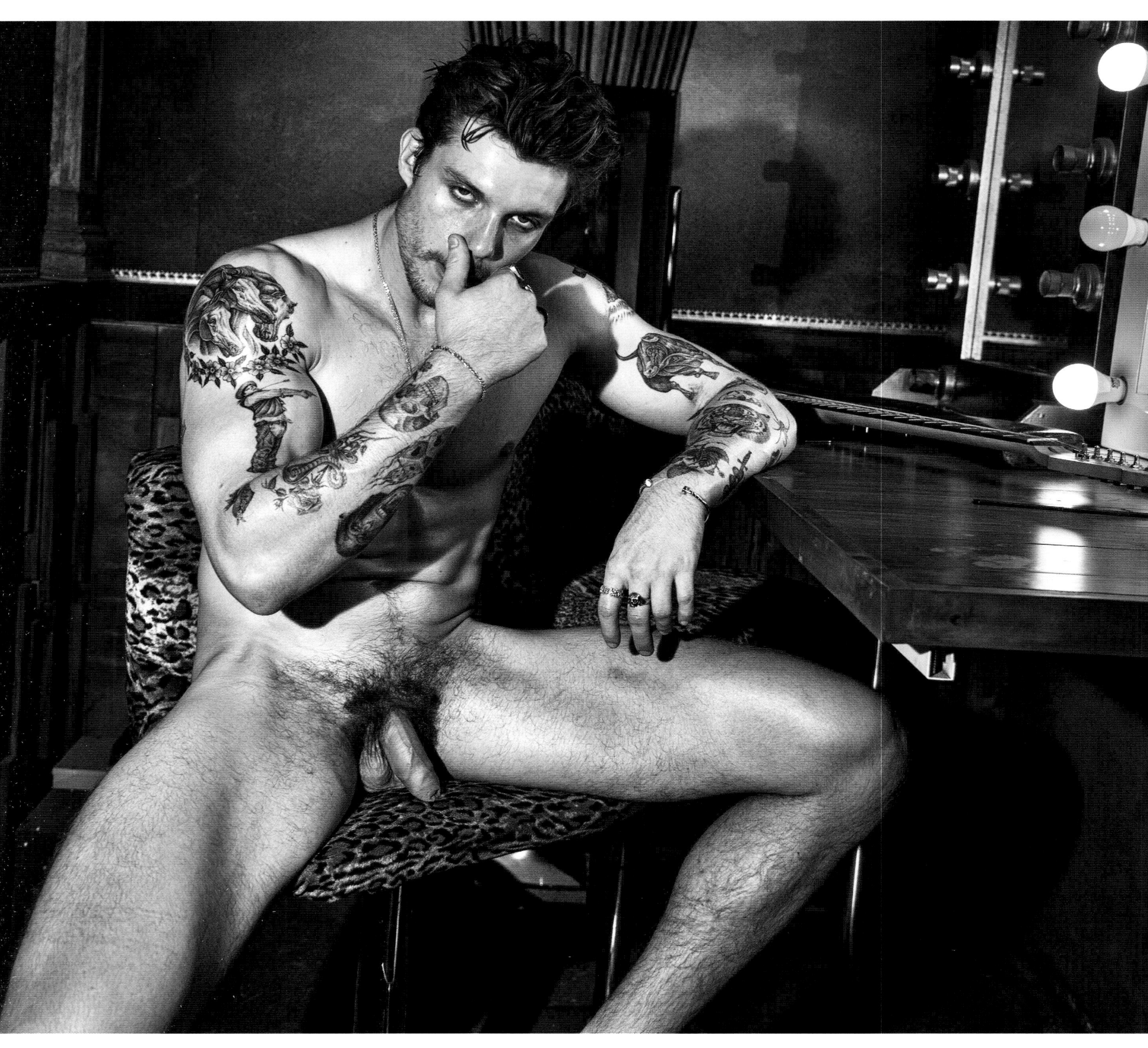

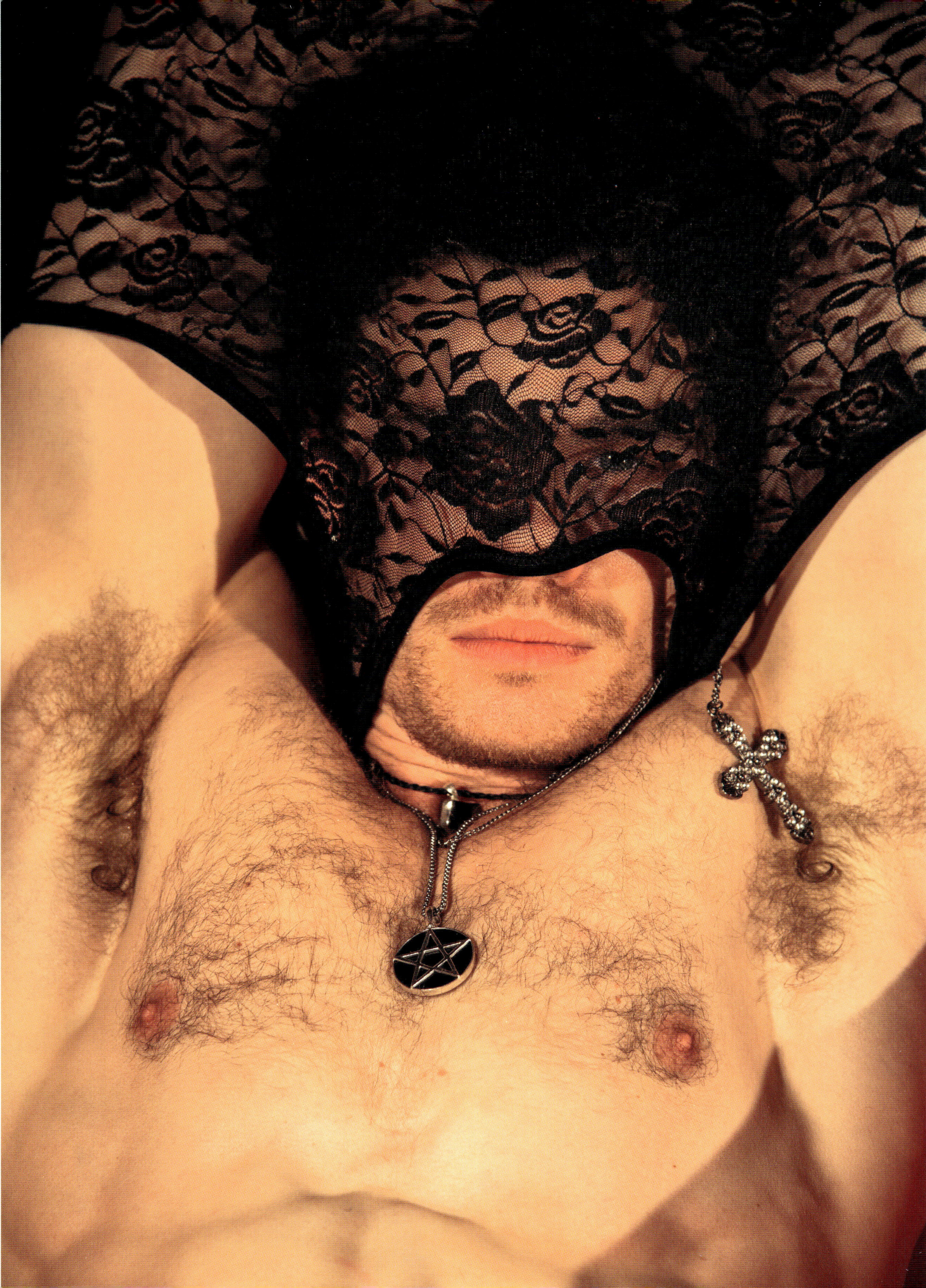

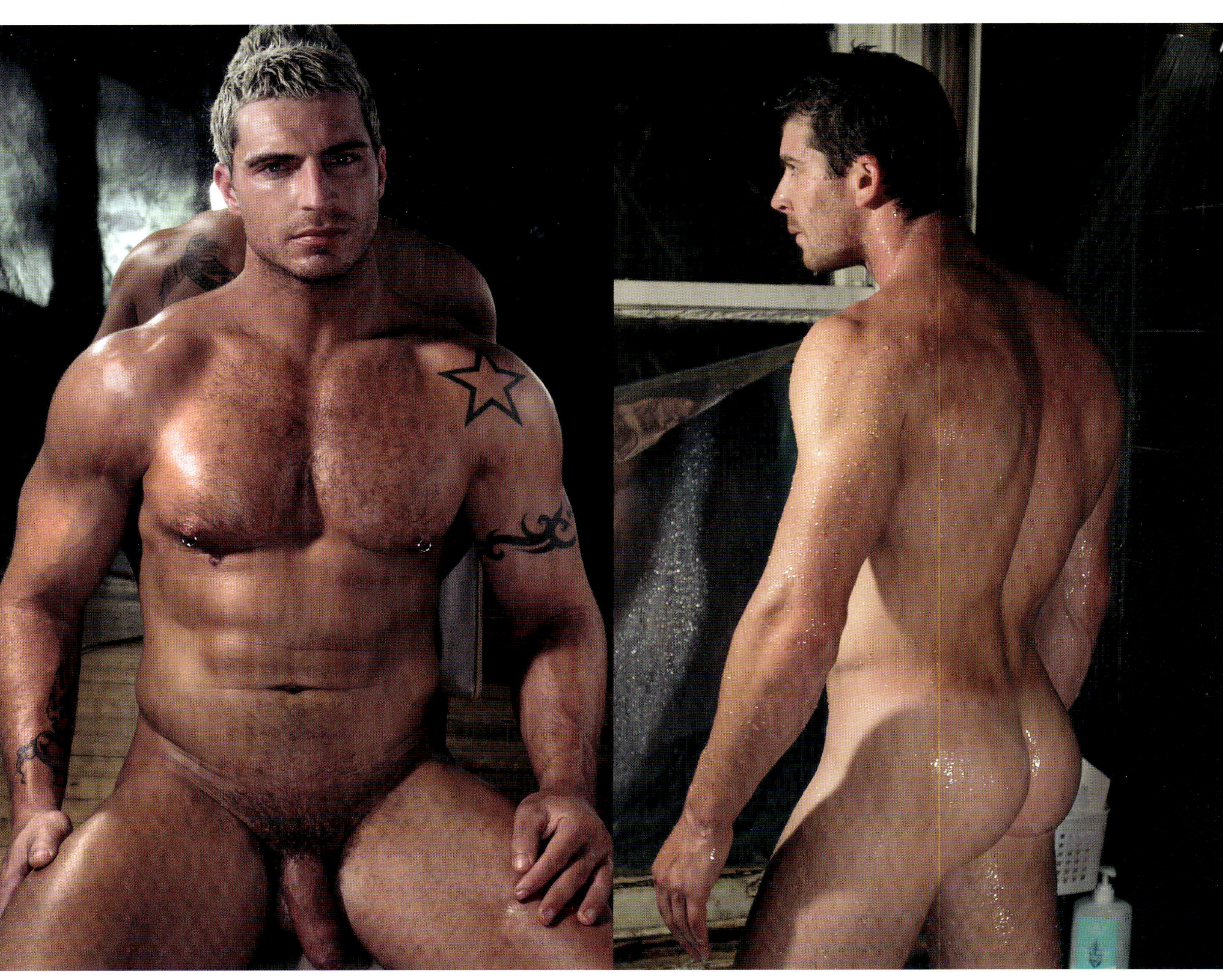

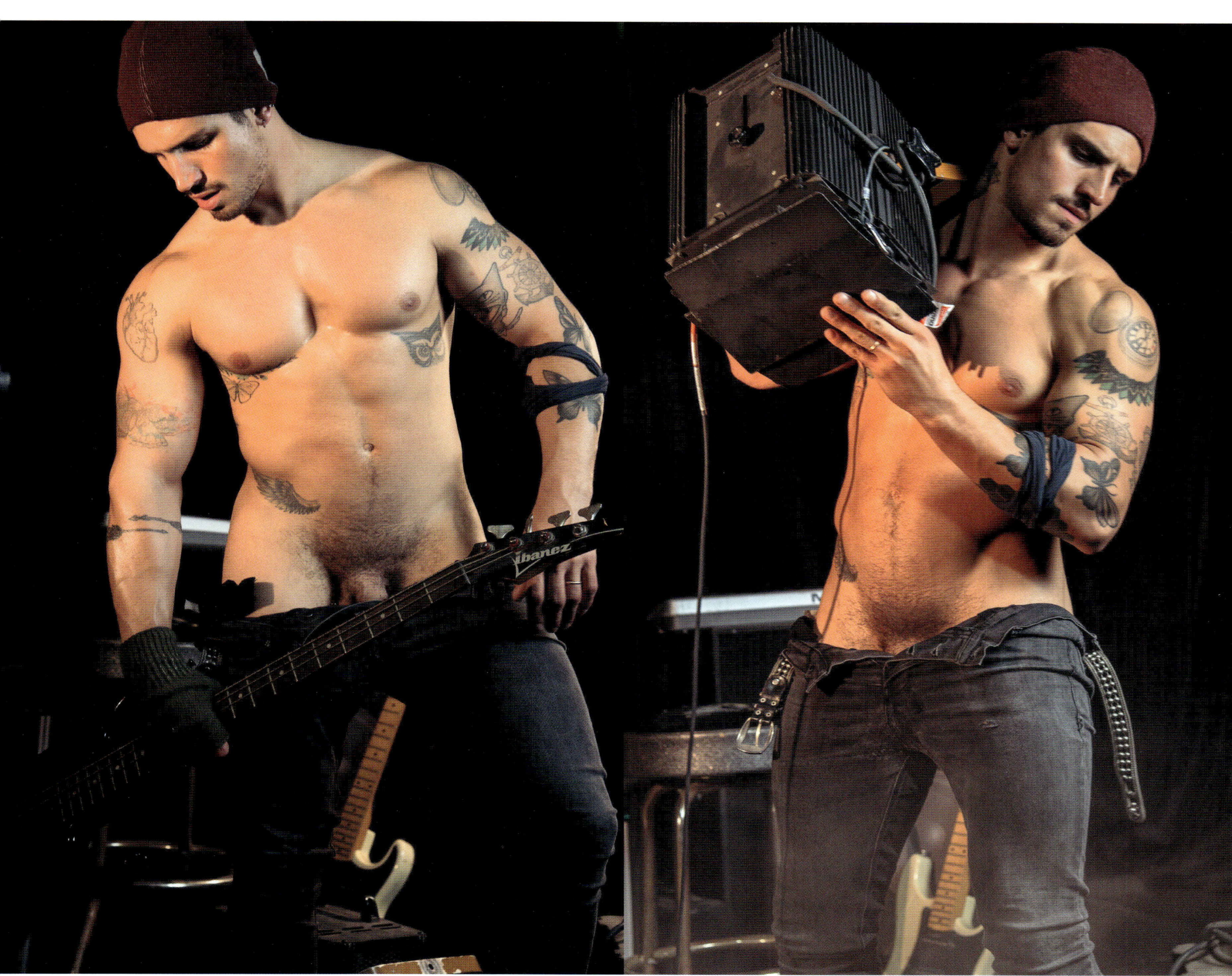
Ibanez

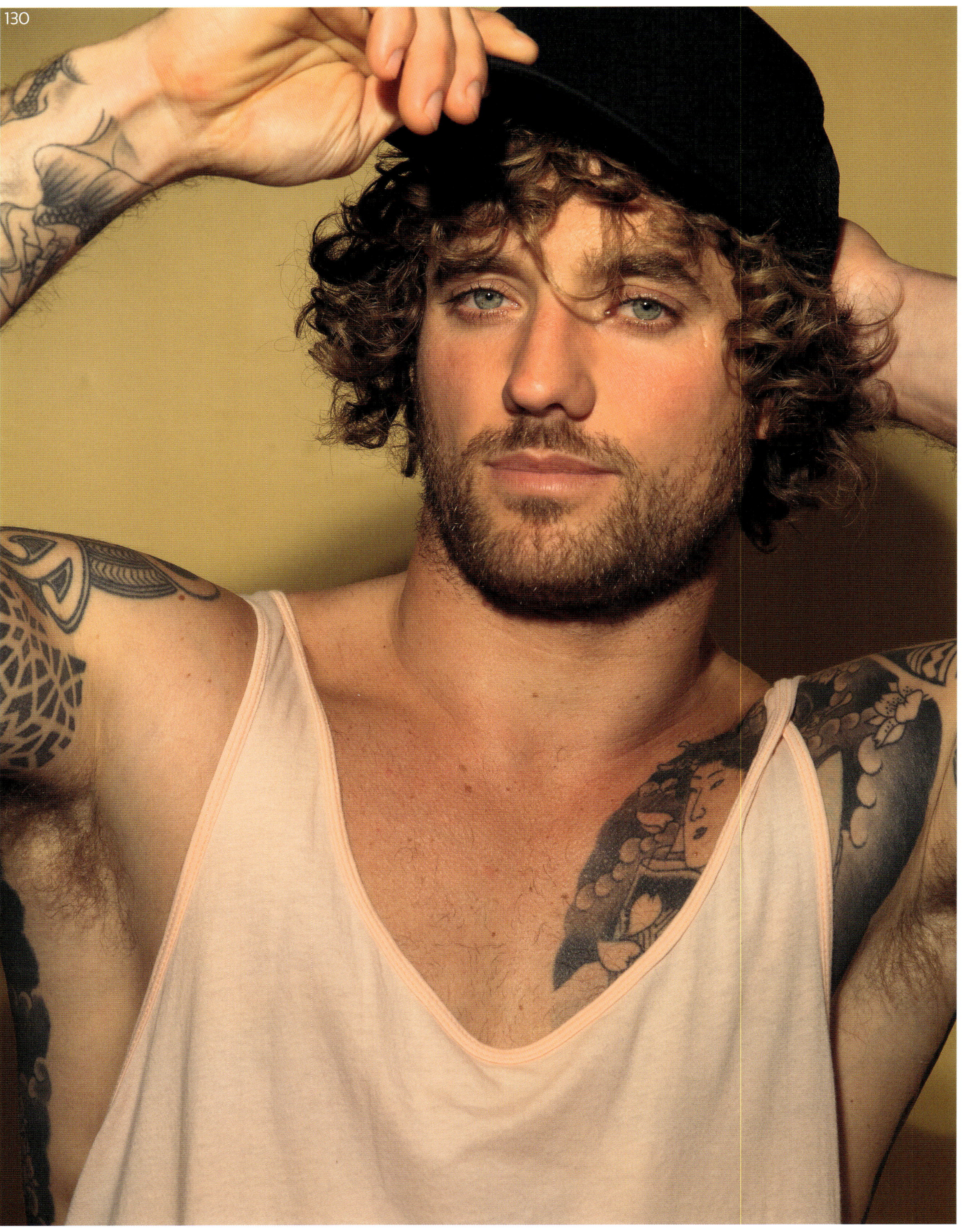

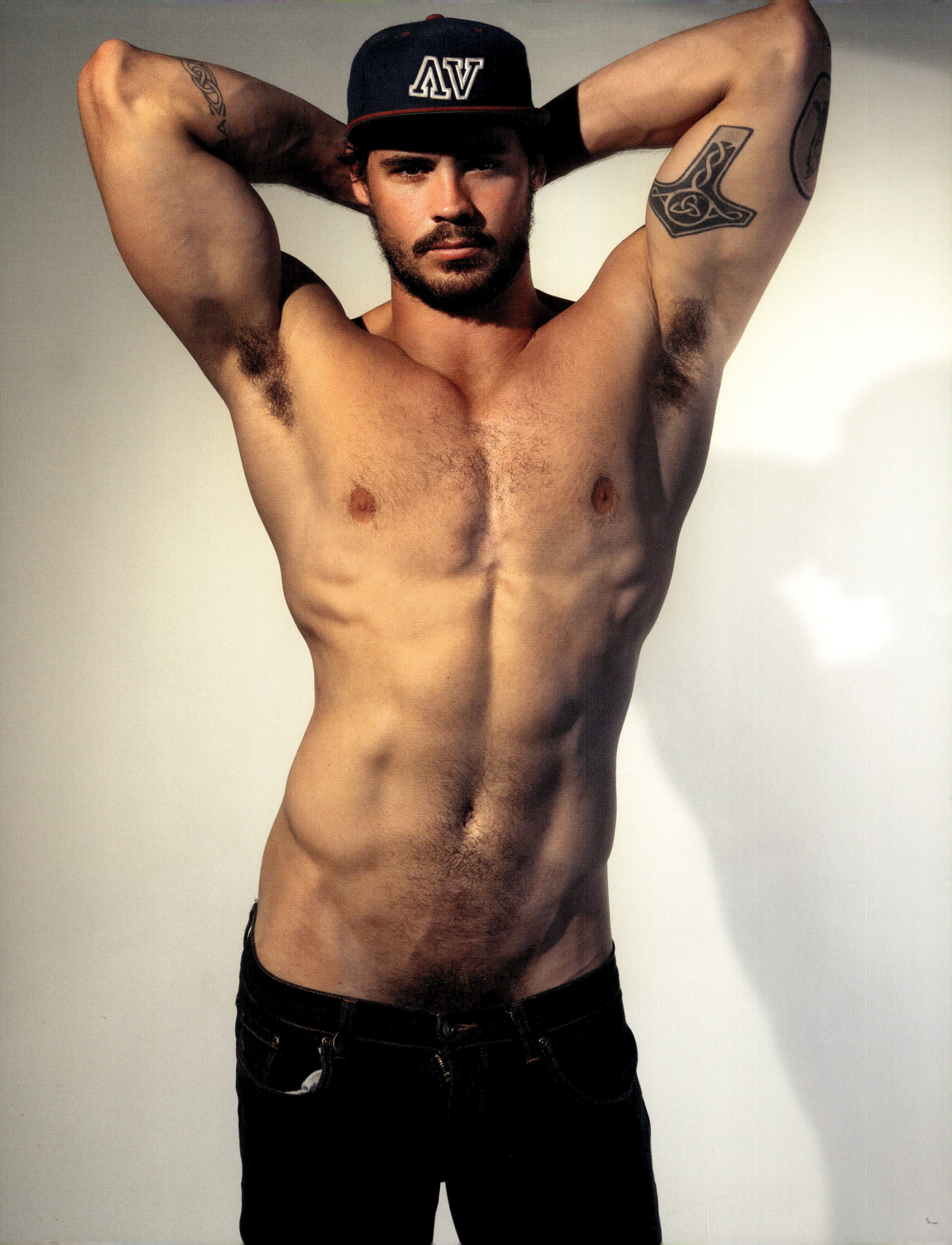
AV

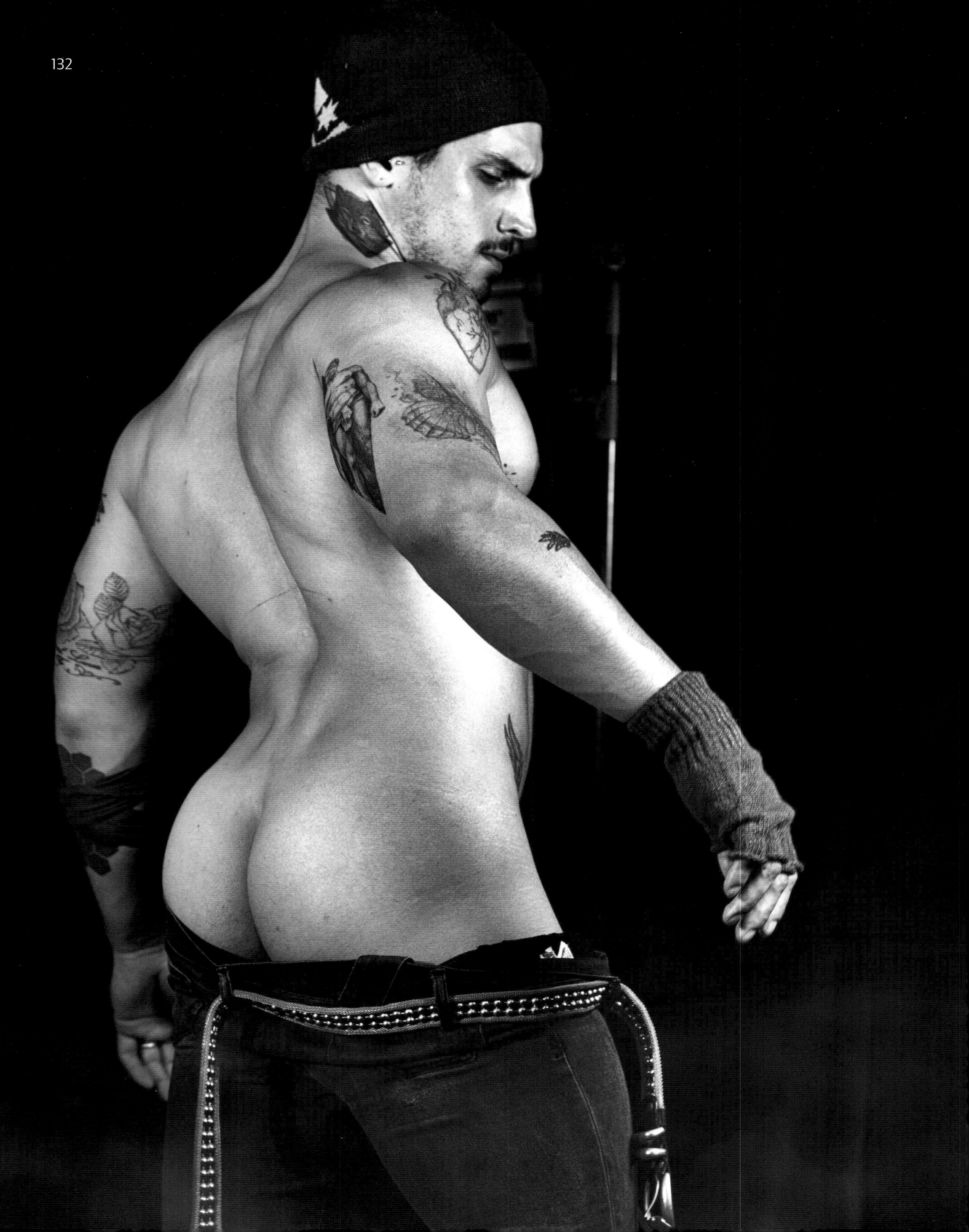

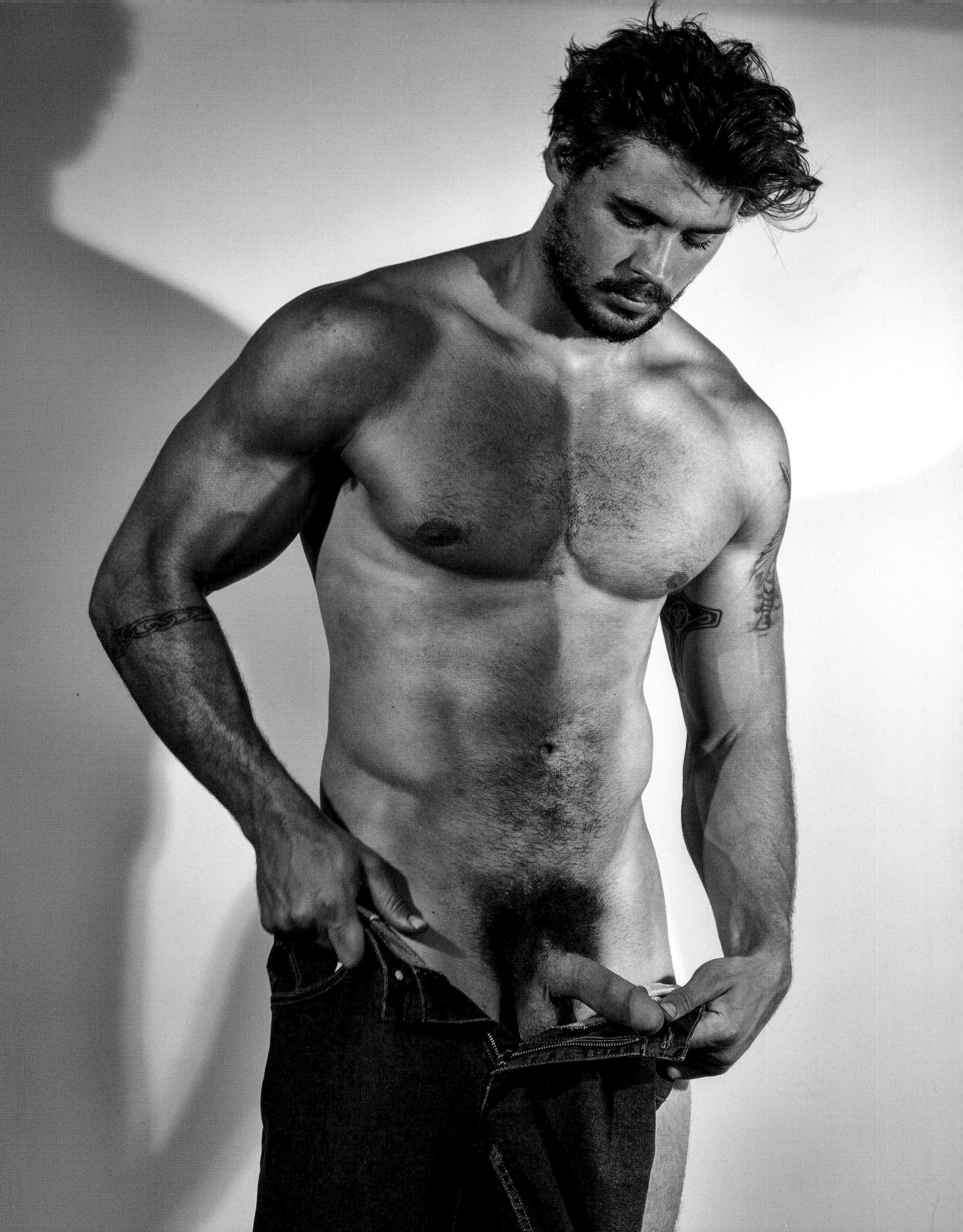

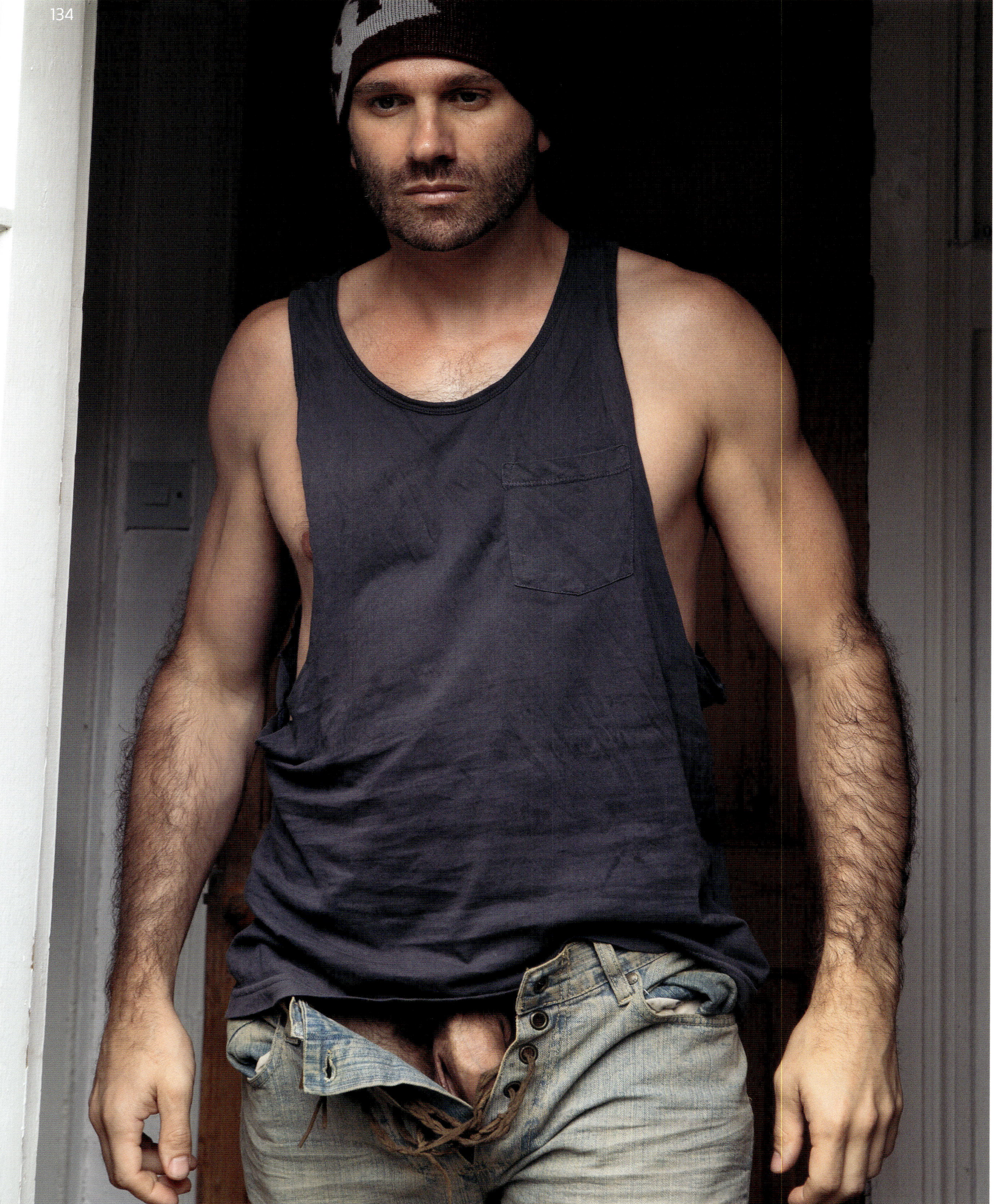

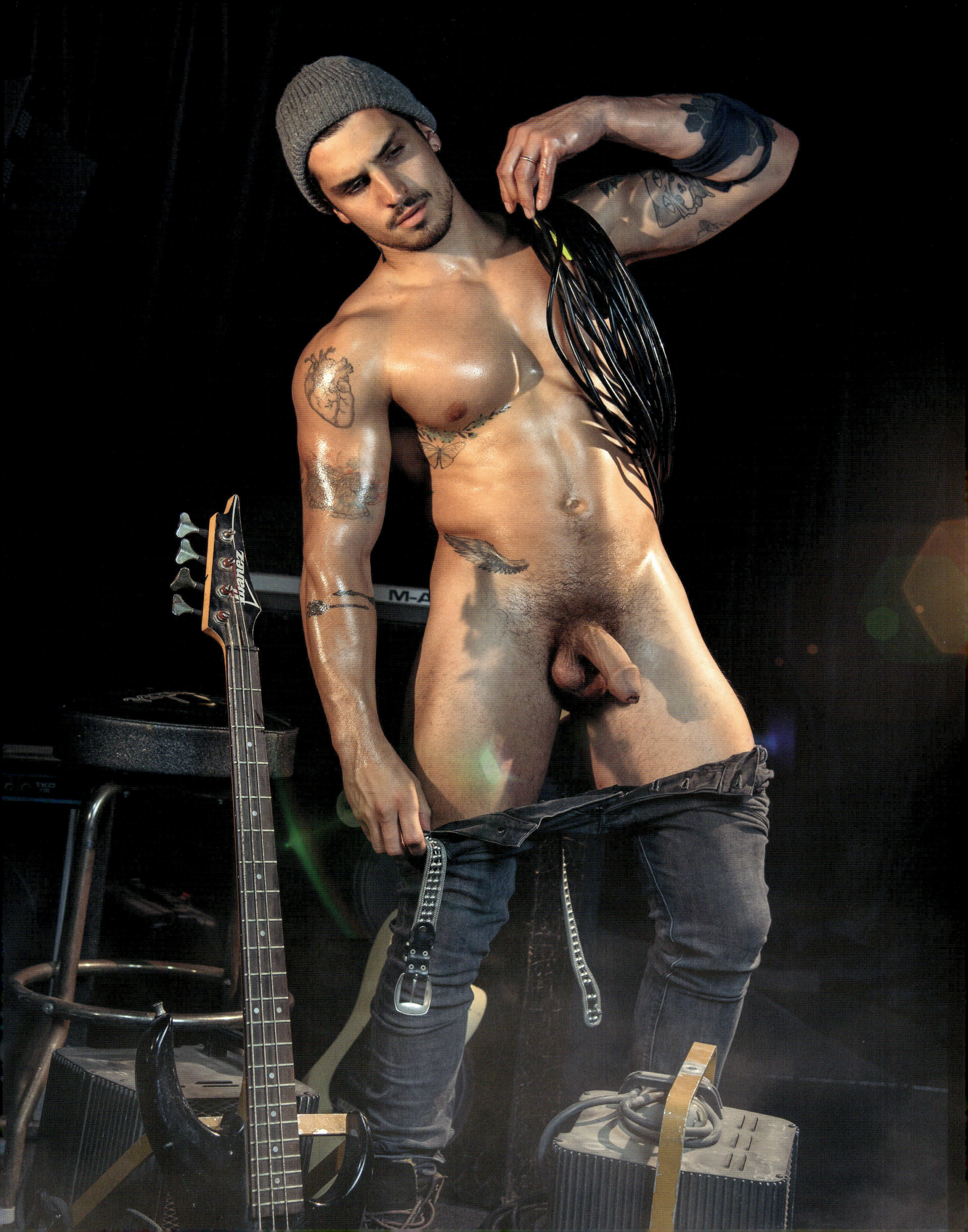

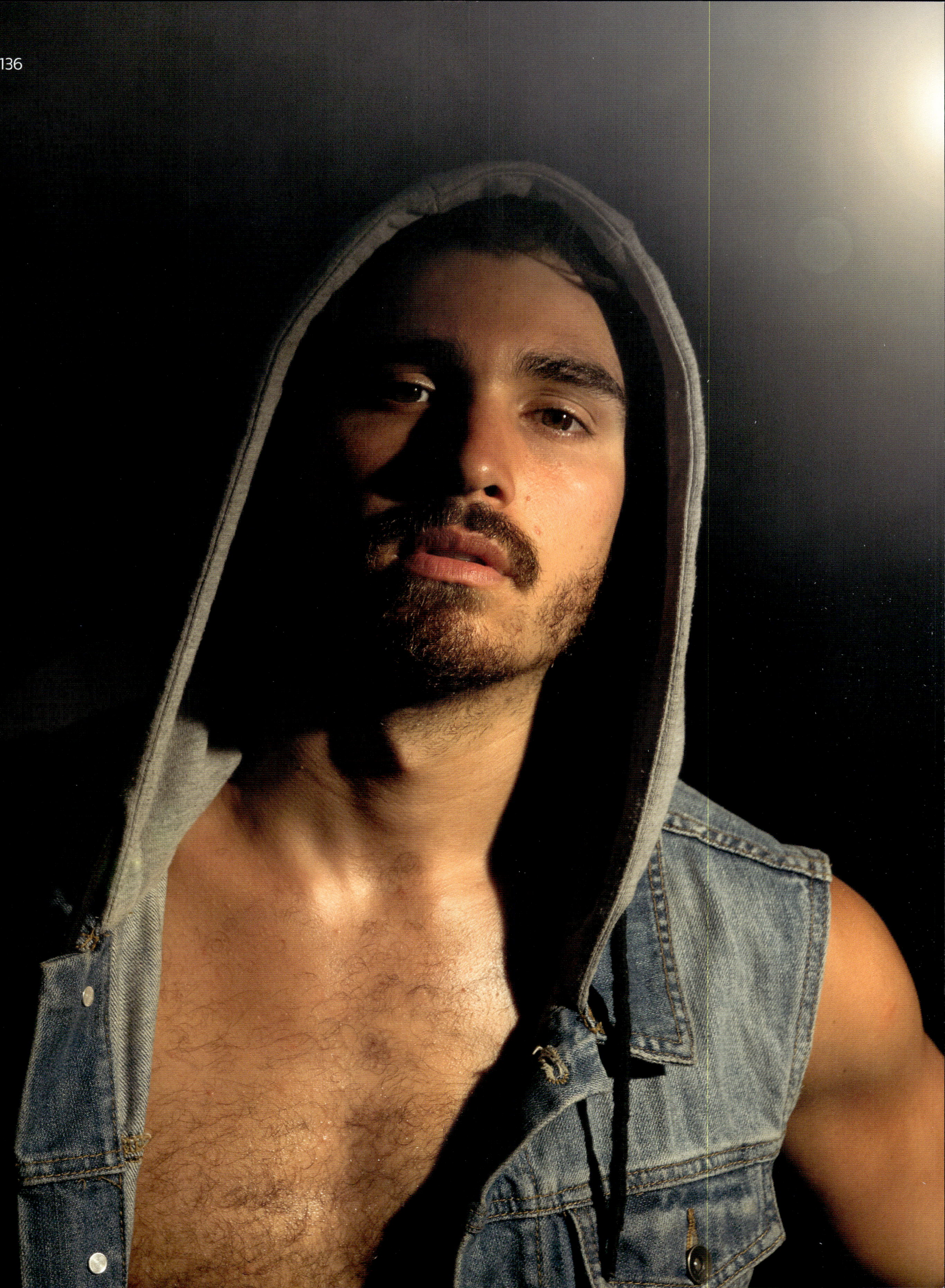

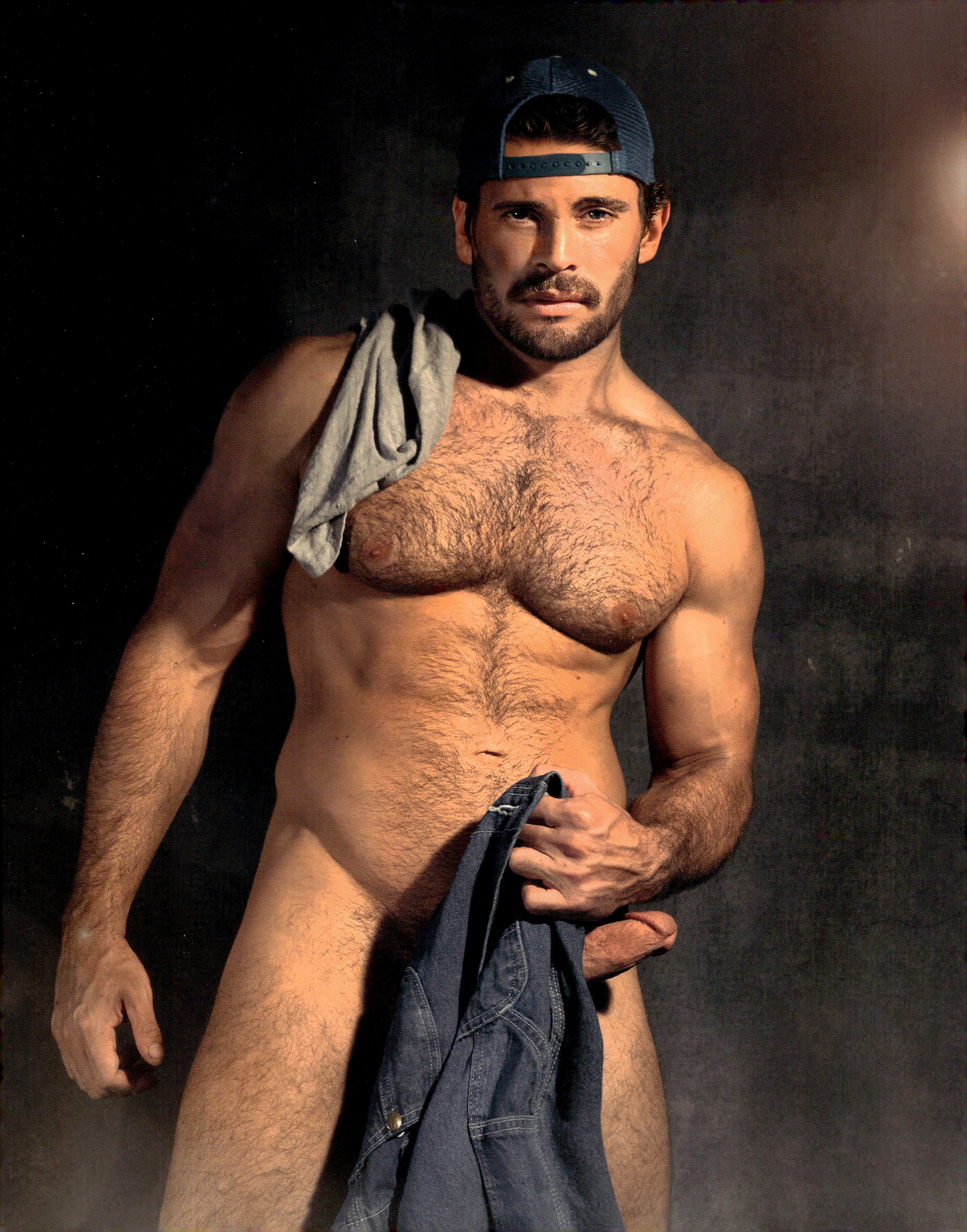

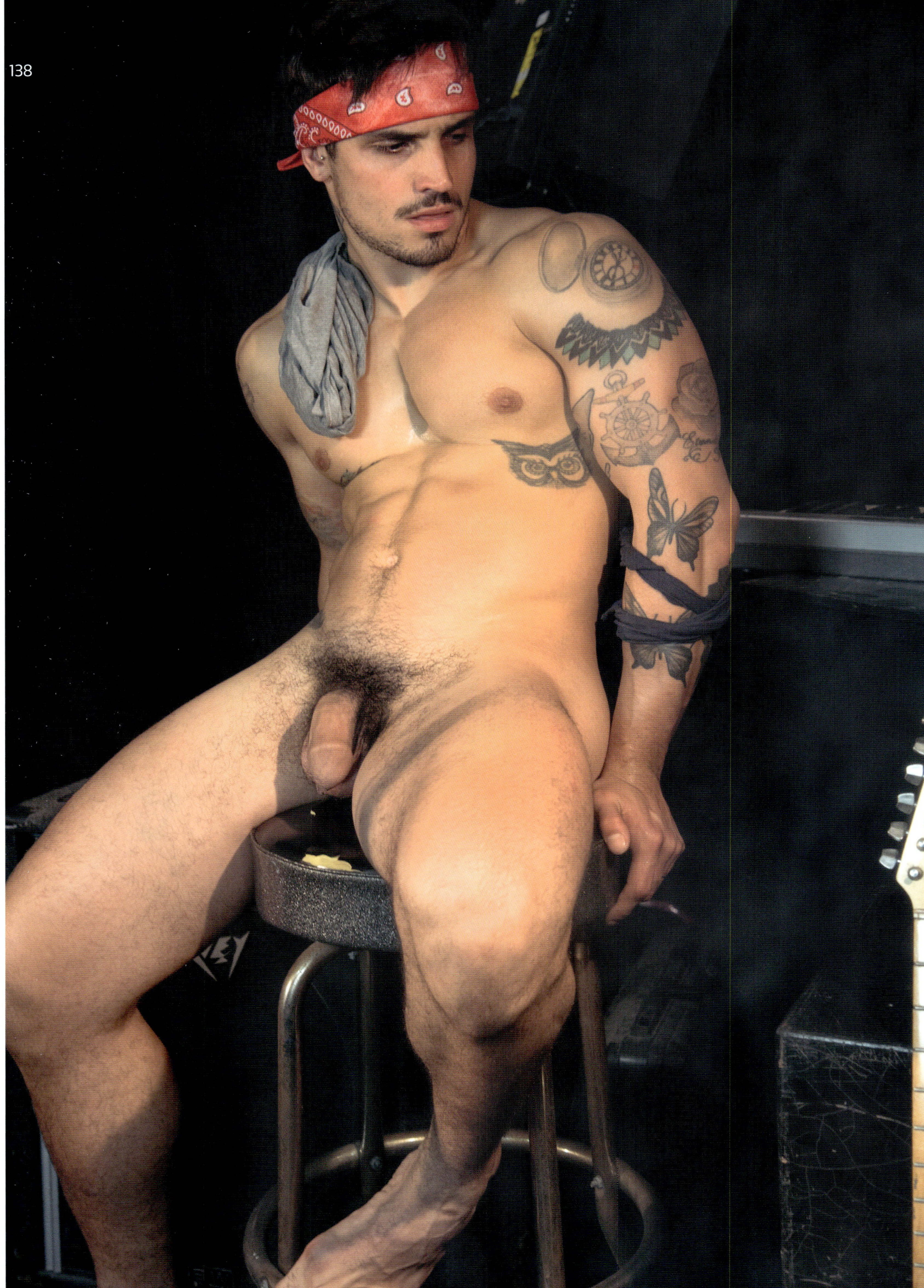

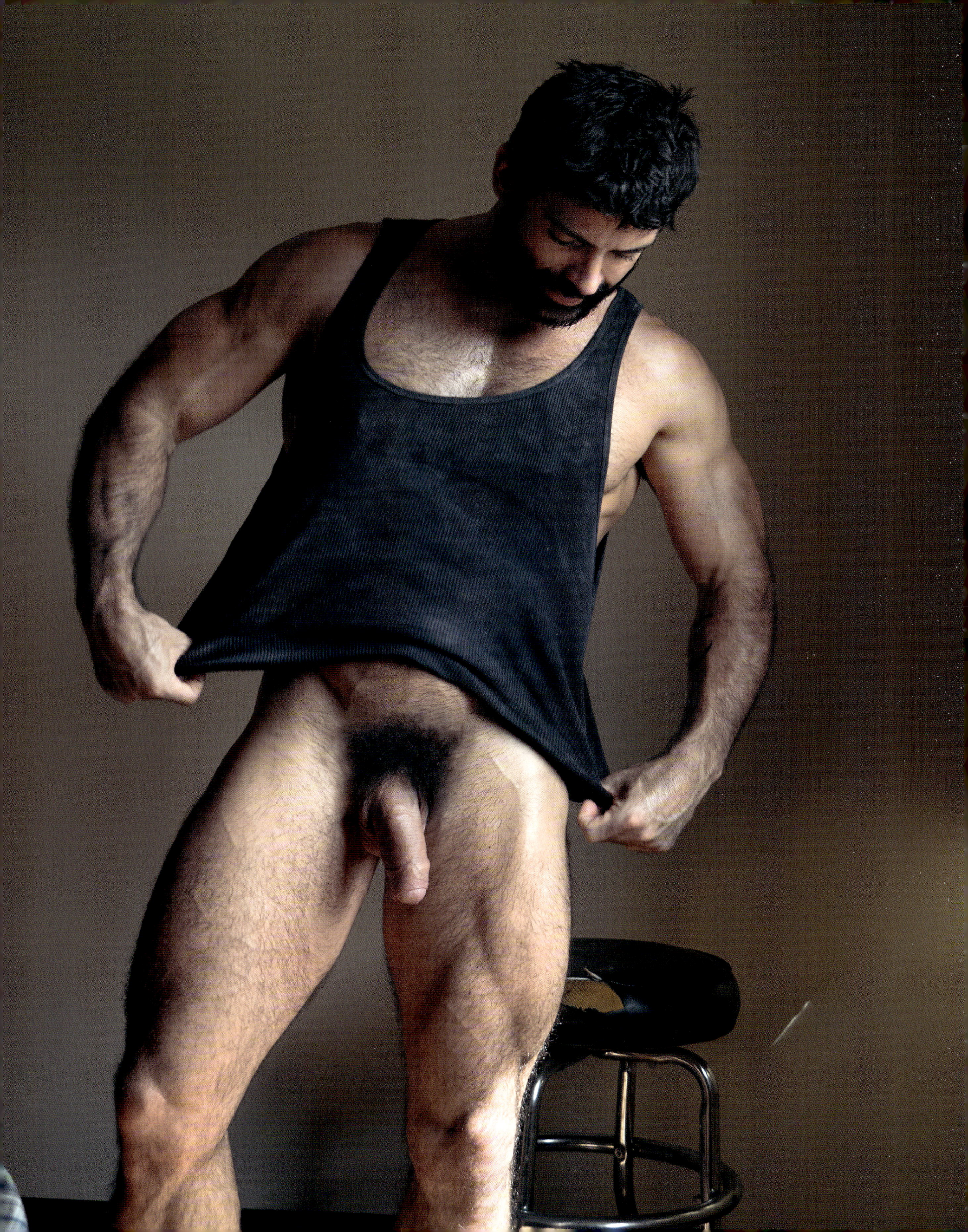

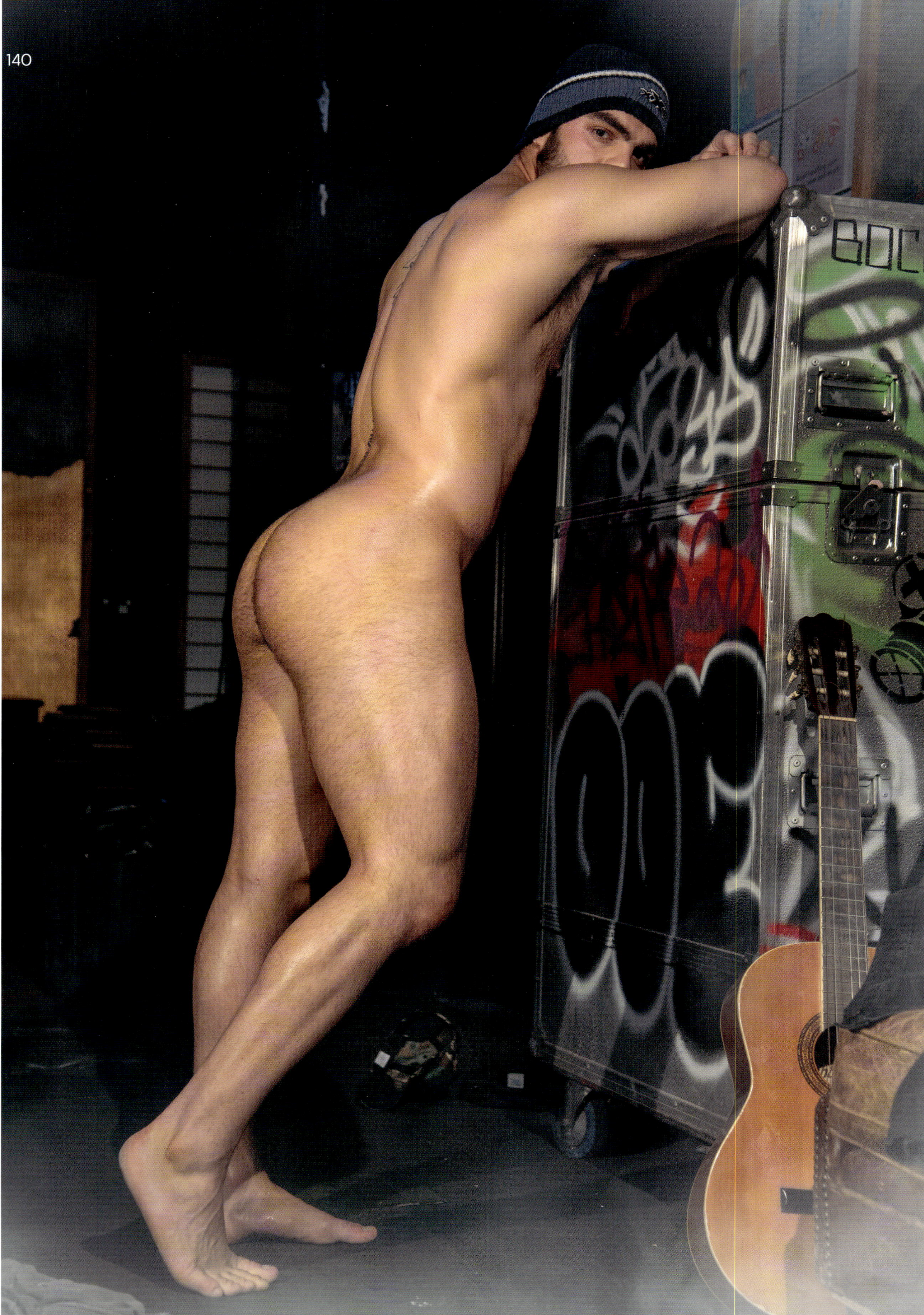

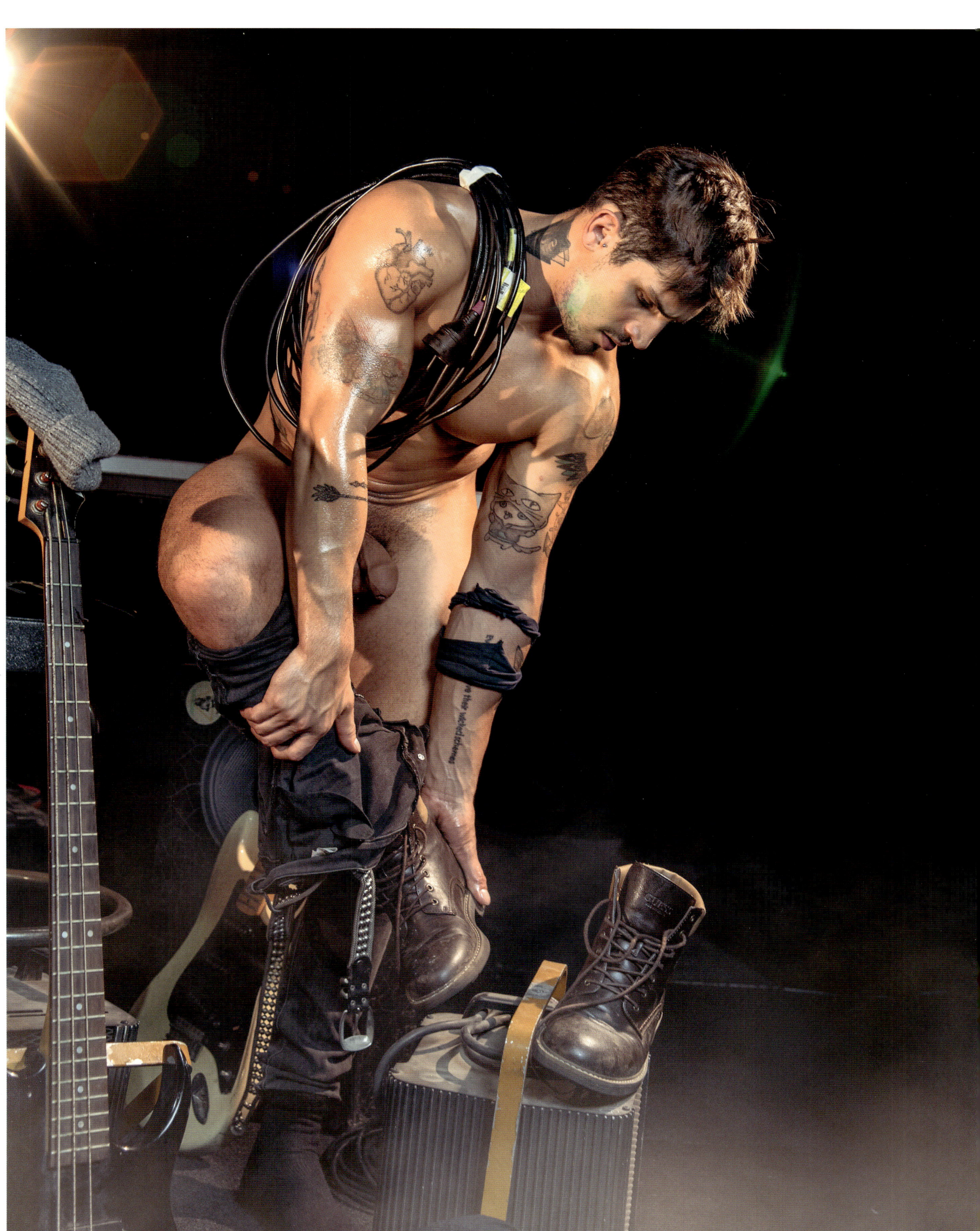

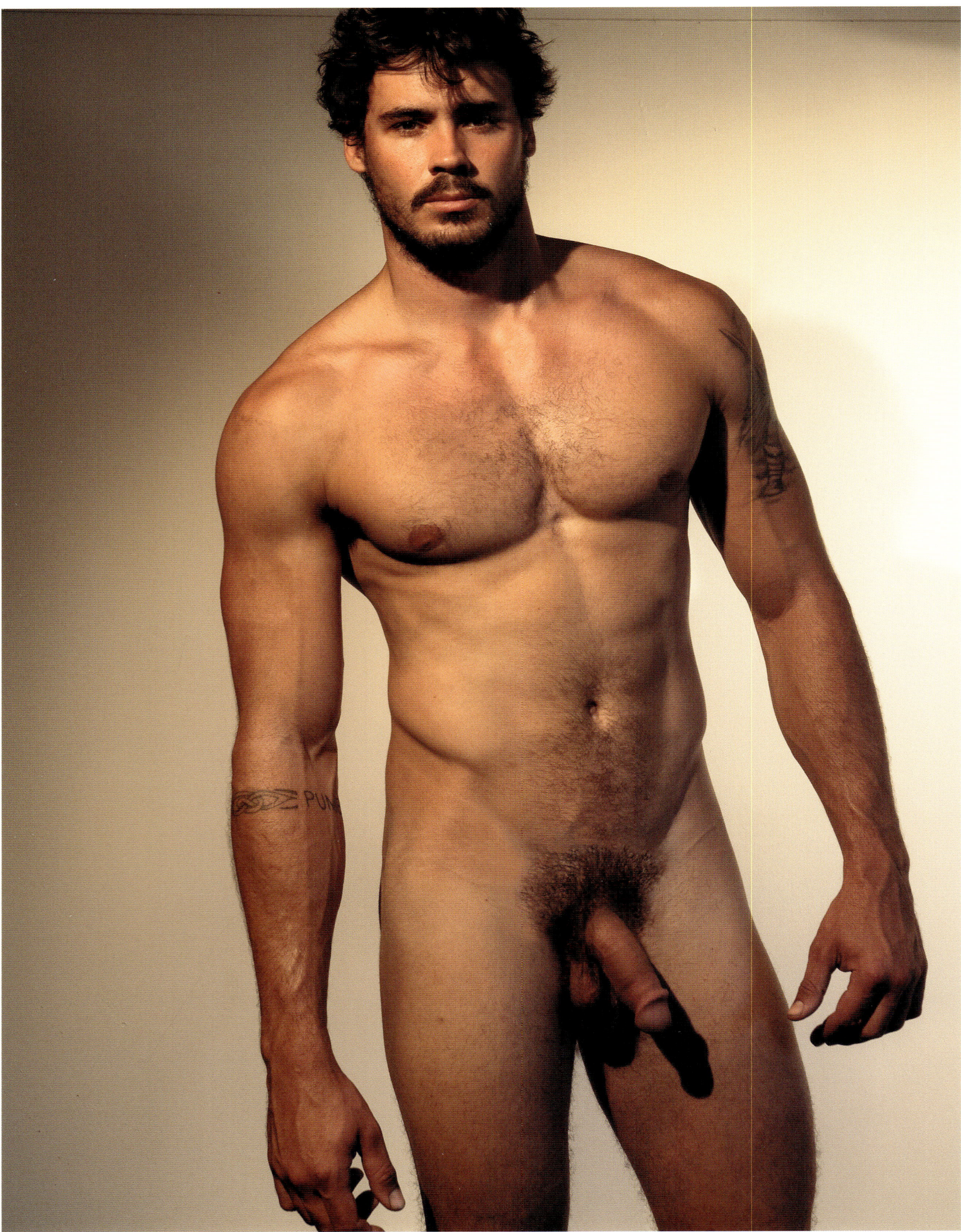

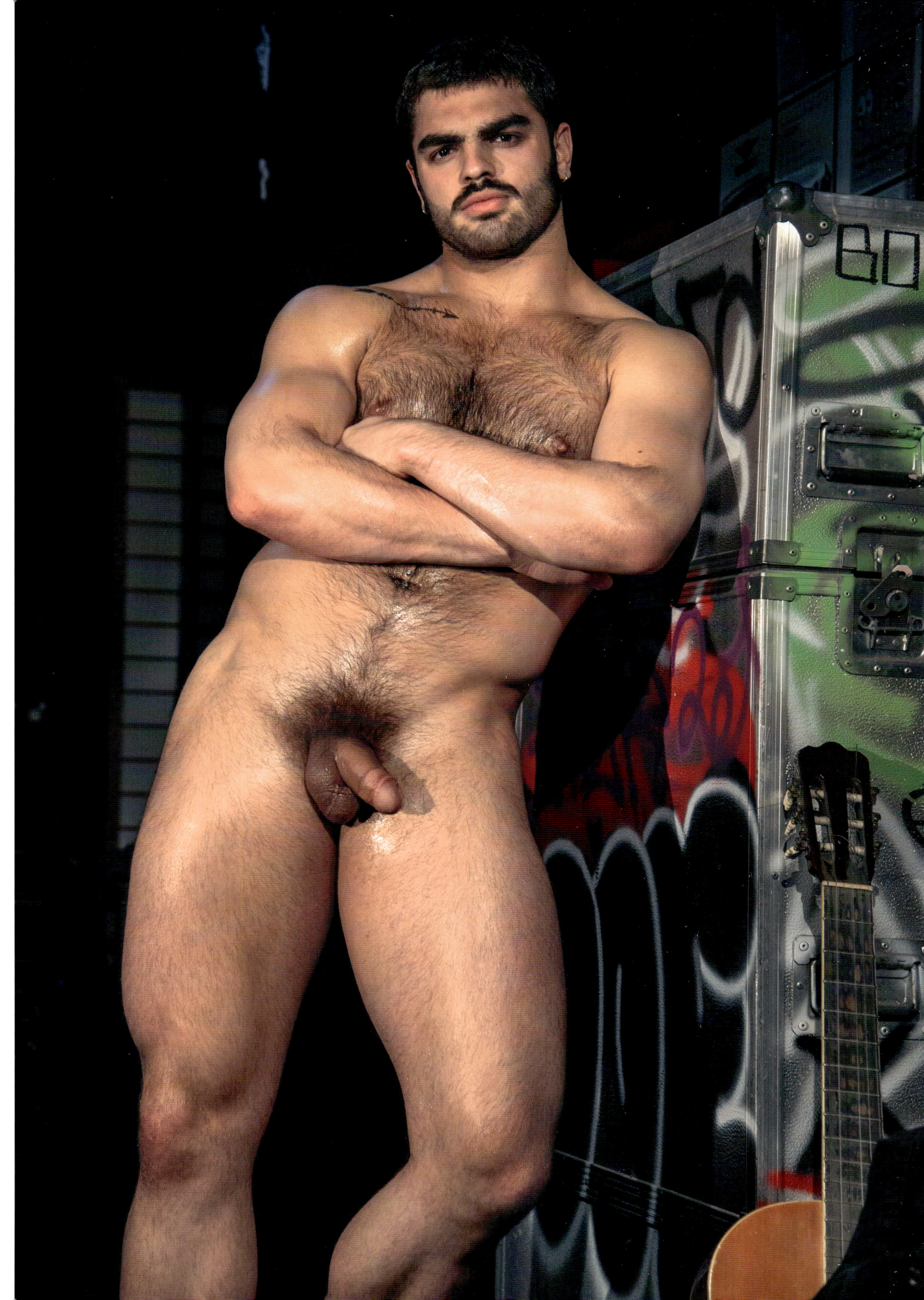

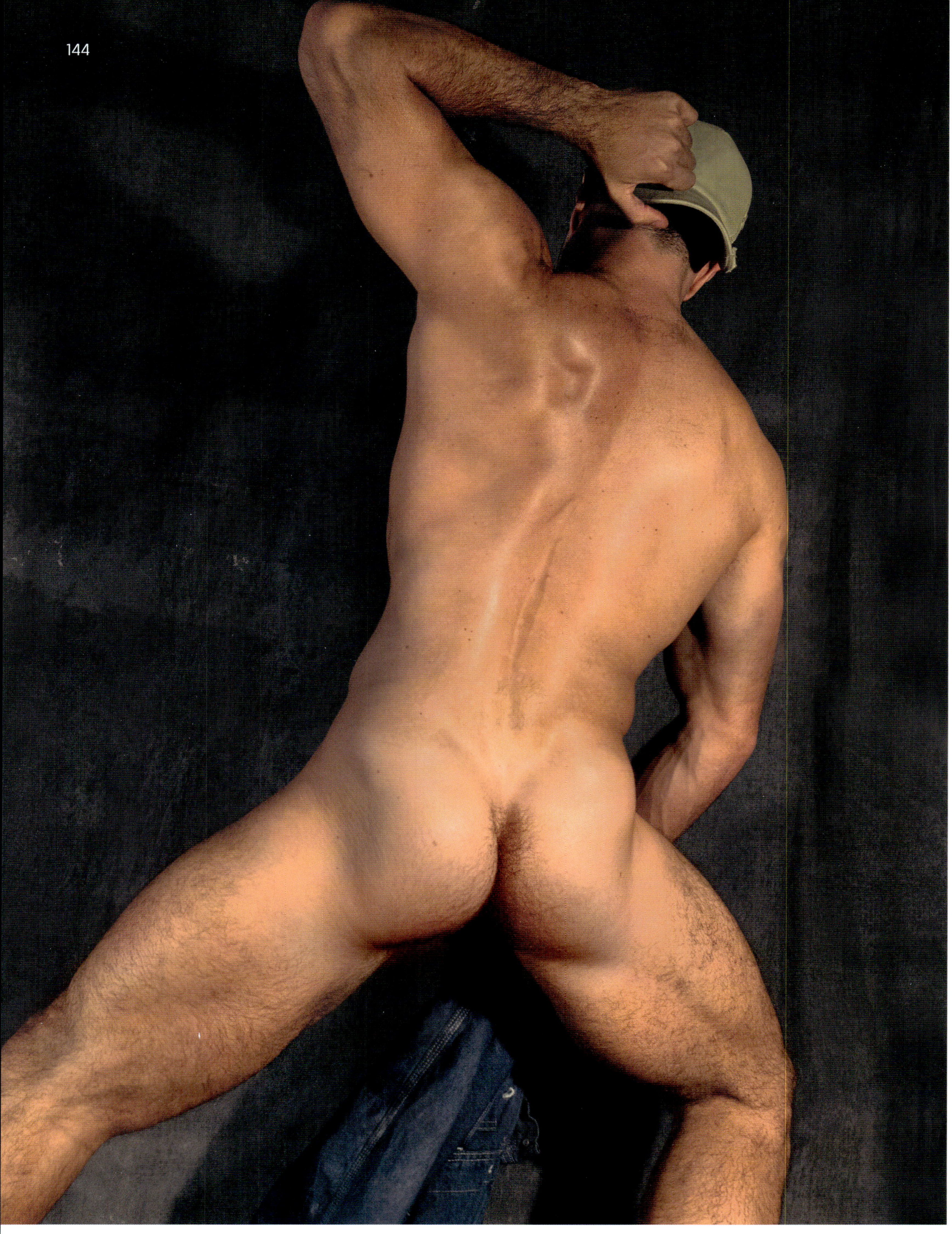

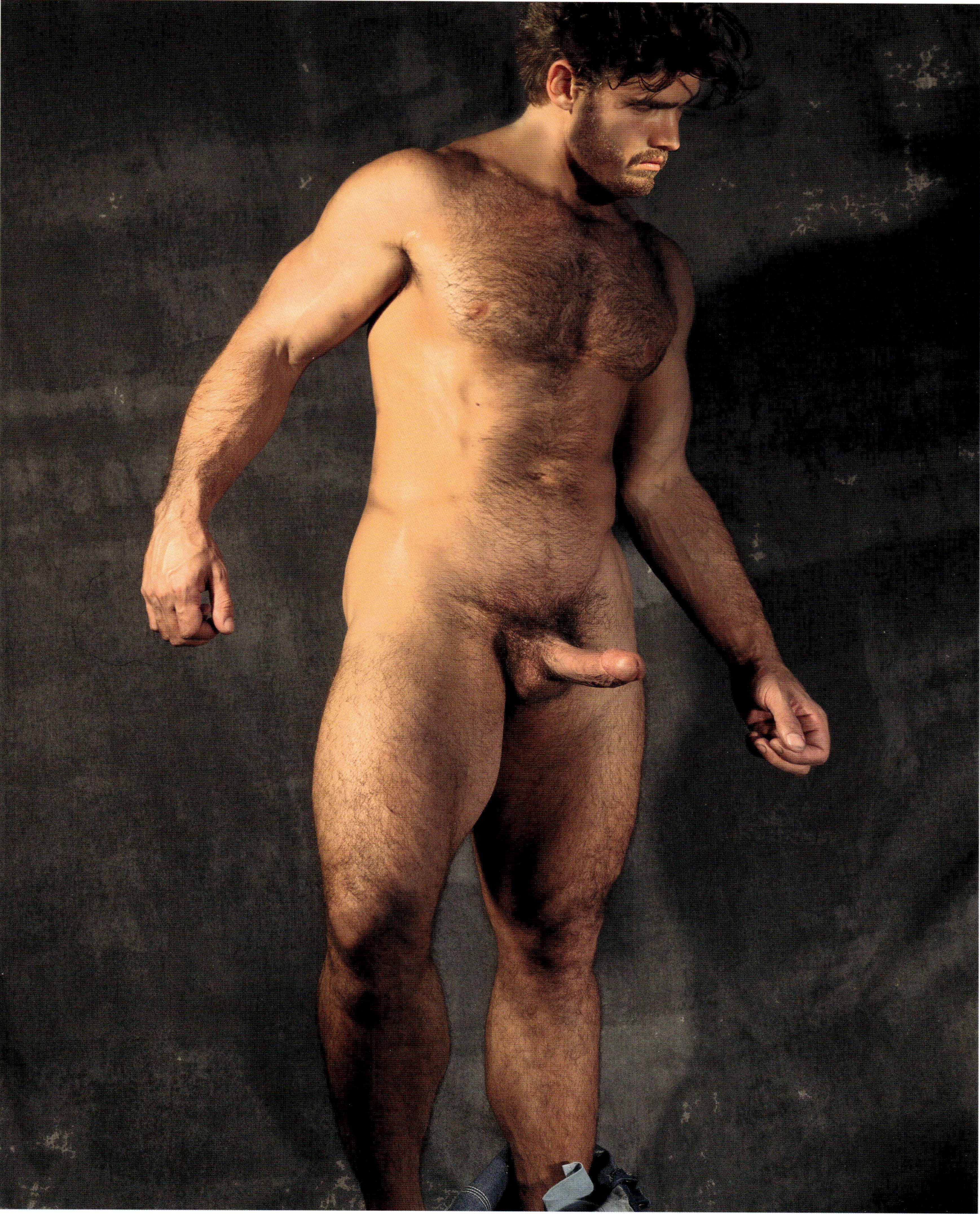

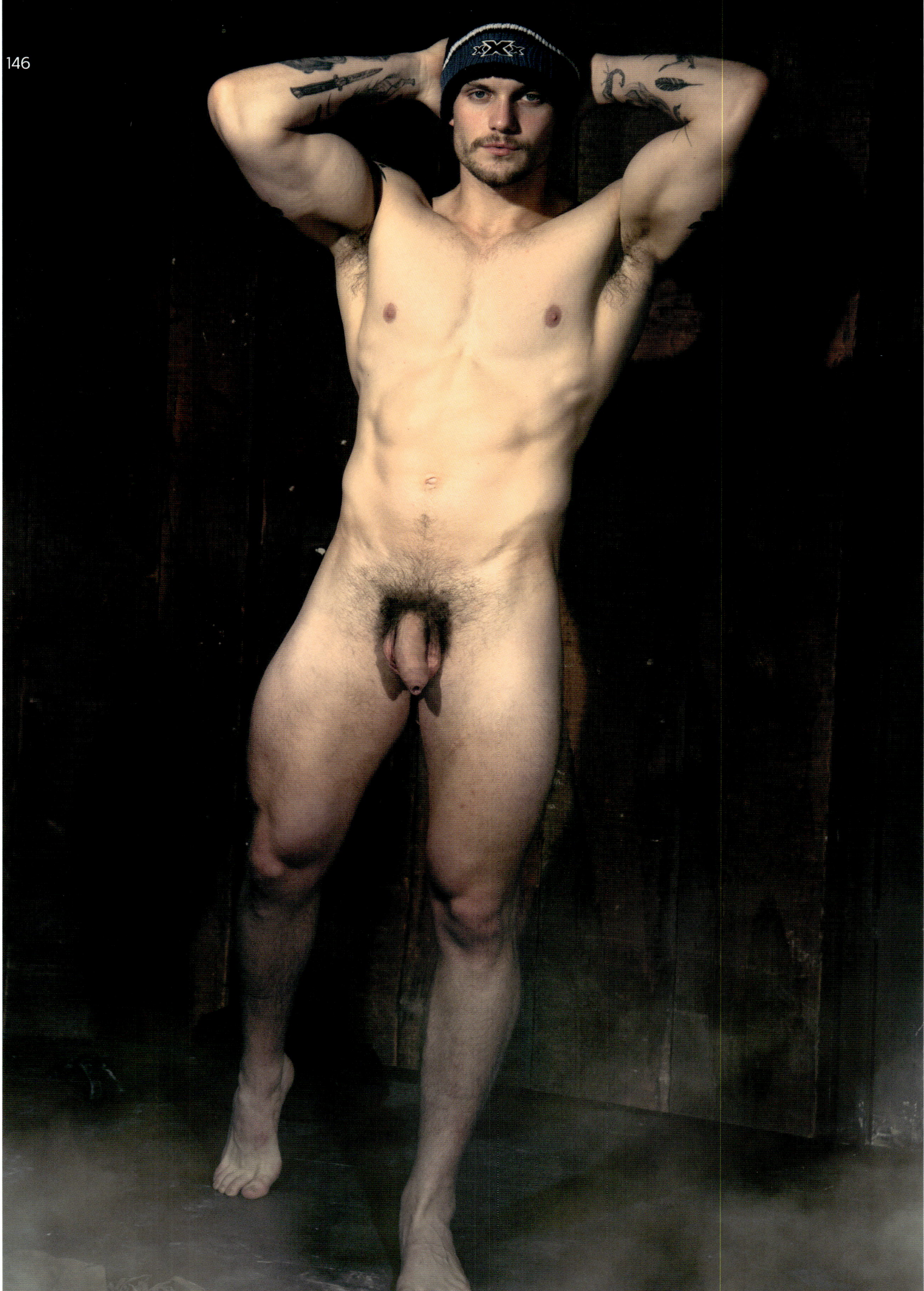

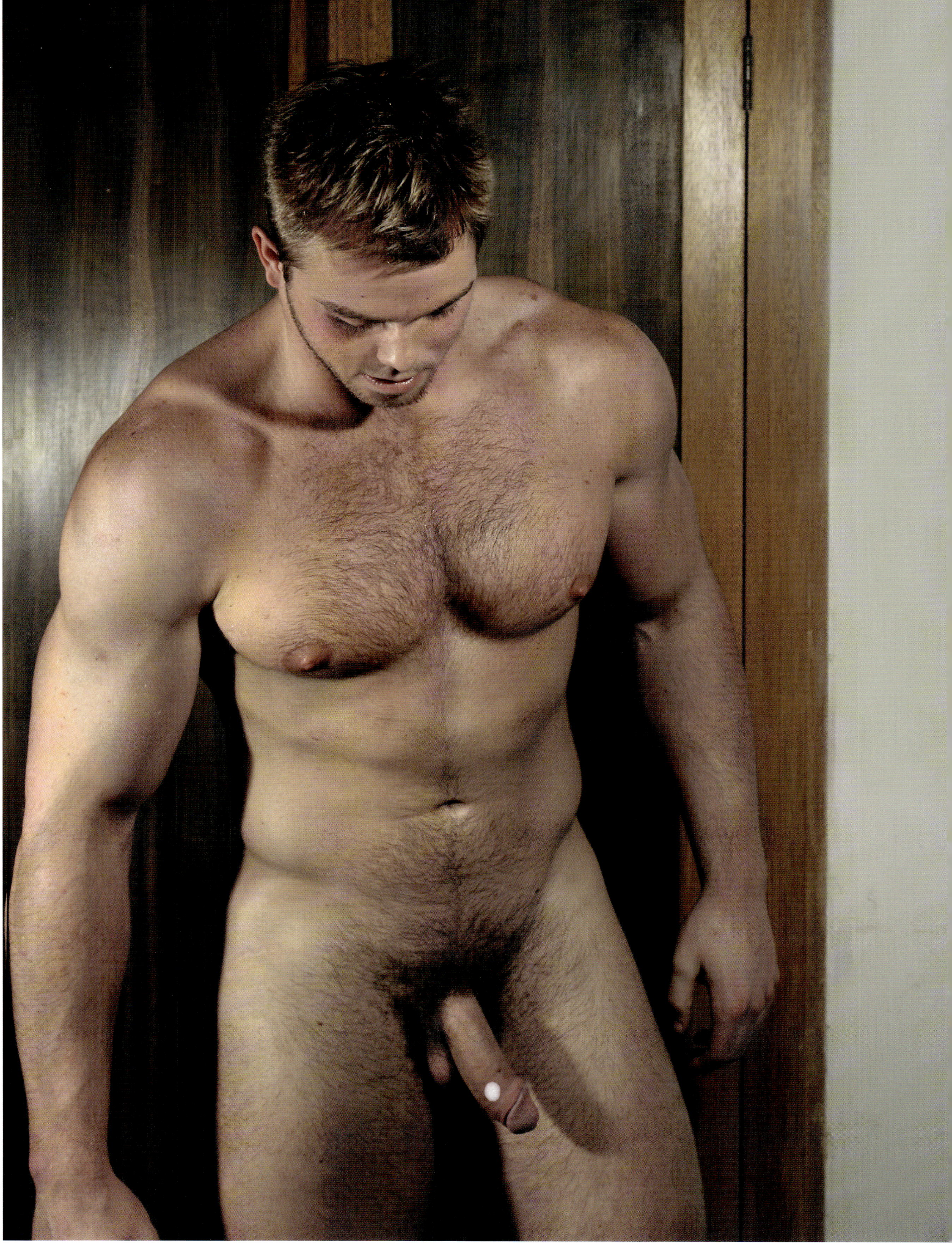

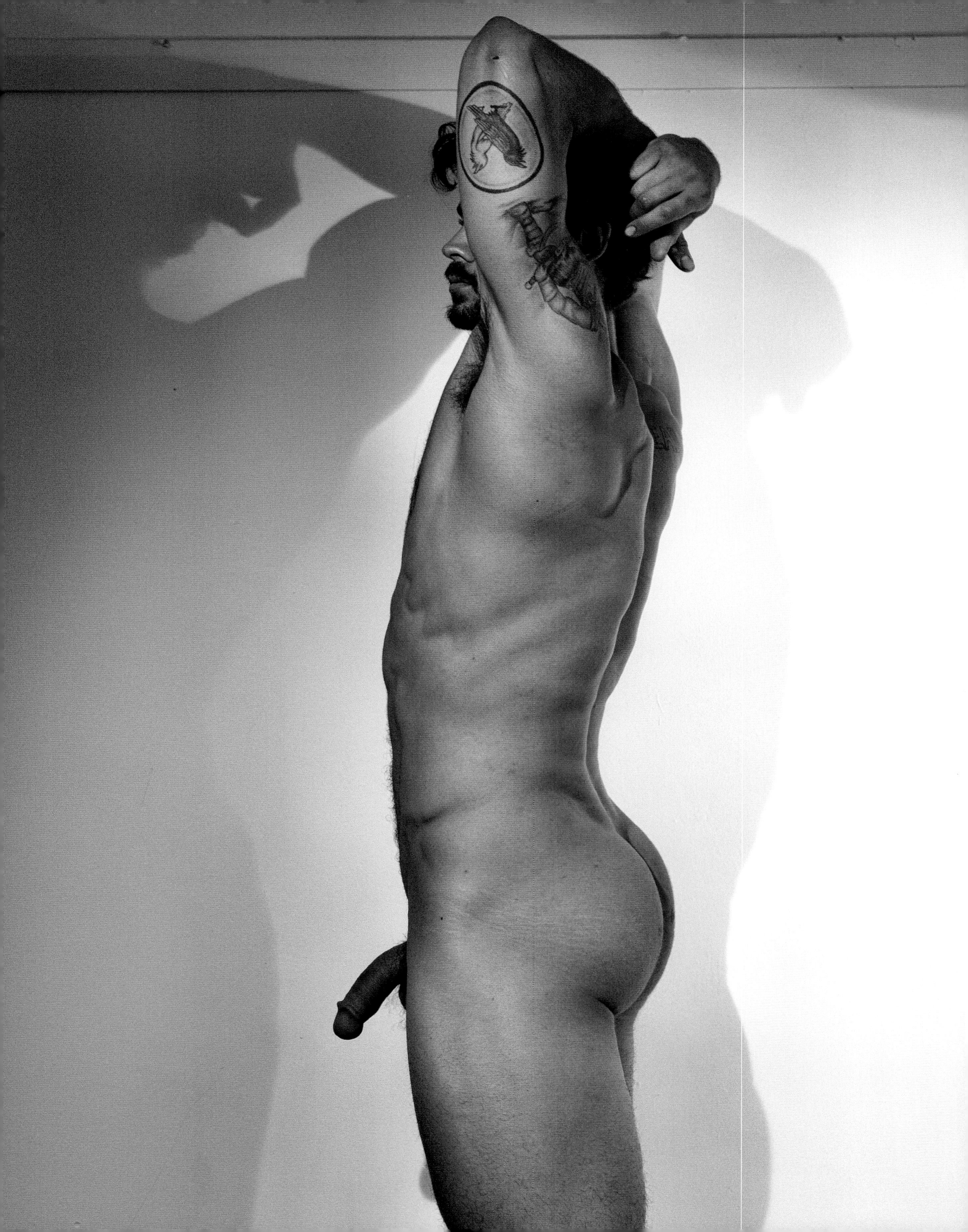

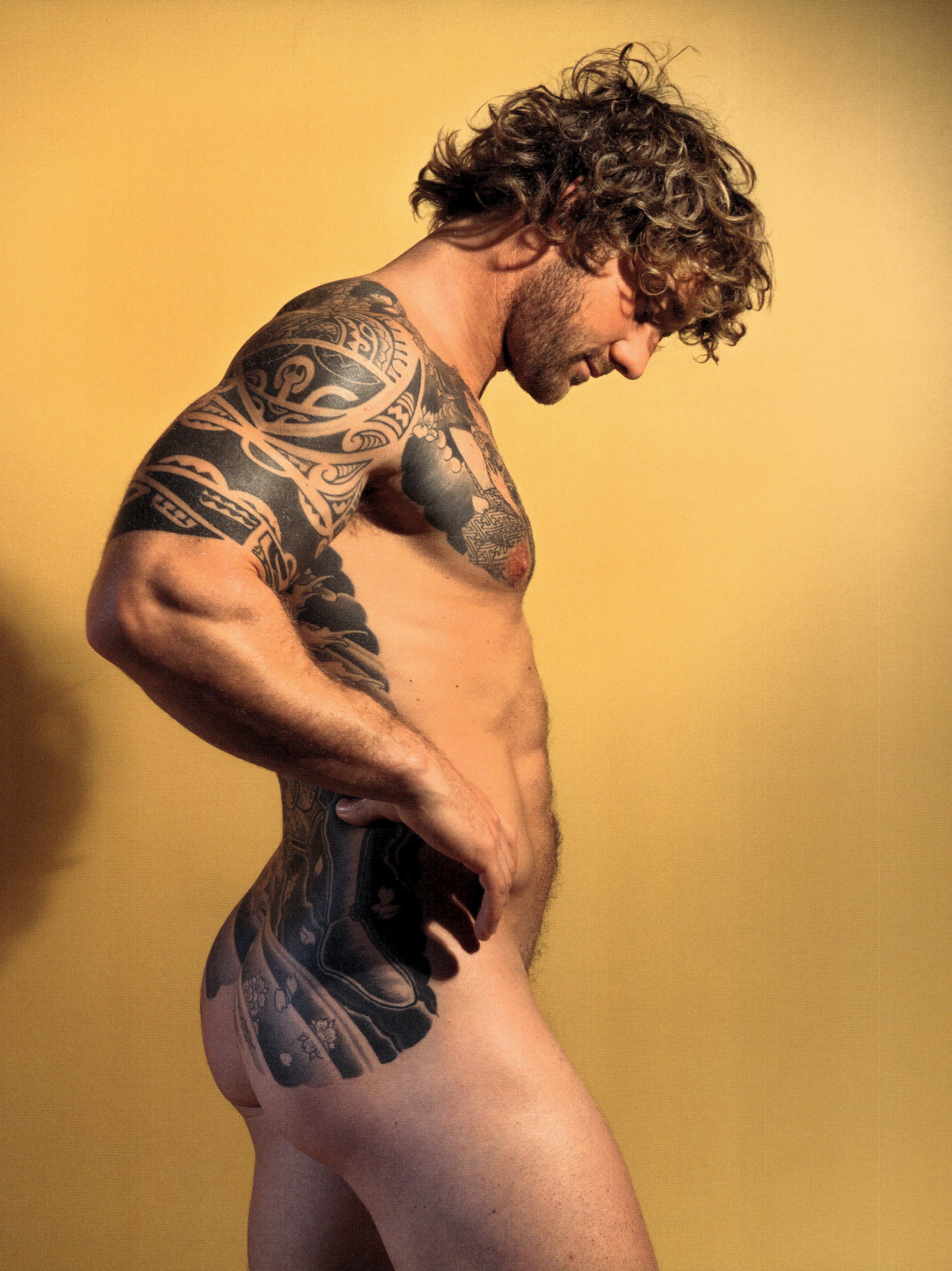

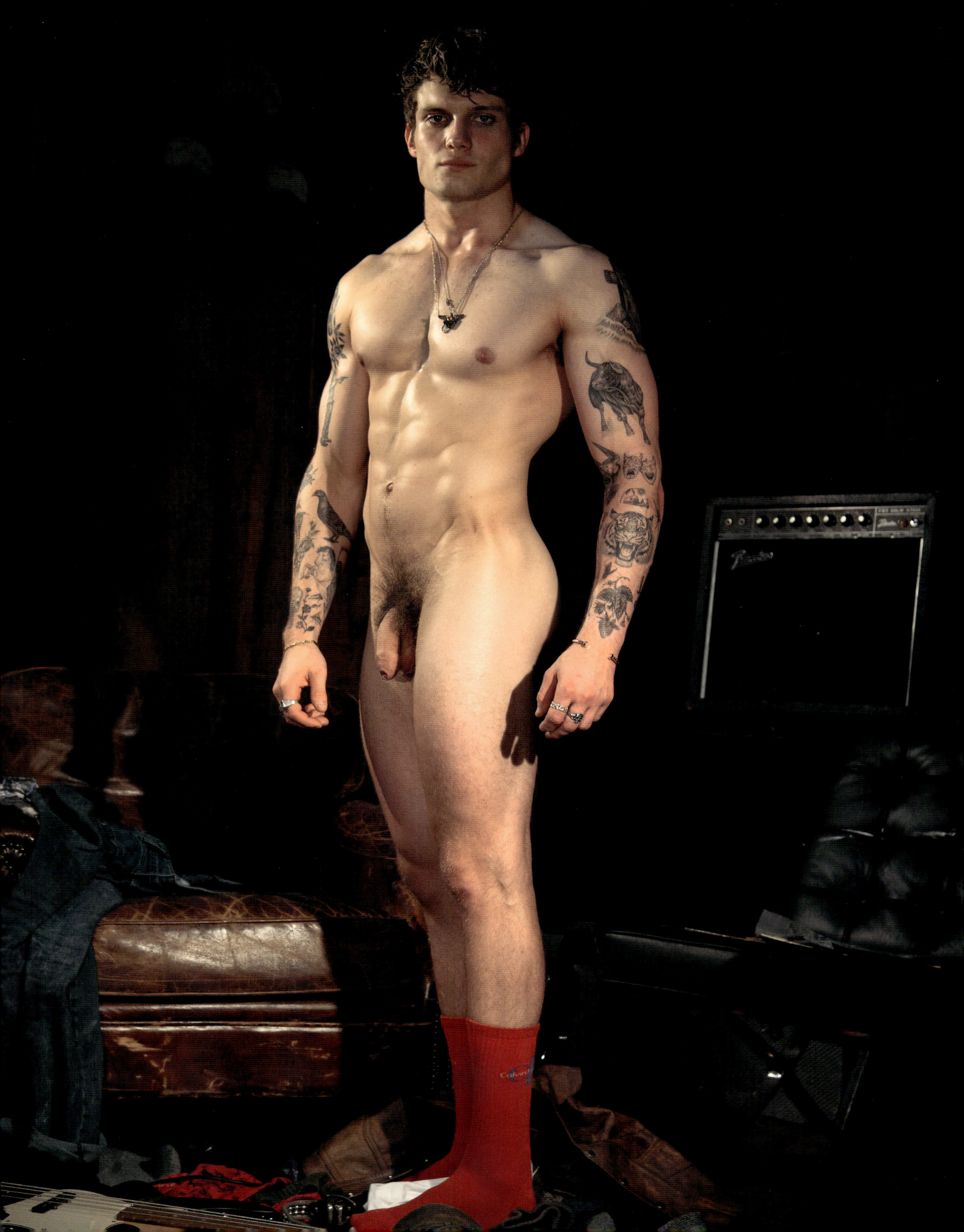
Calvin

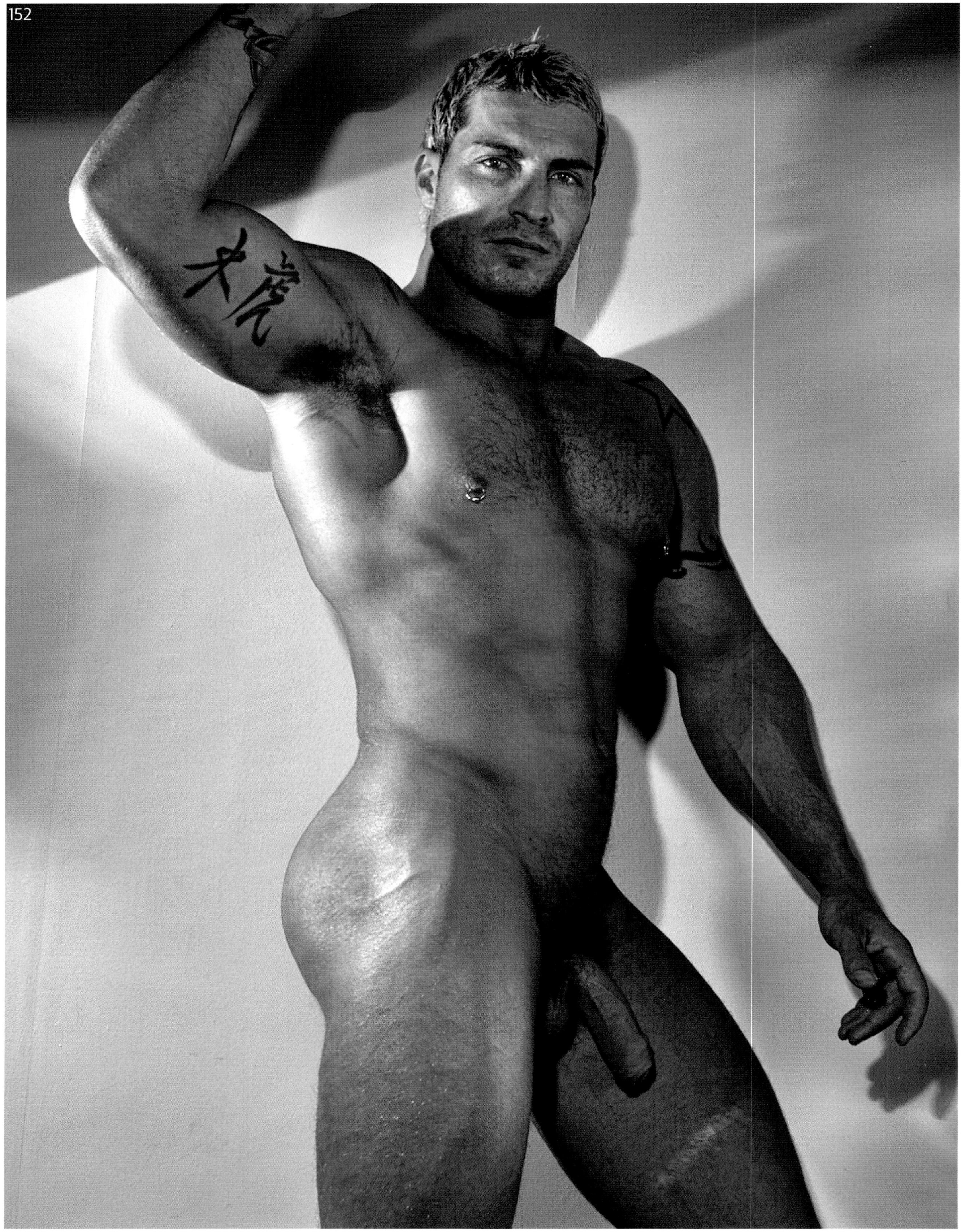

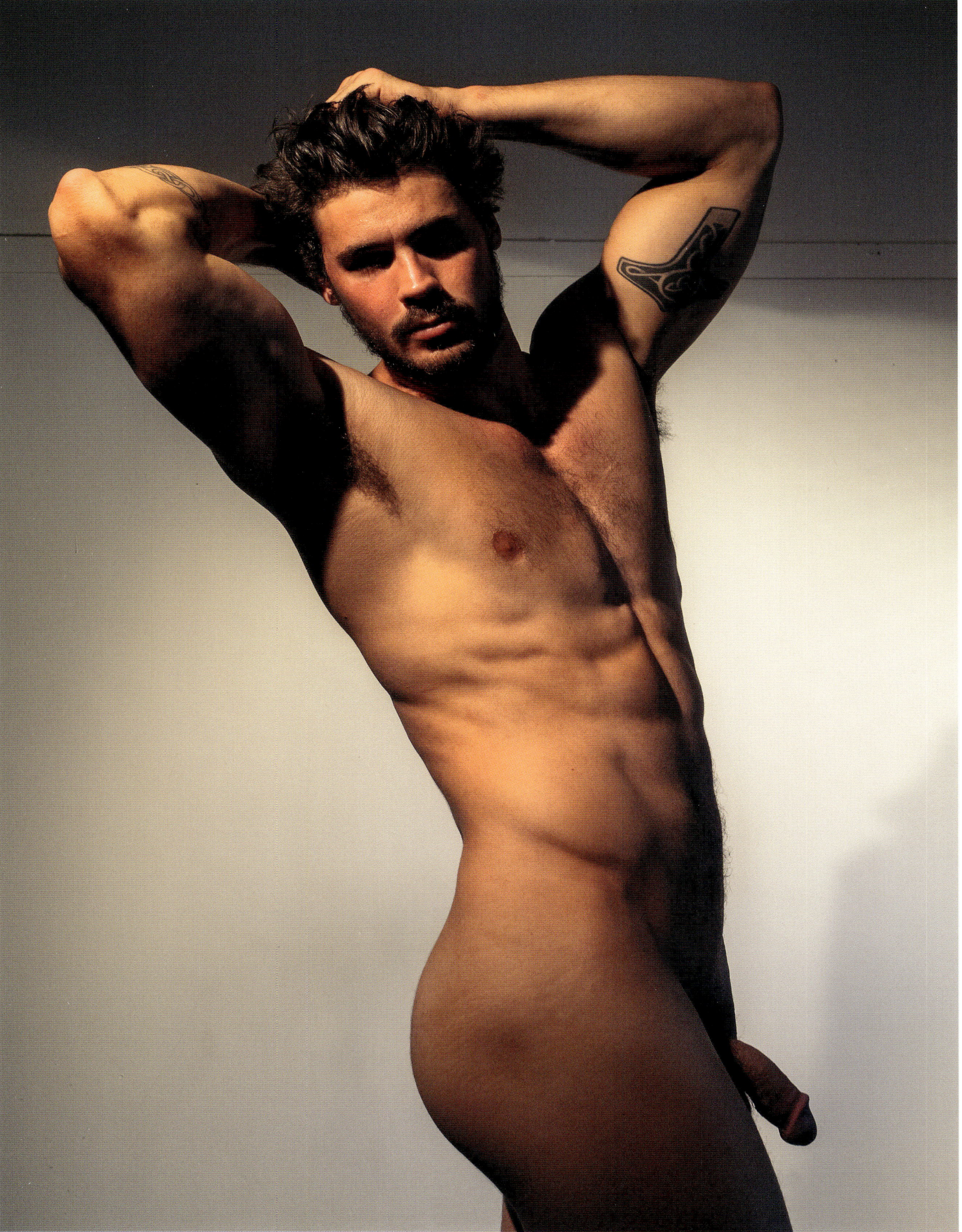

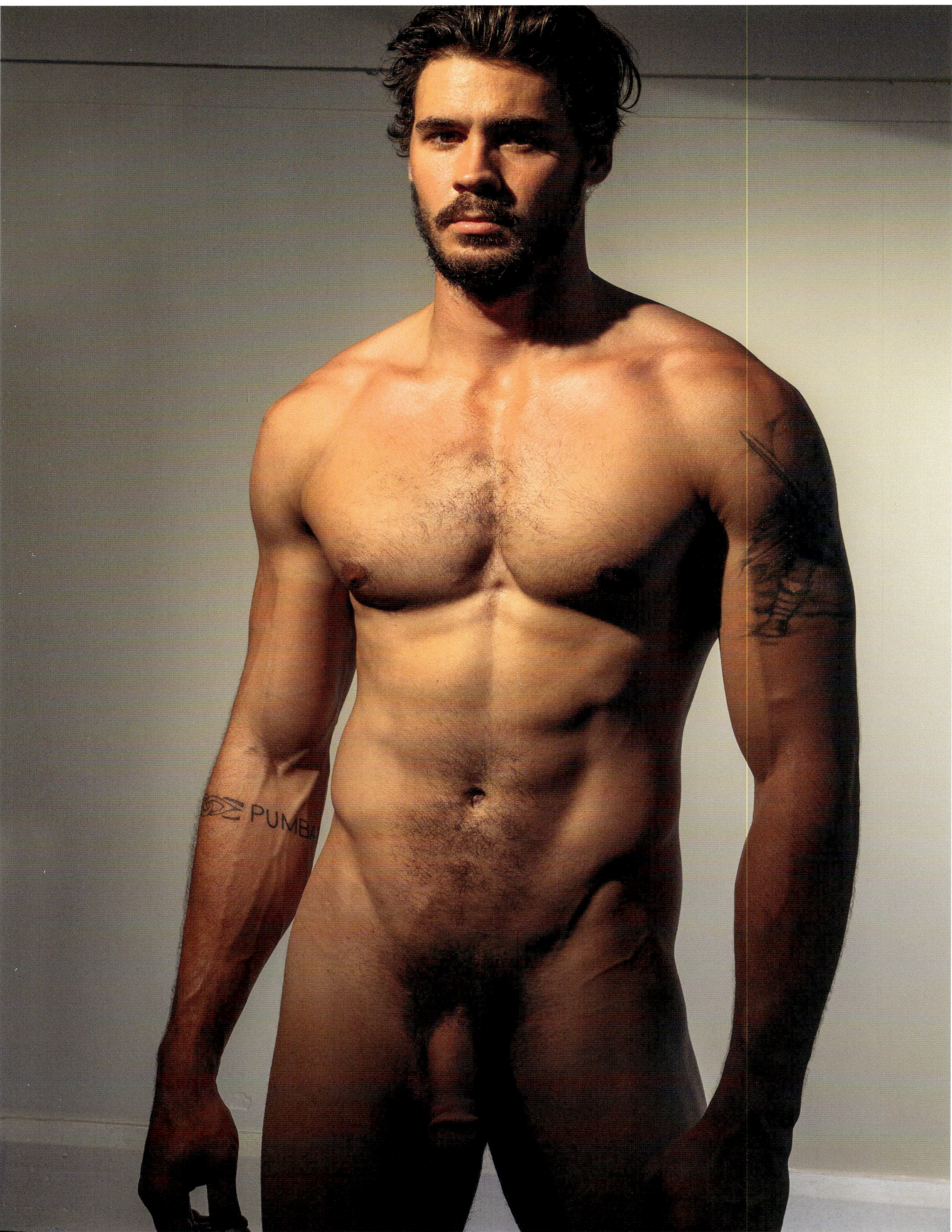

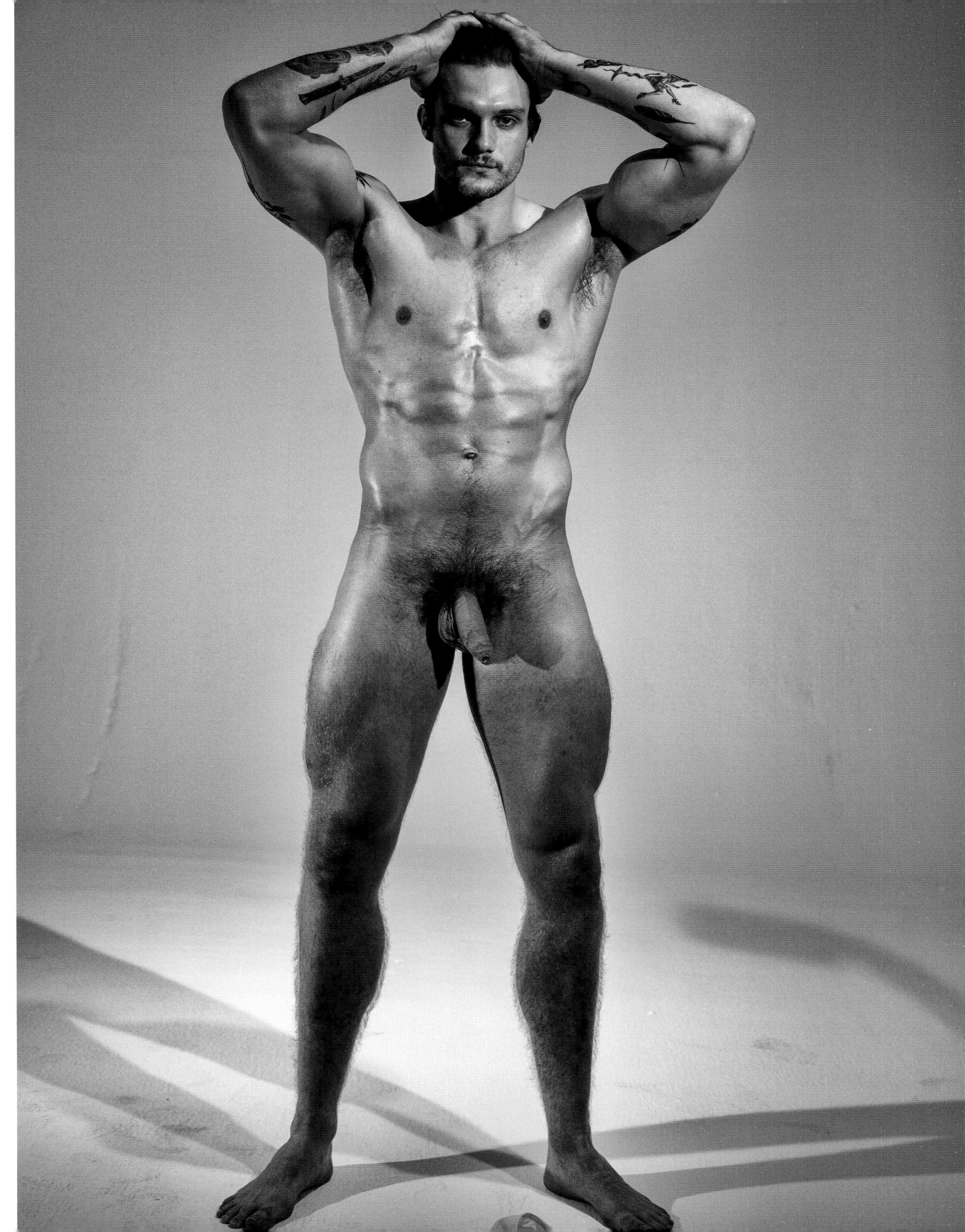

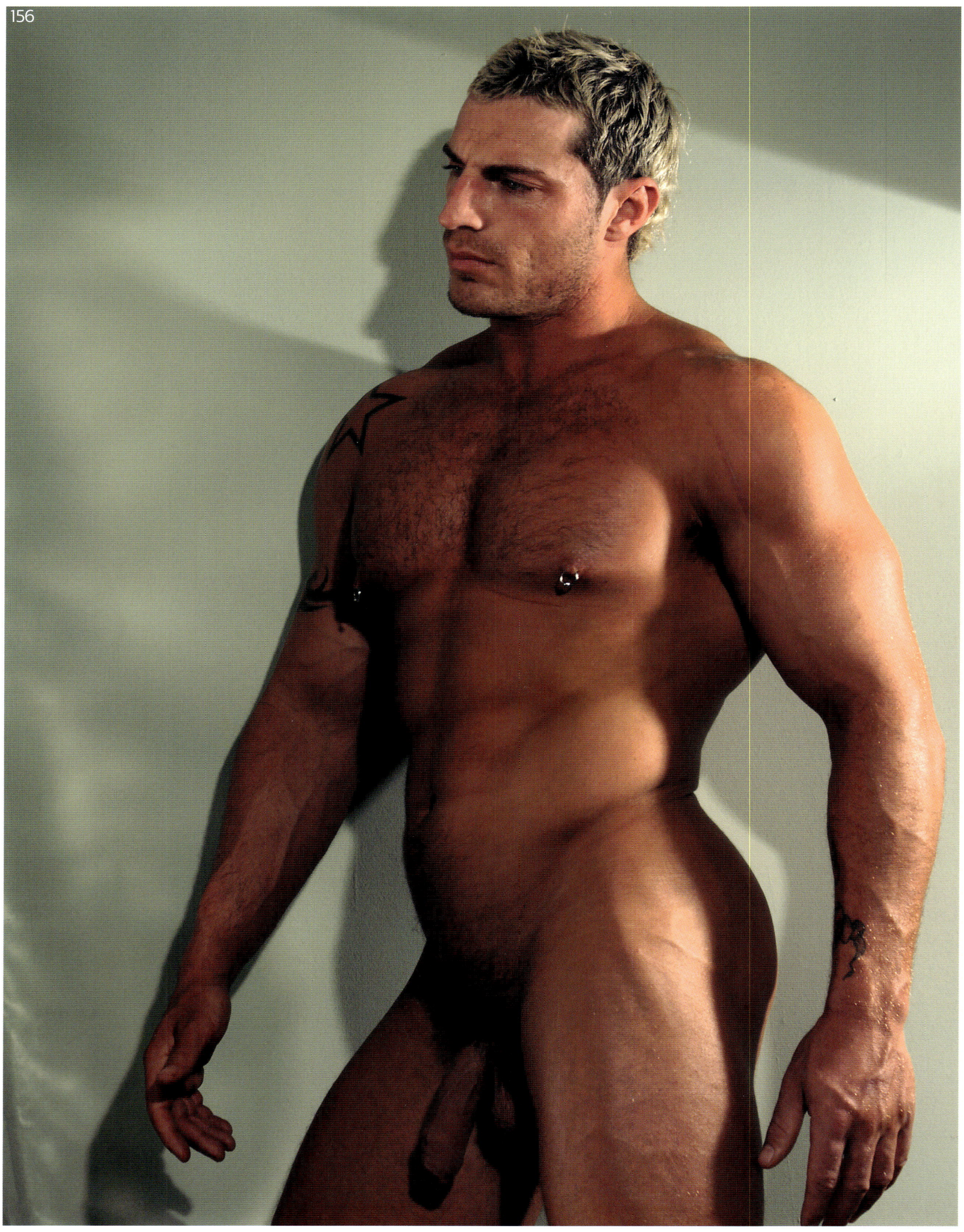

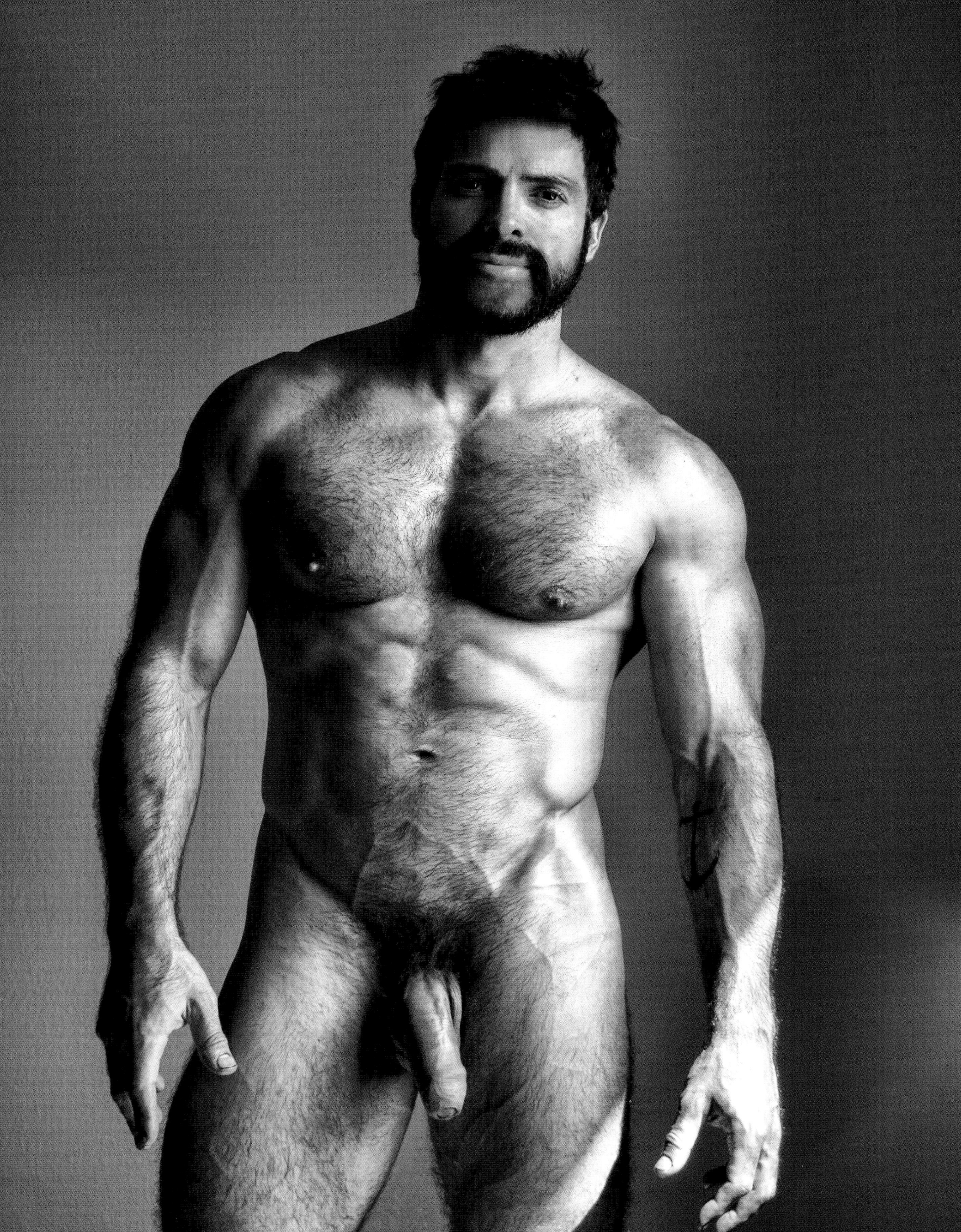

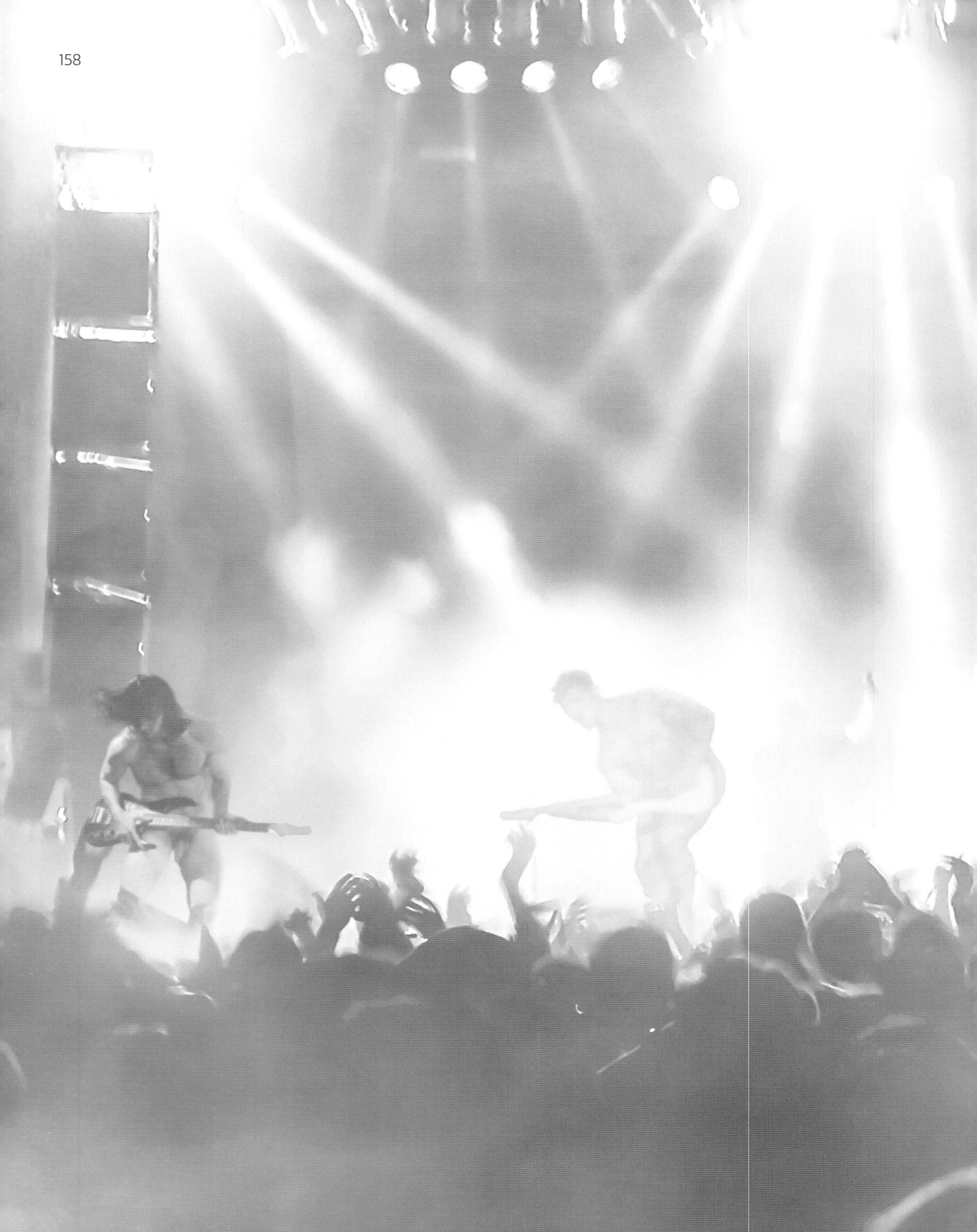

THANK YOU TO MY SPONSORS

Eddy Fang
Moises Uriostegui
Sigfrido Ferrer
Stephen GothardII
Alexander Schulz
Mark Warning
Robert Ostrander
Roberto M Anil
Jorell Bringas
Frank Kuesel
Charles Hobgood
David Baker
Anton Abela
Francis Jason
M Korenberg
Bonny Loo
Jeffery Chan
Gilles Tschopp
Jeremy C Dykes
Kyle Franklin
Jamison Pitcher
Beck Whitmore
John Cassel
Christopher Cornell

Thomas Buthmann
David Novak
Tsen Shian Kai
Ted Bolivar
J Welch
Manuel Morschbach
Rodolphe Salomon
Jean-Yves Ragil
Thomas W Reynolds
Dan Hetti
Lachlan Moore
Jeff Wu
Robert Dena
Massimiliano Pisoni
Wayne Burge
Ryan M
Brandon Erik Mills
Jonathan Ellis
Andrea Vegnaduzzo
Chuck Wallace
John Grassi
Rich Lo + Joe Mayock
Yuka Nishiya
Scott Dennis

William Olsen
Steve Terry
Kevin Newman
Yuyi Nivans
Gary McKenzie
Pablo Saccinto
Andrew Holstein
Matthew Connolly
C Mark Nichols
Tom Leclercq
Pete Boyer
Brian Yambao
Rino Vaccaro
John Crawley
Marco Rinaudo Colombara
David Matthews
Jason Thurber
Todd Berkan
Alex Sanz
Matt Hutson
Eric Dahlberg
Sean Clinton Madison
Mark Clayton
Shane Glaister

Martel Jackson
Mark Walker
Lucas Crawford
Kevin Lambert
Jeffrey Delaney
Marcus Chan
Lee Alex
Travis M
Tony Giampetruzzi
Marcel Rupp
Jim Vivyan
Josh Pacheco
Joshua HK Li
Oscar Carrillo
Yuhuang Cai
Marius Fritjof
Scott Tyson
Mark Brittain
Alan James
Michael Rodriguez
Andrew Taylor
Brad Irwin
Mark Murray

CONTRIBUTORS

Barry J Walmsley & Jesse G McMaster, Peter D Kelly, Terry Jiang, Kéri Viktor, Michael Yung, Rich Zappala, Stuart Burk, Jarrod Lehman, Jackson & Jake, Andrew Gordon, Shaun Waterman, Adrian Levy, Nysha, Steven Harris, Mark Stephanz, Timothy Hilder, Sean Snell, Jerry T. Henning, Mick Elliott, Andrei Pick, Nevets Faulkner, Martin Moch, Ferg Byrne, Alex Marin, Zachary Danneman, Philip Tanner, Lyndon Lovell, Mark Plant, Raphael Thunus, John Mercer, Mitsuru Hirao, Kendall Lao, Michael Mafrici, Dave Mutton, Bill Nugent, Brian Holden, Jonathan Acevedo, Jason Severino, Stephen Martin, Patrick Camilleri, Charlie Sthapanachai, Greg McDougall, Bill Murray, John H. Bookwalter Jr., Christopher + Jeremy Barks-Herrod, Songmao Zheng, Richard Fowler, Jim Cassaro, Matt Sammels, Ribert Liow, Ron + Roy, James P Schuetter, Robert Andrews, Patrick A. Moore, Stephen Messham, Lawerence Robinson, Robbie Nyaguy, Henry Kuah, Roy Semerdjian, Jeremy Staie, Ryan Ricketts, Gary Cannon, Corbin Talley, John Johnson, Ralph Natter, Brad Stephens, Jermaine Thompson, J Wenham, Bobby Pinter, Thomas West, Ed Galloway, Derek Wilkins, Bradley Trotter, Lee Wrona, Andrew Simon, Gary M Heath, Frank Sherbondy, Donald Gortner, Jr, Andrew Scannell, Robert Montario, Louis Rowles, Eric Thomas, Lyle D Marcks, Matthew Katz, James Jernigan, Jon Kerwin, Jeremy Freitas, Peter M, Wesley Boozer, Grant Elder, Dennis Lui, John Harris, Colm Kinsella, Stephen Pham, Nicholas Roethlisberger, Thomas Reveau, Atsuhiro Meguro, Gary Klockenga, Bob Comstock, Matthew Griffin, Jimmy Anderson Jr, Derrick Daubert, Jakoda Snider, Michael Moser, Kyle Flake, Thomas Zachariason, Michael Mahoney, Alexander Gonzalez, Marcin Mandau, Matthew Ford, Shane Crawley, Mark Reeve, Chris Fletcher, Robert White, Matt Batton, Tyson Gherghetta, Kori Wamser-Berce, Kees Paalvast, Joshua Ballinger, Brad & Paul Nodari-Stewart, Graham & Anthony Dening-Williams, Andre Fiset, Grant MacKinnon, Curt Schade, Cyril Heng and Richard Sullivan, Kris Sorensen, Don Bates, Theo Vasilakos, Josef Garrington, Tim Sauke, Michael Murawski, Mark Farr, Adam Newton, Melenaite Cook, Nigel & Alan, Derek McLaren, Alex Waite, Jeremy Hill, Brendon Bearman, Cédric Joly, Peter Strömberg, James Lew, Daniel Jordison, Jure Podobnik, Jason Farley, Benjamin Tan, Ja Jaques, Greg Brady, Marinus van de Rijdt, Drew McCombs, Pierre Chin, Rob Bellen, Alexander Weems, William Prengaman, Angela Rogers, Justin VarneyBennett, Geoffrey Vandewiele, Eric Pelletier, Dion Y, David Delrie, Garrett Sander, Jarrod Gould, Rick Priest, S Aube, Trevor Frodsham, Ross MacDonald, Barry Greene, Juan A G de Paredes, Benjamin Jordan, Erik, Eric Ueno, Chris Stringfellow, Brian Green, Nicolas Emmanuel-Emile, Marco Vitiello, Will South, Gavin Wong, Andrew Grundy, Richard Novotny, Brett Tizard, Ignacio Orellana, L Weckwerth, Matthew Rhodes, Peter Hunter, John Trujillo, Pan Sukpaladisai, Paul Jones, Ben Burnett, Mark Robinson, Keno Dressel, Stephen Stair, Scott Tasker, Michael Burran, Emmanuel Tsakiris, Kevin Seeger, Mark Sztainbok, Michael Kyffin, Lewis Jones, Ryan de sanary, Richard Lotter, Sam Louie, , Ruben Ceballos, Francis Cox, Robert Giguere, John Thompson, Dave K, David Bridge, Christopher Day, Victor Aguirre, Paul Keevers, Tadashi Ogura, KdeS, Marc Teixeira, Murray Woodall, Daisy Rocco Shoen, Mika Grekin, Jorge Squella, Cody Roberts, Zackory D, David LaPlaca, David Prince, Aron Robert Michael, Carlos Humberto Conde, Thomas F Elsemiller, Wayne Leonard, Tom W Walker, Luis Ibaceta, Tika Bordelon, Reynaldo Velazquez, Francisco Javier Medrano Díaz, Robert Clark, Jon Brown, Tal Harris, Peter Martin, Brian Bennett, Barry McCorkle, Alan Aantonio, Scott Cowan, Richard Willett, Jose Jorquera, K Bygrave, Art Abenoza, Frank Bruno, Ryan Bousquet, Kam Wan, Rick Myers, Manuel Rios, Erick Jacobson, Tanie Mangundayao, Jeremy You, Stephen Bond, Miguel Delpino, Conrad Andrews, Aaron Glenn, Shane Smart, Drew Landis, Marcus Manley, NickGanga, Marvin Brown, Shaun Beecroft, Baron Heinrich, TR Molenda, Chris Hulbert, Chris Klim, Asari Burk, Wade Spark, Alex Malton, Douglas Cano, Scott Huether, Russell Windle, Ian Smith, Gilles Vandendriessche, Keith Jenkins, Chris F, Matt Robbie, William Babcock, Brandon Carrion, Brad Kardux, , Keegan Treadaway, Wesley McCraw, Roger Trottier, William Briere, Chad Tsakissiris, Christopher Hawkins, Branigan C, Simon Foley, Christos Vasiliou, Glenn Meadley, Nicholas Himm, Stefani Barbosa, Douglas Read, Jimi Sweet, Mark Radcliff, Bruno Liddle, Greg Braun, Ferran Giménez, Rich Williams, Alan Burgess, Sergio Sánchez, Jurgen Wagner, Vladimir Contreras, Troy Czabania, Peter Hoyle, Jerona Tate, Jared Harries, Scott J Hendry, Cesar Castillo, Peter Wise, Chris Engelskirger, Nicholas Engler, Andreas Schwarz, Michael Macal, Brian Harman, Juan Flores, Martin Durham, Craig Gibbon, Kevin Henderson, Julien Bertrand, Luca Raciti, Nicolas Moriseau, Bryan Birch, Robert Arnold-Simons, Claudio Malagoni, Jason Salzenstein, R Aukerman, Daniel Gardner, David Cordon, Rylan Reed, Bob Costa, Dylan Michael, Kim DelCarmen, Freddie Lara, David Liston, Luca de Montis, Tobias Wenker, Nick Inglis, Timothy Byrne, Todd Ellis, Robbie Goodall, Christian Schwock, Dustin Holland, John Brown, Randy King, Ronald Cowan, Richard Rabon, Will Arthur, Ken Pinkela, Mark Lancaster, Thomas Hickman, Adam Damian, Vincent Ridgway, York , Michael GK, Zakariya Ziani, David J James, Kerry Croker, Chad Taylor, Norman Balke, Darren Knowler, Neil Johnson, Christian M, Jeffrey Correia, Stefan Hoven, Bruce Billings, Federico de Vera, Kent Meyer, Mike Reid, David Futterrer, Raddy Jarrar, John Simpson, Larry Raymond, Paul Stankovic, Howard Bragman, Lance Vandermark, Gavin B, Gabriel Horn, Josie Angel, Trey McDuffie, Yannick Skrzypacz, Clinton Bird, Anthony + Adrien, Reed Massengill, Harold Cepeda, Jason Hilton, Jouke H Lanning, Duane Chilton, Etienne Guillory, Dale Bramley, Bradley Brady, Gabriel Lucas, Jizhe Li, Juan Carlos Castano, Marlon Fixico, Michael Daferede, Chris McGlamery, Paul Smith, Gene MeltonII, James Moseley, Joe Heidenreich, Michael Horvath, , Keith McWhorter, Cole McKenna, Timothy Watson, Charlie Victor, Randy Porta, Tim Dwyer, Jason MacIntyre, Stephen Conn, Brad Hooper, Eugene Dixon, Oscar Peña, Kieran R, J Campbell, Robert Baggani, Robert Schmidt, Trevor Green, Luke O'Brien, Troy Cashatt, D Tremblay, Arik Pou, Murray Baker, Ta-Chung Ong, RHF, Nathan A, Darien Summers, Wolfgang Treinen, Samuel Dailey, , , Jody Freeman, Trevor B, Scott Byrne, Tony Vo, Hassan Otero, Ricky Organista, Theo Kelegouris, Rayshawn George, Ryan Kohlmyer, Thomas Moretto, Stéphane Dodé, Vern Warner, Alberto Garcia Olivares, Denny Acosta, Abhishek Murudkar, Eheleute Rüd, Tim Miller, Christopher Catchings, John Carvey, Craig Baltimore, Kyle Hardy, Michael Frearson, Scotty Young-Vidal, Roger Morales, Paolo Iacopino, Graeme Simpson, Nigel Maggs, Jason Ashmore, Greg Day, Ross Klee, Danny Orosco, Michael Nachtigal, Joshua Epstein, Denis Fahuet, Gavin Edwards, Raphaël Gallet, Mario Mangaran, Koushiar, Robert Hsieh, Shane Kruger, D. J. Barton, Adam Jarvis, Steven Pitcher, Jericho Trinidad, Matthew Downie, Ben Delorie, Duane Roth, Daniel Torres, Tanner Doggett, Daniel Stimson, None, Clayton Skaggs, Joseph Gray, Glenn Snow, Nellie Neal, Mark Warbrick, Robert Moreira, Jeramy Hamilton, Max Booth, David Stevens, Aaron Luttrell, Derek D, Colt, Ricardo Garcia, Alec Drummond, Rocco Chanel, Mico Mendoza, R Elder, Joshua Cole, Bret Tiderman, w, Clark Cutchin, Simon Thompson, Jake Thompson, Eddie Joo, Brett Byrnes, Ben Allen, Eric Hayes, David Murray, Wynt Curliano, Hanson Wu, Joseph Scaglione, Robdog, Jesse Kivi, Matt Stamp, Dan Noble, Adam B., Josh Roberts, Vinh Nguyen, Christopher Hornyak, David Sherley, David Liu, Bryan Chen, David Martinez, Andy Tan, Magio Madjerec, Hoang Phan, Troy Hansen, Jochen Manninger, Ruben Ruiz, James Leigh, , Scott Wood, Damien Killeen, Alex Toth, Michael Mills, David Rupp, Eric Li, Ryan Derrickson, Daniel Sculli, Mark Phelps, Anthony Scott, Baba, Hermano Lage, Michael Kilgore, Cameron Williams, Nathan McGaughey, Kenneth MacLeod, Reza Tootoonchian, Drew Bishop, Tyson Vick, JB Uchoa, Mauricio Munilla, Nichlas Emmons and Dustin Nelson, Andrea Pane, Gary Mobley, Mark Fichandler, Anselm Lee, Steve Needham, Cameron Pearson, Joey Pesce, Jordan Tyler, Jim Morris, Martin, T Scarpelli, Fred Parham, Darren Comissiong, Anthony Miller, Kieren Erol, Daniel McCarty, Randy Amante, Eilam Adame, David Himmelreich, Geoff Freeman, Luís La Pegna, Robbie Allan, Richard Bao, Simon Haldenby, Kenta Misak, Brandon Spevak, Jonathan Roberts, Josue Castilleja, Will Godwin, Quentin D, Steve Louis-Charles, Jeff Champagne, Nickolis Strafford, Scott Wilkinson, Jack L Northrup, Damon Terrell, Blake Smith, Eugene, Chris Ostgaard, J. David Kopp.